JOINT ENTERPRISES

A VOLUME IN THE SERIES
Massachusetts Studies in Early Modern Culture

Edited by Arthur F. Kinney

JOINT ENTERPRISES

Collaborative Drama and the Institutionalization of the
English Renaissance Theater

HEATHER ANNE HIRSCHFELD

UNIVERSITY OF MASSACHUSETTS PRESS
Amherst and Boston

LC 2003016305
ISBN 1-55849-434-0

Designed by Sally Nichols
Set in Garamond 3 by Binghamton Valley Composition
Printed and bound by The Maple-Vail Book Manufacturing Group

Library of Congress Cataloging-in-Publication Data

Hirschfeld, Heather Anne, 1968–
    Joint enterprises : collaborative drama and the institutionalization
of the English Renaissance theater / Heather Anne Hirschfeld.
        p. cm.—(Massachusetts studies in early modern culture)
Includes bibliographical references and index.
    ISBN 1-55849-434-0 (alk. paper)
1. English drama—17th century—History and criticism. 2.
Authorship—Collaboration—History—17th century. 3. Theater—
England—History—17th century. 4. Playwriting—History—
17th century. 5. Renaissance—England. I. Title. II. Series.
PR68.A9H57 2004
822'.409—dc22
                                        2003016305

British Library Cataloguing in Publication data are available.

FOR A. LEIGH DeNEEF

CONTENTS

ACKNOWLEDGMENTS

It is a pleasure to be able to thank in a public way the many hands that have made this book truly a "joint enterprise." I owe much more than I can repay to exemplary advisers: Annabel Patterson, A. R. Braunmuller, A. Leigh De-Neef, and Sarah Beckwith. I am similarly indebted to colleagues from Duke University, Case Western Reserve University, the Folger Library, and the University of Tennessee, Knoxville, all of whom offered wisdom, time, and encouragement: Natalie Houston, Scott Lucas, Katherine Little, Graham Hammill, Laurie Shannon, Nora Johnson, Eric Wilson, Tom Bishop, Martha Woodmansee, Athena Vrettos, Christopher Flint, Stanton Garner, Jr., Tom Haddox, Honor Wallace, Misty Anderson, Janet Atwill, Joseph Black, Lisa Celovsky, Joe Trahern, John Zomchick, D. Allen Carroll, and Rob Stillman.

This book could not have been completed without various kinds of institutional support: a John Lievsay Scholarship from the English Department at Duke; the Folger Library; and, at the University of Tennessee, the English Department, which has provided funds as well as a wonderfully collegial environment in which to work and teach, the College of Arts and Sciences, and the Office of Research. Readers and editors at the University of Massachusetts Press have been helpful and gracious during a number of stages of production. I would like to thank Arthur Kinney, Bruce Wilcox, Carol Betsch, Amanda Heller for her fastidious editing of the manuscript, and the anonymous reader for insightful comments and suggestions. Michael Cornett and Jeffrey Masten also offered useful suggestions and guidance on chapters of this study.

I am unthinkably lucky in my family and friends. Some have already been mentioned as colleagues; others have offered enthusiasm and care even from outside the academy or the discipline of English. Susan Contente and Kurt Piehler are the source of most things good in Knoxville. Brian Hirschfeld is an ideal brother, Minnie Ames an ideal sister-in-law. My parents, Pamela and Henry Hirschfeld, have provided every kind of support and love at every stage of my work, and I hope to be able to honor their love and kindness. Finally, three people have guided this project in ways as incalculable as they are essential. Emery and Frances Lee—and especially Frances—have been the friends I did not know to dream to have. And Leigh DeNeef was and continues to be a model of the generosity, patience, and faith without which this book would have been impossible. It is to him that it is dedicated.

I am grateful to University of Oklahoma Press for permission to publish a revised version of chapter 2, which first appeared in *Genre* 32 (1999); and to Duke University Press for permission to publish a revised version of chapter 5, first published in the *Journal of Medieval and Early Modern Studies* 30 (2000).

Introduction
Cases of Collaborative Production

Over half of the plays of the English Renaissance were scripted by more than one dramatist.[1] Such scripting, what we refer to casually today as "dramatic collaboration," was thus a significant, though by no means exclusive, form of writing for the Elizabethan and Jacobean theater.[2] In this book I analyze the institutional frameworks that undergirded such joint composition as well as the interpersonal dynamics that characterized it. Looking at discrete instances of joint writing in the form of "case histories," I elaborate the diverse socio-professional and personal energies driving particular collaborative relationships and assess how these relationships could change in concert with theatrical "professionalization" or the "rising strength of playing" in the late sixteenth century and the first half of the seventeenth.[3] I thus treat dramatic collaboration as a historically embedded but personally inflected creative phenomenon with distinct forms and implications which reinforce a view of early modern dramatists' exceptional awareness of the interests and stakes involved in their work.

By such an approach I seek to enter and extend contemporary scholarship on the significance of joint work in paradigms of early modern authorship. Much of this scholarship has been devoted to analyzing and theorizing the literary practices of elite circles of writers and patrons sharing manuscript volumes and letters; and in it the term "collaboration" has been used to designate a range of writerly interactions, from the efforts of two writers working closely together to the activities of scribes, printers, patrons, and readers in shaping the meaning and significance of a text.[4] Less systematic consideration, however, has been afforded to the joint endeavors of commercial dramatists. Of course, the early modern theater has for a long time been understood as a community whose organization both necessitated and facilitated close relationships among players as well as writers. As T. W. Baldwin noted in his influential early study, the theater business "was founded, especially in Shakespeare's day, both in theory and in practice on a closely knit, self-propagating society of friends, whose whole aim in life was to make their mystery a success."[5] Such a view has licensed a highly generalized approach to collaborative composition grounded in the necessarily communal nature of the drama itself. As John Cox and David Kastan suggest in their introduction to *A New History of Early English Drama*, "drama is always radically collaborative, both on stage and in print"; it is therefore "motivated and sustained" by "networks of dependency, both discursive and institutional."[6] Similarly, Andrew Gurr submits that "the companies worked collectively, as teams, making joint decisions about everything from the plays in the repertory to the direction of their tours. . . . Plays in performance are the product of teamwork, and all the companies' operations were done as a team."[7] And Douglas Brooks, in *From Playhouse to Printing-House*, offers an "analysis of dramatic authorship [that] suggests that play-texts were increasingly shaped not by individual authors, but rather by various networks of engagement that both enabled and inhibited the materialization of plays as they passed from the stage to the page."[8]

But while such assertions certainly reflect the practical reality of dramatic production as an enterprise involving multiple interactions between numerous invested parties, they rely on a deliberately broad definition of collaboration as any kind of cooperative endeavor behind a literary or performative text, and therefore they inadvertently risk neglecting the very particular activity of shared composition as an object of study.[9] I focus on this very particular activity in order to investigate its contexts, rationales, and consequences. While not denying the importance of composition or production processes that accrue around or alongside a text's written creation, and while not insisting on any idealized notions of dramatic creativity,[10] I address joint writing as a form within but also distinct from other kinds of communal work done for and in the early modern theater.

I do so in ways not broached by a wide spectrum of attribution studies, which have for a long time dominated the study of collaborative dramatic texts. Such studies attempt to determine who wrote what play or what part of a play, using various external or internal criteria.[11] Whereas the external approach relies on documentary evidence to indicate the presence of multiple authors of a text, internal analysis—grounded in a core belief in the existence and discernibility of distinct writing habits—attempts to identify authorial hands on the basis of predilections for stylistic identifiers such as metrical form, feminine or masculine line endings, length of sentences, the collocation of words, or idiosyncratic diction. Earlier versions of such scholarship, perhaps most magisterially exemplified in Cyrus Hoy's mid-century work on the Beaumont and Fletcher canon, have been critiqued by Samuel Schoenbaum and Jeffrey Masten for either their evidentiary unreliability or their methodological anachronism.[12] But such methods still proceed today in modified, modernized forms that depend either on historicized approaches to stylistic choice or on new, seemingly more "objective," computational technologies. Jonathan Hope's work is a strong example of the former; his book *The Authorship of Shakespeare's Plays* is a socio-linguistic study that assigns acts to Shakespeare or Fletcher based on each author's use of historically shifting variables such as auxiliary verbs and relative markers. He explains that "socio-historical linguistic evidence attempts to use the predictable patterning of incoming and recessive variants during language change in order to detect the hand of a chosen author," and distinguishes such work from stylometry—the statistical analysis of literary style—in either its early forms, such as Hoy's, or its contemporary incarnation, which relies heavily on computational methods and powers.[13] Indeed, stylometry today, influenced by advances in statistics and pattern recognition, uses various forms of multivariate analysis to examine authorial habits at lexical, syntactic, or semantic levels, and has become, especially with the availability of machine-readable texts, almost its own industry.[14]

But no matter how advanced and subtle their tactics, attribution studies from Hoy to Hope assay the historical practice of joint writing with relatively limited assumptions and goals: identifying or classifying authorial hands without addressing the implications of combined work. Even a contextualized approach like Hope's, which takes into consideration the historically shifting use of key words, does not account for other contextual issues such as the changing status of dramatic authorship in the period. Such a lack, which is much more acute in analyses by statisticians looking, for instance, at the repetition of function words or the differences between writers in vowel collocation, subverts what I consider a respectable premise of attribution studies: that writers have personal, identifiable stylistic "fingerprints."[15] In fact, one of my guiding claims in this book, which I discuss in chapter 1, is that early modern writers operated according to various conceptions of authorial identity and identification—however different from ours today—and that collaborative work would have been affected by them.

But contemporary stylometrics and other attribution studies lack the historical background either to account for such conceptions or to assess the institutional situation that would have helped determine the shape and meaning of joint work. So although I rely on some of their conclusions concerning authorial hands, my intentions and interests are quite distinct from theirs. In the chapters that follow, I consider who wrote with whom not to assign responsibility for specific lines but in order to examine *why, for what purpose*, or *with what effects* particular dramatists joined forces. The paradox here is worth pausing over: I am concerned with the identification of authors of a given collaborative play, but these identifications are not an end in themselves. Rather, they serve a broader interest of assessing the contexts and meanings of the collaboration. My enterprise is thus a materialist and interpretive rather than a bibliographical one. Its materialism, however, is of a piece with the kind described by Luke Wilson in his study of early modern intentionality: it is "more concerned with what it is like to produce and consume things than with things in or as themselves; and it explores ways of working backward from text to work."[16]

In its turn from attribution studies, my project follows the lead of Jeffrey Masten, the most comprehensive theorist of collaborative work for the stage. In *Textual Intercourse*, he questions reigning orthodoxies about the indelible hand of the singular playwright by calling fresh attention to the prevalence of collaborative writing within the early modern theatrical community. His work, in other words, poses "historical and theoretical challenges . . . to the ideology of the Author. Collaboration is . . . a dispersal of author/ity, rather than a simple doubling of it; to revise the aphorism, two heads are different than one."[17] In order to do so, Masten situates the practice of collaborative work within larger cultural discourses of sex and gender, what he terms "the socially sanctioned bonds among men within the institutions of the theatre and . . . the more widespread bonds in the culture among those who were, or desired to be, English gentlemen." By describing collaborative work as a manifestation of aristocratic male friendship through readings of homoerotic bonds in Shakespearean comedies and in the commendatory poems to the 1647 Beaumont and Fletcher folio, Masten "suggests the ways in which collaboration is . . . implicated in and enabled by Renaissance discourses of eroticism, gender and power."[18]

Such a program has rightly been extremely influential in reconfiguring anachronistic notions of early modern authorship inherited from a post-Romantic veneration of the singular, isolated author and in demonstrating the intersections between joint writing and broader cultural formations. But the strength of Masten's work—its reliance on an explicitly "discursive argu-ment"—is also its weakness, and so his study needs to be qualified as an adequate barometer of collaborative work during the period. Because he views collaboration largely as a discourse or a rhetoric to be inserted into and com-pared with others, Masten cannot account for specific "shapes" or instances of collaboration; for him they all become, ultimately, part of writers' strategies to forge "bonds" among "English gentlemen." Masten himself gestures to this limitation when he observes that "the collaborative production of play-texts . . . was manifold, and it is important to note that collaborations between (or among) writers had differing valences. Further investigation might detail both the differences and similarities of collaborations . . . that resulted from differ-ent positionings within the institution of the theatre and outside it."[19]

My project picks up on this exhortation. Its "case study" approach, which details the institutional setting for specific joint enterprises, allows me to trace different kinds of collaborative endeavors as they were determined by concrete fields of production—by the material contexts as well as the personal interests that structured the choices and chances of participants embedded in an evolv-ing theatrical milieu. By identifying specific models of joint work, this ap-proach marks a distinct corrective to Masten's study, which, even as it focuses on joint writing, is more a genealogy of authorship—a study of an arc from non-proprietary to possessive composition—than a study of forms of collabo-ration itself.[20] It is precisely the latter that I am attempting in this book. Whereas Masten's genealogy leads him to conclude that the very idea of "in-dividual" composition for the stage is an anachronism, I argue throughout that early modern playwrights assumed the existence and consequences, if not the priority, of identifiable hands in particular texts, and these assumptions, rooted in Renaissance rhetorical theories and practices, mark the particular configu-rations of collaborative writers and texts.[21] The discussions that follow thus offer a survey of different modes of collaborative writing as a compositional tradition within the theater. Although they do not presume to map to a progressive or teleological history of joint work, whereby one mode or form cedes to another in a preordained fashion, they do set individual cases of collaborative enterprises in their historical, and particularly their theatrical, contexts, and they attend to the changes in those contexts as they reflect what can be called the "institutionalization" of the Renaissance stage in early modern London.[22]

Institutionalization is a term that denotes the development of the early modern theater as a discrete infrastructure with its own history. A number of local and general studies have shed fresh light on this development, particularly in London, offering new insights into and new formulations of the ways the theater operated not only as an anthropological phenomenon, but also as a more comprehensively commercial enterprise, with its own particular commercial and theatrical procedures as well as associations with the court and the city.[23] What emerges from these studies is a picture of a self-sustaining entertainment industry that, growing out of both popular and aristocratic troupe traditions and reliant on both royal patronage and popular acclaim, cannot be explained strictly in terms of economic, social, or political determinants. Rather, such a milieu is best construed as what we might call, borrowing a useful term from Pierre Bourdieu, a "cultural field," a semi-autonomous realm dedicated to the making of textual or performative objects. A cultural field, even as it is affected by, and operates in ways homologous to, other social, political, and economic realms, is fundamentally characterized by internal rules that orient its participants' activity—what Bourdieu calls the participants' "position-takings." I consider the dramatists' collaborative work as a species of such "position-takings," as moves or strategies made by agents both responding to and affecting the cultural grid in which they work. Furthermore, the rules Bourdieu traces are part of an "economy" that is based not only on the value and exchange of material goods but also on the accumulation and distribution of "symbolic" or "cultural capital." Artistic producers or consumers may or may not invariably behave (take positions) so as to unerringly maximize their cultural capital; but their endeavors in a cultural field always figure a symbolic event or action meant to represent their own interests or investments.[24] Collaborative activity, in the context of the early modern theater, represents such figurative action; joint work is not only a pragmatic expedient for the rapid manufacture of plays, the customary explanation for joint work, but also a symbolic practice with distinct meanings for the world of, as well as beyond, the drama.[25] In the chapters that follow, I offer readings that challenge accepted rationales for collaboration by exploring the diverse implications of joint work, both for a given play as well as for the broader theatrical infrastructure.

As I suggested earlier, these readings take the form of a series of case studies of collaborative plays. This methodology is designed to situate specific collaborative experiences in terms of the competing economic, political, intellectual, and emotional interests that characterized Renaissance dramatic production as well as in terms of a wider historical and cultural moment. As Curtis Perry has written, the case study can account for the ways in which particular texts are "mediated by more localized, idiosyncratic factors" while acknowledging how they are simultaneously set in a broader cultural milieu.[26] Each of the case studies addresses a basic set of questions concerning the particular "shape" or "mode" of a specific writing group, setting these questions against personal as well as institutional backdrops. How and why did certain writers join together? What kind of relationships might they have shared? How did these relationships affect their writing? In sum, what particular kind of collaborative grouping did they represent, and what could their grouping *mean*? Such questions may be seen as a variation on Neil Carson's more pragmatic queries: "Who determined which playwright or playwrights would dramatize a particular story? Was the association of collaborators arranged by the actors who commissioned the play . . . or did the playwrighting syndicates evolve for other reasons? What were the conditions that made collaboration such a prominent feature?"[27] My answers to these questions, unlike Masten's, are materialist rather than discursive. To address them I pursue a tripartite program: I map the institutional conditions of particular joint productions; I consider how "prescient dramatists"—David Bradley's phrase to recognize the playwrights' agency, their awareness of their roles in the theater—might have understood these conditions and responded to the collaborative undertaking; and I chart the ways these understandings are encoded in the rhetorical and metacritical strategies of the plays themselves.[28]

In sketching the institutional environment of each collaborative endeavor, I consider a variety of historical elements, including the personal and professional affiliations of the writers in the dramatic community, the composition and economic prosperity of their acting companies in comparison to competitors, the changing sociocultural status of playing and playgoing in London. I thus draw on a variety of documentary, biographical, and literary sources and range over multiple companies and venues. Each study then explores the kinds of authorial investments in—or divestments from—collaborative work this setting might have provoked. It is at this point that I begin to indicate the reasons for, as well as the ideological stakes in, the grouping of particular playwrights; I propose, in other words, the kinds of strategizing, at both conscious and unconscious levels, which motivated the team. I then suggest that such strategizing can be seen as marked by one predominant (though by no means exclusive) interpersonal affect: competitive animosity, for instance, or mutual friendliness. The move here—to associate a strategic position with an emotional state or investment—represents a shift away from frames of reference provided by Bourdieu, who shies away from psychological assessment. But my interpretations do not reflect a transhistoricizing perspective; rather, they posit a connection between the writers' institutional positions and the emotional dynamics of their collaborative enterprise. And it is on the basis of these dynamics that I discuss how a particular writing relationship might simultaneously have shaped and been exposed by the rhetorical effects and thematic purposes of a play itself. In other words, I read the plays against the collaborative relationship I have defined, so that each case study centers on a rhetorical or thematic analysis of a collaborative text and charts both the links and the dislocations between the play's modes of production and its forms of representation. My reading procedures therefore are disynchronic: I use my sense of the collaborative context to inform my reading of the text, but I also use the text to inform my sense of the collaborative context. The readings that result suggest new ways of approaching standard concerns of Renaissance drama criticism: the status of theatrical impersonation; the use and effects of metadrama; the relations of court, city, and stage; and the role of patronage in the existence of the acting companies.

Such case studies reflect several interpretive emphases which devolve from recurrent issues in theater history—such as the relationship between public and private theaters—here reconfigured in their relation specifically to collaborative enterprises. I broadly outline these emphases in the remainder of this chapter, then specify their terms for particular plays in the chapters that follow. The first focus of attention is the local, material context of joint work, including its venue and auspices. Studies of the London stage have made scholars increasingly aware of the complex relations not only among the city, court, and stage but also among theaters, audience members, players, actors, owners, and censors. Collaborating dramatists affected and were affected by the specific stage and audience for which they wrote, as well as by the company or theater owner that employed them. For instance, as chapter 2 on the collaborative *Hoe* trilogy shows, writers perceived a difference between venues and audiences as well as playing periods, and they seem to have understood that collaborative work would assume different connotations based on the very literal "place of the stage" for which they were writing. Likewise, collaborative work might vary according to the professionals involved: joint writing was shaped by company members whose corporate profile, as Scott McMillin and Sally-Beth MacLean have suggested for the Queen's Company, was as important as company venue.[29] Robert Daborne, for example, relied on what must have been a strained relationship with the financier Philip Henslowe to explain, post hoc, his sharing of a text with Cyril Tourneur: "J have not only labord my own play which shall be ready before they [Elizabeth's company] come over but given Cyrill Tourneur an act of ye Arreignment of london to write y^t we may have y^t likewise ready for them, J wish y^u had spoken wth them to know thear resolution for they depend vpon y^r purpose, J hav sent y^u 2 sheets more fayr written vpon my ffayth s^r they shall not stay one howr for me, whearfor J beseech y^u as heatherto."[30] Clearly, Daborne was comfortable (or desperate) enough to apportion part of a play to a colleague, and by his own accord. Daborne must also have been confident (or simply hopeful) of Henslowe's approval of the choice of Tourneur as collaborator; such approval was by no means a specious point, as Henslowe was paying Daborne even if it was the acting company that performed the play. Daborne's behavior presupposes assumptions about both Tourneur's abilities as a collaborator—and about his abilities as a collaborator with or for Daborne in particular—and Henslowe's response to this collaboration. For another manager or with another potential collaborator, Daborne's approach might have been very different. We do not know Henslowe's precise response (although it is clear from the obsequious touches in Daborne's communications that he did continue to give the insolvent Daborne money); but the exchange does give us a glimpse of the effects of distinct personnel and personalities on collaborative production. Such effects and their implications will be a persistent concern in this book.

The second principle of the case studies is the theater's proximity, both literally and figuratively, to London guild life. Players, dramatists, and other professionals affiliated with the theater were not simply surrounded by civic companies but were intimately involved with them. They performed plays for them on special occasions; they focused on them in their plays (Dekker's 1599 comedy *The Shoemaker's Holiday* is the most obvious example); they were hired to write and perform in pageants for them; and in what has become a commonplace of theater history, they often belonged to them.[31] Insofar as Renaissance scholars have come to see the organization of the London theater as increasingly "guildlike," the structure of the trade companies have come to serve as a central coordinating paradigm for various kinds of literary work.[32] Alexandra Halasz, for instance, makes such a methodological claim when she stresses how connections between professional writers and the Stationers' Company affected their creative visions, and Roslyn Knutson has suggested that the model for the theater's "development of a business protocol and repertory practices . . . was the guild."[33] In what follows, then, I view the organizational similarities as well as the differences between the theater and the trade companies, what one historian terms the "key institutions" of London's civic life, as particularly instructive for thinking about joint writing.[34]

So, rather than measuring the work of collaborating dramatists solely in terms of "gentlemanly" interaction at court,[35] I suggest that joint work would have been, and should be now, understood at least in part in terms of guild relations. These relations, because of the immense diversity of particular guilds and their histories, were extremely complex and multifarious. They were nevertheless marked by patterns of harmonization and stratification, of alliances and frictions: between the liveried members, with their own shops and the right to hold company or civic office; the journeymen and yeomen, who were free of the company yet not entitled to wear livery; and the apprentices, who were not yet free of the company.[36] There were other alliances and frictions as well, for example, between the twelve most powerful livery companies and the lesser crafts, especially in the late sixteenth and seventeenth centuries, which saw the incorporation of an unprecedented number of new companies and the amalgamation of smaller trades by larger, related ones.[37] Even more striking was the bifurcation during the Elizabethan and Stuart years between craft and mercantile interests, as the companies split between artisans, liveried traders, and what Robert Ashton calls a "business elite."[38]

Whether or not such disparate interests rendered the guilds "oligarchical," and whether or not they contributed to what some historians see as their decline into solely symbolic institutions, are historiographic conundrums.[39] What is clear, however, is that the early modern companies were an elaborate and advanced, not simply an ideally egalitarian, form of trade. Company rhetoric might insist on the unambiguously reinforcing relationship between members, corporation, and nation, as the Grocers did when they defended the proper "art" of garbelling (sifting) spices against corruption and thus the destruction of "a bond of great unities [between] the retailers with the merchants, and of no less service for the Common-wealth."[40] But the companies were exclusive: their "major economic ambitions" were not only to "regulate the conditions of production, to promote the quality of goods in their trade, to insure honesty in weights and measures, and to provide for the training of future generations of craftsmen and merchants," but "to create a monopoly over their branch of the town's trade and to prevent the incursion of foreign artisans and capitalists" as well.[41] They were self-interested, at both the group and the personal level: "The corporations were too closely linked with particular interest groups to act for the whole community."[42] So at the same time that individual guilds may have fostered company loyalty through dinners and pageants, and at the same time that groups of companies may have been united against municipal governments antagonistic to their privileges, there "is no reason to assume that [financial opportunities] prevented friction from arising between . . . groups."[43] Company interaction, then, in its communal as well as competitive forms, offers an important paradigm by which to understand joint writing, not only because it was a palpable context for the playwrights' work but also because it was the object of their approval and critique.[44]

But equally illuminating for understanding collaborative work are the ways in which the early modern theater contrasted with the livery companies. For there were, as W. R. Streitberger says, "some important differences between the companies and the London guilds."[45] Perhaps the most important difference was that the early modern theater was not itself a liveried company; it was neither legally chartered nor incorporated. Rather, individual companies were patronized: they wore the regalia of an aristocratic or royal patron whose endorsement enabled them to acquire the licenses necessary to perform on the road or in London, and who might champion their cause to or in the Privy Council.[46] Although certainly, as Stephen Orgel shows, the players' and dramatists' memberships in other civic guilds helped to "relat[e] the work of acting to the crafts and professions, and thereby implicitly la[id] claim to their rights and privileges," theater professionals did not share, as a community, in the kind of corporate personality and permanence afforded by chartering and incorporation, both of which, William Kahl writes, helped make possible a company's "complete control over their trade for the economic advantage of their members."[47] So although the playing companies received licenses or patents, and even though they were financed by sharers with inheritable interests in them, they were not given the powers and privileges of self-administration that came with incorporation.[48]

The most salient point about legal incorporation of a trade was that it "endow[ed] the guild with the personality of the perpetual corporation."[49] Insofar as there was no effort to charter or incorporate the theatrical enterprise, or even to charter or incorporate a particular troupe, we must see members of the theater industry, despite their investment in permanent playhouses, as at least partially unable, or unwilling, to pursue for themselves a certain kind of corporate civic status and permanence. There are several potential explanations for this difference, which may or may have not been an intentional outcome of the playing troupes. "Non-incorporation" of the theater might have been the result of an inability to conceive of playing as a true "trade," commensurate with those of the guilds and thus requiring legitimation and recognition by charter and livery. It might have been the result of antitheatrical prejudice, which pitted the theater against civic institutions; it might have been the result of the association of ludic activity with amateur acting in schools, the Inns of Court, or festival display rather than with professional endeavors. It also might have been the intentional goal of theater professionals—or their noble sponsors—who, given the theater's long history of noble patronage, saw advantages accruing from the specific relation of the drama with the aristocracy and from its distance from the legal organization as well as the encumbrances of the guild.[50]

Whatever the rationale, the result was that the companies were in the position to *improvise* on guild structures: they were both allied with and separate from the trade organizations in significant ways.[51] And this freedom to improvise is in the service, whether intentional or not, of individuation. Improvisation on guild structures maintained distinctions or "charismatic" differences—between writers, players, troupes—which could have been either an aspect of professional success or, in the case of the amalgamation of the Queen's Men in 1583 from the leading players of multiple companies, an aspect of professional vulnerability. The point to recognize here is a vision of the acting profession as a set of discrete companies which, despite their connections to the crafts and trades, remained distinct—"unincorporated," as it were—from city, crown, and, most important, one another. Although contemporary scholarship has tried to downplay theatrical rivalry and dissension,[52] successful theater work must have been understood to depend on the identifiable differences between companies, whether such differences fostered fellowship, combativeness, or some combination of the two. Of course the boundaries were crossed and distinctions dissolved at various moments. But the relevant question for the dramatists concerns the institutional situation resulting from the formalized civic presence of distinct acting troupes whose personalities were not determined by overarching affiliations and responsibilities. Playwrights, some of whom were actors or sharers in a company, some of whom were under "contract" with a company, and some of whom were more or less loosely aligned with a company or multiple companies, would have been subject and responsive to a variety of pressures resulting from this configuration. The groupings and writings of collaborating dramatists must be understood in relation to these pressures, and I assess them in their particularities in the chapters that follow.

The final interpretive basis of the case studies involves the agency of the dramatists in the orchestration and effects of their collaborative work. Although I do not assume a naïve and transparent notion of authorial intentionality which affords unequivocal access to what the dramatists wanted or meant, I discuss collaborating playwrights in Bourdieu's terms, as "position-takers" in a cultural field, as actors involved, at both conscious and unconscious levels, in the purpose, meaning, and stakes of their scripts' production as well as content. For although playwrights were participants in a novel profession for which the contours of what we now think of as proprietary authorship were not in place, their work is informed, as I elaborate in detail in chapter 1, by investments in writerly and performative styles that connected the dramatist to his work in both anticipated and unanticipated ways.[53] Such connections were part of their strategic designs for, as well as their affective responses to, writing with one another for the public stage. And such designs and responses could change over time.

Furthermore, these designs and emotions cannot be evaluated in terms of a narrow sense of financial motivation and reward. Rather, they need to be assessed as part of the symbolic, and not simply literal, economy of the early modern theater, where purely monetary gain or loss was simply "one field among a plurality of fields which are not reducible to one another."[54] Too often, scholars and critics of the drama, particularly collaborative drama, assume that writers and players were interested only in maximizing financial profits. Roslyn Knutson, for instance, argues that collaborating dramatists "cooperated" in order to ensure their own and the companies' box office success.[55] This argument, while productive, nevertheless overlooks the possibility that writers may have banded together for non-material or extra-material reasons. Even if writers collaborated to ensure a profit, their efforts would not have guaranteed "cooperation" in an unambiguous or unequivocal sense, that is, cooperation as mutually beneficial or gratifying. Collaborative work, whether in the service of literal or symbolic profit, would have involved a variety of relations deriving from professional, political, and emotional as well as financial desires. To approach these other motives and their significance, in the case studies that follow I infer the variety of interests underlying seemingly "cooperative" pairs. I do so by considering the dramatists' experience with collaborative work, including their regular and occasional partners; the various kinds of professional writing they did both for the stage and off stage; and their statements, both explicit and metatheatrical, about their understanding of authorship. These experiences, as well as the institutional context in which they were embedded, constitute the grounds for the playwrights' position-takings vis-à-vis collaborative work. I thus demonstrate the complex ways in which these positions translated into the form and the substance of particular plays. Each of the case studies therefore articulates a specific relation between the dramatists' "positions" and the joint plays that they created.

In chapter 1, I analyze trends in *Henslowe's Diary* and other contemporary sources in order to establish "baselines" with which to compare other instances of joint work and the notions of authorship they represent. The discussion also connects these trends with Renaissance treatments of rhetorical style; the object here is to make clear the dramatists' potential investments in, if not a post-copyright, proprietary notion of authorship, a connection between professional identity and style. Each subsequent chapter treats a collaborative play that I consider a "representative" product of, as well as an intervention in, the theatrical conditions and concerns of each of the first four decades of the seventeenth century. In chapter 2, I discuss a trio of collaborative comedies, *Westward Hoe* (performed 1604, published 1607), *Eastward Hoe* (1605), and *Northward Hoe* (performed 1606, published 1607), and argue for the aggressive impulses behind their joint composition, suggesting that they are both the products and the emblems of the competitive environment of the private theaters at the time of the Stuart succession. Such competitiveness allows for what I see as *Eastward Hoe's* rhetorical program of "anti–self-fashioning," a system of verbal mimicry by which each author eliminates his own playwriting style in order to protect his linguistic signature from the collaborative endeavor. Chapter 3 explores the joint activity of Francis Beaumont, John Fletcher, and William Shakespeare in relation to the development of the Stuart court masque during the first half of the 1610s. Focusing on inset masques in *The Maid's Tragedy* by Beaumont and Fletcher (performed 1612, published 1619) and Fletcher and Shakespeare's *Two Noble Kinsmen* (performed 1613, published 1634), I argue that joint work for these dramatists represents a response to what I consider a vexed relation between the hermeneutic possibilities of the court masque and those of the public drama at a time when their institutional boundaries were coming into closer and closer contact. In Chapter 4, I discuss records of Thomas Middleton and William Rowley's collaborative habits to argue that they enjoyed a friendship that influenced the linguistic density of their play *The Changeling* (performed 1622, published 1653), allowing them to "change" their own experience of a mutual, intimate relationship or "fellowship" within the theatrical community into a devastating portrayal of its opposite at court, where the friendly sharing of texts is perverted into the frightening inhabitation of another's conscience. The final chapter concerns the effects on collaboration of the hardening of distinctions between elite and popular cultures in Caroline London. Looking at the pairing of Thomas Heywood and Richard Brome, dramatists who represented different eras of theatrical expertise, I suggest that *The Late Lancashire Witches* (1634) hints at a shift—or at least the dramatists' fear of a shift—in the role of the commercial theater in the 1630s. Their joint work "across generations," I argue, both challenges the polarities drawn by and between Caroline writers and playgoers and defends the endangered integrity of the theatrical institution.

In these case studies, I consider how the strains and rewards of collaborative playwriting were shaped by a variety of theatrical conditions, and how these strains and rewards registered in the plays themselves. I also attempt to specify different forms and concepts of authorship articulated in particular joint ventures. Ultimately, I seek to deepen the contextualizing project of recent work on collaborative writing by tempering its emphasis on radical collectivity and its skepticism toward individual input with attention to the roles or stakes of distinct "position-takings" in the construction of joint texts. My interests here are not in charting who wrote what lines, and I do not base my analyses on a positivistic faith in stylometric or linguistic analysis as the final arbiter of collaborative work. Nor do I assert either the formative or hermeneutic primacy of the singular author. Rather, my effort is to attend to the *psychic* dimensions of collaborative work—dimensions that are best understood when considered as fashioned within the institutional contexts of literary production. It is my hope that these case studies, precisely because they allow for the analysis, in tandem, of material conditions and psychic investments, can offer a compelling approach to understanding collaborative work and the models of authorship it underwrites.

ONE

Scenes of Collaborative Production

T he focus of this study falls on specific collaborative groupings and plays written for the Stuart stage. To make sense of them, we must recognize them as permutations of, or innovations on, earlier forms of collaborative activity dating from the heyday of the Elizabethan popular theater in the last two decades of the sixteenth century and the first years of the seventeenth. Such collaborative work, as one element of the general flourishing of the professional drama, would have been conditioned by and understood according to a variety of dominant and emergent meanings of authorship, particularly dramatic authorship, in the early modern period. These have received a large amount of critical attention in recent years, with studies focusing on the relations between authorial sensibilities and classical education, manuscript or scribal practices, gender, the law, government regulation of writers and writing, print culture and the book trade, and religious prescriptions and proscriptions.[1] The general outcome of these wide-ranging studies has been to emphasize both the multiplicity and historicity of notions of authorship and the embeddedness of the author in cultural or institutional environments that conditioned his or her work as well as the ways he or she apprehended it.

My goal here is to supply a historical framework for understanding early modern collaborative strains of authorship by stressing the "place" of the stage—that is, the theatrical venue—as a guiding constraint on models of authorial practice and collaborative work in particular. I consider the different configurations of late-sixteenth-century collaborative playwriting in relation to distinctions between public and private theaters, which contrasted not only in terms of size but also by the presence of adult as opposed to boy acting companies. Because these models of collaborative work depend on a particular approach to Renaissance notions of personal expression, I assess joint writing for the stage in light of the connection between rhetorical performance and selfhood (a connection made eloquently by Stephen Greenblatt in *Renaissance Self-Fashioning*). Surveying classical and early modern rhetorical treatises, especially the metatheatrical plays of the *Parnassus* trilogy and the Poets' War, I consider how early modern dramatists depicted relations between rhetorical style and selfhood and the ways in which they were invested in authorial personality and its recognition.

THE PLACE OF COLLABORATION

Although there is no absolute agreement among theater scholars as to the extent or implications of the disparity between public and private theaters, a fundamental difference between them—whether in terms of size, protection from the elements, and location in the city—has been widely accepted. (Although Thomas Dekker suggests that it does not matter "whether therefore the gatherers of the publique or private Play-house stand to receive the afternoones rent," the satiric logic of his sentence rests on the implicit, assumed distinction between the two.)[2] I sketch what appear to be the accepted authorial programs of the two venues in order to underscore that, for various material reasons, different types of theaters promoted different versions or modes of theatrical authorship, at least in those decades when boy companies played at the private theaters in Blackfriars and St. Paul's churchyard.

As documents such as *Henslowe's Diary* suggest, the Elizabethan public amphitheaters inclined toward collaborative work. The record of the diary is clear: almost all of the dramatists, including names such as Ben Jonson and George Chapman which now seem "singular," participated in joint work. Neil Carson demonstrates that in the playing seasons between 1597 and 1600, for instance, the number of collaborative scripts varied between 25 and 62 percent of total plays negotiated for. During these seasons collaborative plays accounted for as much as 82 percent of total plays finished.[3] Particularly extensive and impressive is the consistent activity of various groupings among Henry Chettle, John Day, Thomas Dekker, Michael Drayton, Richard Hathaway, William Haughton, Thomas Middleton, Anthony Munday, and Robert Wilson, which Philip Henslowe records in his account book of expenditures for the Rose and Fortune playhouses during 1592–1604.

Carson calls these groups "syndicates" and pronounces them "anything but random."[4] Indeed, he describes particular patterns of collaborative activity for these playwrights: Drayton, Middleton, Munday, and Wilson wrote together, and exclusively, for the Admiral's Men; Chettle, Dekker, and Heywood wrote with one another, usually but not solely for Worcester's Men, but never with Day, Hathaway, or Haughton, who also wrote for both companies. As Carson suggests, the syndicates' patterns "give the impression of some kind of formal or informal understanding on the part of the playwrights," rendering "the assumption that collaboration was forced on players and dramatists alike by the pressure of the performance schedule . . . seem unsupported by the evidence."[5] Although the diary does record some one-time-only teams such as Jonson, Henry Porter, and Chettle, who collaborated on a lost play titled *Hot Anger Soon Cold*, many groups worked together on a regular and recurrent basis.[6] And though it is not possible to be sure, as it was in the case of Robert Daborne and Cyril Tourneur, whether the writers themselves arranged these groupings or whether it was the acting companies or financiers who commissioned them, it is clear that collaborative work for the Admiral's and Worcester's Men—adult companies playing in large amphitheaters on a near-daily basis—was characterized in this period by consistency and repetition.

These patterns provide an important glimpse of early methods or schemes of collaboration. They indicate that writers worked not only in pairs but also, more frequently, in groups of three, four, and even five, and the groups observed hierarchies, as some writers were paid more than others for what appears to be the same amount of work on a play. (Of course, the difference in payment may reflect different contributions.) More striking is the way they demonstrate how these collaborators participated in the construction of multipart—what we now call serialized—plays (see table 1). Serialized titles are recorded by Henslowe in his payments to the writers as well as in his collections after performances, and they testify to an implicit or explicit respect for certain principles of group effort, including those of creative, aesthetic, or personal compatibility and accountability. Between the late 1590s and early 1600s, the diary records nineteen play sequences specifically identified as "parts": "part one" or "second part" or "introduction to." Thirteen of these sequences have at least one writer documented for each of the corresponding parts. And in eleven out of these thirteen serials—or 84 percent—at least one of the writers carries over from part to part. In other words, all collaborative groups engaged in writing serials shared at least one writer in common for each play in the set. For instance, Munday is listed as the sole author of *1 Robin Hood*; Munday and

Serial Productions, Their Companies, and Their Writers, 1592–1603

TITLE	COMPANY	YEAR	WRITERS PAID
Tamar Cham (2 parts)	Strange's	1592	
Godfrey (2 parts)	Admiral's	1594	
Tamberlan (2 parts)	Admiral's	1594/5	(Marlowe)
Hercoles (2 parts)	Admiral's	1595	
Seasore (2 parts)	Admiral's	1595	
Robin Hood (2 parts)	Admiral's	1598	Munday/Munday, Chettle
Goodwin and Sons (2 parts)	Admiral's	1598	?/Chettle, Dekker, Drayton, Wilson
Black Batman of the North (2 parts)	Admiral's	1598	Chettle, Dekker, Wilson, Drayton/Chettle, Wilson
Civil Wars in France (4 parts)	Admiral's	1598	Drayton, Dekker/Drayton, Dekker/Dekker/Dekker
Henry I (2 parts: *Life and Death, Famous Wars*)	Admiral's	1597/1598	?/Drayton, Dekker, Chettle
Oldcastle (2 parts)	Admiral's	1599	Munday, Drayton, Wilson, Hathway/Munday, Drayton, Wilson, Hathway
Henry Richmond (2 parts only)	Admiral's	1599	Wilson
Fayre Constance of Rome (2 parts)	Admiral's	1600	Drayton, Hathway, Munday, Dekker/Drayton, Hathway, Munday, Dekker
Blind Beggar of Bednall Green (3 parts)	Admiral's	1600/1601	Chettle, Day/Day, Haughton/Day, Haughton
Cardinal Wolsey (2 parts: *Life & Rising*)	Admiral's	1601	Chettle/Chettle, Munday, Drayton, Smith
VI Clothers (2 parts)	Admiral's	1601	Hathway, Smith, Haughton/Hathway, Smith, Haughton
London Florentyne (2 parts)	Admiral's	1602	Chettle, Heywood/Chettle
Black Dog of Newgate (2 parts)	Worcester's	1602	Day, Smith, Hathway, other poet/ Day, Smith, Hathway, other poet
Lady Jane (2 parts)	Worcester's	1602	Dekker, Chettle, Heywood, Smith, Webster/Dekker

Source: Henslowe's Diary, ed. R. A. Foakes and R. T. Rickert (Cambridge: Cambridge University Press, 1961).

Chettle are listed as the joint authors of the second part of the play, *2 Robin Hood*. The three parts of *The Blind Beggar of Bednall Green* follow an even more interesting pattern: John Day participates in the writing of all three of them, the first with Chettle and the next two with Haughton. Furthermore, of the thirteen sets of author-identified plays, seven—or 53 percent—conserve at least two collaborators across the series. For instance, Chettle, Dekker, Wilson, and Drayton are paid for *1 Black Batman of the North*, with Chettle and Wilson being played for the second part. The two parts of both *Oldcastle* and *The Black Dog of Newgate* are the most consistent: the same collaborative groups wrote both segments of the set—Munday, Drayton, Wilson, and Hathaway for *Oldcastle* and Day, Smith, Hathaway, and the "other poet" for *Black Dog*.

These numbers suggest a "conservation of collaborators" across serialized plays. Such conservation testifies, in turn, to the ways dramatists, and the companies that employed them, may have recognized a kind of "right" to the multiple parts of a serialized story line. That is, they might be said to have approved a version of intellectual property which, though not a program for individual economic entitlement, nevertheless acknowledged the investments of particular writers—and, more important for my purposes, of particular writing groups—in related plots.[7] The members of specific groups must have been understood as sharing affinities that needed to be reproduced for the success, however measured, of serial plays. And their joint writing must have been considered a compositional form that bore a direct relationship to the plays scripted. As we shall see, later Stuart groups, for whom there is more or different information, pose a contrast to this profile of the early syndicates' writing patterns and their implications.

The later groups also contrast to an alternative approach—or lack of an approach—to collaborative writing in the early boy companies, particularly the earlier and later Paul's Boys and the Chapel and Blackfriars children who played, respectively, at Paul's and two different playhouses in Blackfriars prior to 1590 and again after 1600.[8] These boy companies seem to have relied on plays written solo. Although many of their early plays remain anonymous, John Lyly emerged in the 1580s as the dominant writer for Paul's, and after the resumption of child acting at the turn of the century, Ben Jonson, George Chapman, John Marston, and Thomas Middleton became the regular, and solo, writers for the boys. That the majority of these dramatists all had connections to collaborative plays for adult companies only makes their individual work for the children more significant.[9]

Of course, forms of collaborative work for the boy companies and their theaters was an essential part of their production. For instance, the plays involved the efforts of multiple hands unique to these venues, especially musicians. But if the music and singing at the private theaters de-emphasized the role of the playwright in favor of the composer and his music, other conditions of the Elizabethan private theaters nevertheless helped make possible the establishment there of an authorial model different from those for the adult companies at their theaters—that of the solo company playwright. For though playing by children, like playing by adults, became increasingly commercialized in the mid-1570s,[10] its conditions and practices—company routine, status, and repertory—differed from those of their adult peers in ways that must have affected the conception of authorship for children's troupes. (The closure of the boy companies but not the adults' after the Marprelate controversy should be seen, among other interpretations, as a sign of the children's unique status.)

At perhaps the most basic level of difference, the boy companies played only once a week, indoors, to small audience; they therefore needed fewer new plays than the adult companies, which played as often as six times a week at the relatively larger amphitheaters and often, though not always, to larger audiences. If one of the motives for joint work was to increase productivity, the need for fewer plays for Paul's and the Blackfriars children may have translated into the need for fewer dramatists and fewer collaborative undertakings. The joint mode was thus neither an economically nor a practically necessary model of composition at the private theaters.

There are reasons for the absence of collaborative writing at the private theaters beyond those of supply and demand, however. Scholars have noted various features of the Elizabethan private stages and their boy players which gave the venue a particularly "literary" as well as "individualistic" sensibility.[11] Such features and such a sensibility may also have fostered singular as opposed to composite or syndicated authorship. The location and the audience of the private theaters would have been crucial: set in the heart of London, close to either the Inns of Court or the other swelling literary enterprises around St. Paul's Cathedral, these theaters were more likely to draw, even before their prices increased to six times those of the public theaters, educated men from the Inns, including those with literary aspirations and investments in the expression of individual style.[12] In addition to their location, the smaller size of the private theaters facilitated a kind of "coterie" experience even for a mixed crowd: the private theaters' restricted space and audience capacity (estimates put Paul's capacity at 50–100 persons and the amphitheaters at 2,500) as well as their enclosure indoors contributed to a sense of intimacy that would have heightened the identification among and between playgoers and those connected with the performance.[13] While such identification was certainly a part of the outdoor experience—it was at least part of the raison d'être for certain gallery seats—its potential pervasiveness at the indoor playhouses may have contributed to a writerly ethos that favored the "individual," or singular, dramatist whose works for the boys were his "own."

Finally, the playwrights were writing for performance by child actors, and the boys, as E. K. Chambers reminds us, were "much more under the influence of their poets than were their adult rivals."[14] Writing for the boy companies was an invitation to exercise authorial force on the more malleable child actors; and it was an invitation that was likely to be realized in stagings more faithful to the script than those of the adult performers. Ben Jonson's *Cynthia's Revels* (1601) suggests this kind of writer-actor relation in an induction in which the boys argue with one another for rights to speak the prologue. Boy number two says, "I thinke I haue most right to it; I am sure I studied it first," to which number three responds, "Thats all one, if the *Author* think I can speake it better."[15] Partly the result of the privilege of boy company managers to "impress" boys at will, it is this kind of setting that Alfred Harbage recognizes when he says that the private theaters, upon their reopening, were "more nearly a musicians' and authors' theatre . . . Literary men like Chapman and Jonson must have had great hopes of it."[16] Later in the Stuart reign, and for a variety of complicated reasons I discuss in chapter 3, the private theater setting would reward the precise opposite form of dramatic authorship, evidenced especially in joint works by Francis Beaumont and John Fletcher. But in the late 1500s and in the first few years of the new century, the conditions of the children's troupes at Paul's and Blackfriars recommended and benefited a model of dramatic authorship that is best understood under the rubric of the solo writer.

It is not at all my goal to depict this "solo" writer as a version of the singular author now associated with post-copyright, Romantic theories of authorship. Nor do I mean to insist that all boy company plays were written by a single hand; there are too many anonymous ones to make such an assertion with complete certainty, and title pages from this period are not always reliable. Rather, I am highlighting material differences between the public and private stages and suggesting that, whether or not an objective verity, the nature of the boys' companies and their private theater performances must have seemed particularly hospitable to plays written by a single writer. Indeed, as chapter 2 on the *Hoe* plays notes, records and title pages suggest that it was not until

1604 that the first collaborative play since the reopening of the boy companies was brought to the boards of one of the private theaters. At the very least, even if there were collaborative plays from the 1580s or early 1600s being written and performed at Paul's or the Blackfriars, that work would have had a different meaning or implication from that of collaborative work for the Rose, Fortune, Theatre, or Globe. As Bourdieu asserts, "The same practices may receive opposite meanings and values in different fields, in different configurations, or in opposing sectors of the same field."[17] So although Mary Bly has shown convincingly that collaboration, broadly construed, was the dominant mode for the boy company the King's Revels playing at the Whitefriars theater, this joint work needs to be understood as a mode unique to this troupe during its brief existence (1608–9) and to its plays, composed largely by amateur rather than long-term professional dramatists.[18] While my case studies are committed to the notion Bly articulates, that certain playhouses and companies fostered certain writing and production strategies, I do not read her model for the Whitefriars boys backwards to explain turn-of-the-century playing at Paul's and Blackfriars. Writing solo for a boy company represented one available form of dramatic authorship at the time, and I use it as a model against which to measure later collaborations both for the boy companies and for adult troupes when they began performing at the private theaters.

Such a model, like those for the adult companies, would have operated because the dramatists had specific investments in their work. And these investments are linked predominantly to Renaissance notions of rhetorical style: of the particular, idiosyncratic writing of performance predilections and abilities. In the remainder of this chapter, I underscore the importance of stylistic expression for early modern dramatists and its relation to concepts of professional and personal identity. These remarks provide a foundation for later arguments about collaborative work by formulating a historicized sense of individual investment in writing style and by making clear what was at stake for writers who pursued joint work.

"THE PHRASE, STILE AND COMPOSITION OF ANY AUTHOR"

Notions of individual style were a mainstay of early modern rhetorical theory and the various cultural practices it informed. As scholars have shown, such notions were nurtured by grammar school training and the demands of an increasingly performative culture that inculcated a notion of self-differentiation through stylistic imitation of the classics and the court. As Richard Halpern sums up, "Humanist methods of teaching Latin style partake

of a . . . global process for ideological production of social subjects.[19] Arthur
Marotti has discussed this kind of "self-differentiation" not for playwrights but
for the coterie circle centered on John Donne. Marotti's discussion of Elizabethan manuscript practice, which emphasizes the essentially shared nature of
this kind of writing, is designed precisely to deconstruct conventional notions
about singular authorship and style; he argues, in fact, that a Foucauldian
notion of "authorless discourse" is the most appropriate way of thinking about
manuscript culture since its poetry was "subject to reader emendation, to
answer-poem response, to parody, unconscious and conscious revision."[20] But
such "authorless discourse" works only because it is, ultimately, *author-
identified*. As Marotti himself shows, Donne's early poetry depends on the fact
that he "consistently exploited his readers' knowledge of his personal style and
social circumstances to fashion distinctive utterances from literary and cultur-
ally familiar material."[21] The identity of the writer, an identity distinguished
by "personal style," often remained the basis of hermeneutic and creative activity, even in venues or conditions that are now seen to de-emphasize it.

The theater, too, was fueled by concepts of writer- and player-based stylistic
personality and charisma.[22] These concepts are observable in the deference
afforded collaborators on multipart plays which, as I have explained, can be
seen as a concession by writers and companies not only to a nascent form of
intellectual property but also to a notion of compositional integrity based on
consistency of playwright. Such an assumption represents an understanding of
style in the broadest sense of the term. But playwrights and players were noted
for more precise, specific stylistic features. Players, for instance, particularly
the clowns, achieved notoriety that afforded them recognition by both dramatists and audiences based on certain playing idiosyncrasies.[23] Dramatists, too,
were noted for specific ways of writing. The terms used to talk about them
tend to be ones we recognize as tonal, as when John Weever praises "Honie-
tong'd *Shakespeare*" in his *Epigrammes* (1599).[24] A scene from the second part of
Return from Parnassus, third in a trilogy of Cambridge plays, makes the point
particularly well. In one scene, various characters comment on the writers of
the day. They speak of the authors' poetry and drama in impressionistic terms.
Ingenioso is asked to show to the crowd his commonplace book, which con-
tains "sentences gathered out of all kinds of Poetts," including Spenser, Drayton, Lodge, Daniel, Marston, John Davies, Marlowe, and Thomas Watson.[25]
The young men proceed to "censure" them in ways that indicate familiarity
with the writers' generic as well as stylistic affinities:

> INGENIOSO. What's thy iudgement of *Spencer?*
> IUDICIO. A sweeter Swan than euer sung in Poe,
> A shriller Nightingale then euer blest
> The prouder groues of selfe admiring Rome.
> Blith was each vally, and each sheapeard proud,
> While he did chaunt his rurall mistralsye.
>
> (1.2.209–14)

When they discuss John Marston they invoke a nickname, "Monsieur Kinsay-der," and then complain about his style explicitly:

> Me thinks he is a Ruffian in his *stile*,
> Withouten bands or garters ornament.
> He quaffes a cup of Frenchmans Helicon,
> Then royster doyster in his oylie tearmes,
> Cutts, thrusts, and foines at whomsoeuer he meets,
> And strewes about Ram-ally meditations."
>
> (1.2.269–74); emphasis added)

Of Marlowe it is said that he "was happy in his buskind muse, / Alas vnhappy in his life and end. / Pitty it is that wit so ill should dwell, / Wit lent from heauen, but vices sent from hell" (1.2.286–89). And they comment on Ben Jonson:

> IUDICIO. The wittiest fellow of a Bricklayer in England.
>
> INGENIOSO. A meere Empyrick, one that gets what he hath by obseruation, and makes onely nature priuy to what he endites; so slow an Inuentor, that he were better betake himselfe to his old trade of Bricklaying; a bould whorson, as confident now in making of a booke, as he was in times past in laying of a brick.   (1.2.293–99).

In these scenes the authors of the *Parnassus* plays recognize and categorize writers according to an implicit, assumed sense of what constitutes writerly style; they conflate biographical detail and linguistic proclivities into a measure of authorial "personality." The commonplace book of Abraham Wright, from the 1630s, shows its writer to be informed by a similar notion of characteristic style; his assessments of plays suggest that he expects, and judges according to, particular writing habits. The book, "Excerpta Quaedam per A. W. Adolescentem," paraphrases and quotes extended passages from published plays before providing a critical commentary, appraisals that compare the plays within a given author's oeuvre rather than against those of another dramatist. Wright remarks, for instance, that *The Wedding* by James Shirley is "a very good play: both for yᵉ plot and *lines truely Shirley's*" and decries *Hyde Park* because its "lines [are] but ordinary in respect of yᵉ Authors other plaies."[26] Wright and the *Parnassus* dramatists rely on different criteria of judgment, but they share an impulse to recognize a writer's distinct character or persona in terms of identifiable—or, in Wright's terms, "true"—ways of writing.

The Poets' War, or "Poetomachia," as it was termed by Thomas Dekker at the end of the sixteenth century, makes this impulse especially explicit.[27] The Poetomachia was a series of plays in which a set of dramatists mocked one another by, in Jonson's words, "bring[ing] them in a play," that is, by staging them in various caricatures that capitalized on particular writing habits.[28] Whether or not it represented a genuine brawl among writers or an early modern advertising stunt, the Poets' War testifies to a belief—shared by the dramatists and posited for their audience—in the existence and distinctiveness of authorial style.[29] It was a belief about philosophical and professional commitments as much as grammatical tendencies. As James Bednarz notes, the Poetomachia was "a vehicle for aggressively expressing differences . . . in literary theory" and a "basic philosophical debate on the status of literary and dramatic authorship."[30]

The general rhetorical program of the Poetomachia is encapsulated in Jonson's *Poetaster* (1602), which impersonated living Renaissance writers under classical names and credentials according to their contemporary professional identities. These identities are based on the writers' style, again broadly construed: an amalgam of education and behavior as well as linguistic tendencies. The character Horace, based on an ideal of Renaissance rhetorical decorum, is meant to be a stand-in for Jonson; the character Crispinus spews neologisms meant to imitate the diction of Marston. The play reaches its climax when Crispinus, along with his colleague Demetrius, is put on trial for trying to "abuse Horace" since "it will get [the acting company] a huge deal of money, and we have need on't" (3.4.32–37). Crispinus is eventually given a purgative, which forces him to vomit up his personalized terms.

> CRISPINUS. O, I am sicke—
> HORACE. A bason, a bason, quickly; our physick works.
> CRISPINUS. O—*retrograde, reciprocall—incubus.*
> CAESAR. What's that, HORACE?
> HOR. *Retrograde, reciprocall* and *Incubus* are come up.
> . . . .

CRIS. *Childblaind—o—o—clumsie—*

HOR. That *clumsie* stuck terribly.

....

GALL*{us}*. Who would have thought, there should ha' beene such a deale of filth in a poet?

....

TIBU*{llus}*. O, terrible, windie wordes!

GALL. A signe of a windie braine.   (5.3.465–98)

The logic of the purgation represents in heightened form the logic of the other plays of the Poets' War: they all operate according to the expectation that an audience will connect the characters to real writers, based on their characteristic use of language. Style in the Poets' War is explicitly and consciously equated with distinct personhood or personality.

Of course, this equation, grounded in an Aristotelian commitment to rhetorical *ethos*, governed dramatic characterization itself, as when Hieronimo, for instance, is deliberately marked in *The Spanish Tragedy* by his ornate antistrophe meant to stand for and evoke great, weighty passion, or when Tamburlaine's habit of declamation, what the prologue calls his "high astounding terms," portrays a linguistic power equivalent to martial prowess.[31] Indeed, on the early modern stage, style *became* character. Thus, in *Love's Labor's Lost*, Boyet recognizes a disguised Armado because of the latter's curious speech: "I am much deceived," Boyet says, "but I remember the *style*"[32] The existence of the Poetomachia indicates, however, that by the end of the sixteenth century, it was not just fictive characters but the playwrights themselves who were "remembered" in their styles.

This remembrance of style and self has a long history in Renaissance rhetorical texts and courtly guidebooks, which promoted a belief that "you are what you speak." Such a notion was inherited from classical authors such as Cicero, who recommends in *De oratore* that "so much is done by good taste and style in speaking, that the speech seems to depict the speaker's character [*mores oratoris*]," and it was shaped for contemporaries by humanists such as Julius Scaliger, who remarks at the opening of his *Poetices Libri Septem*, "Our speech is, as it were, the postman of the mind."[33] Such functioning did not mean that style was not malleable, that style and self did not change; indeed, as John Hoskyns, the author of *Directions for Speech and Style* (1599), noted, "I have used and outworn six several styles since I was first Fellow of New College." [34] The point here is not the *permanence* or *stability* of stylistic selfhood (although, as I will show, that precise issue could be at stake in a collaborative enterprise like *Eastward Hoe*). Rather, the point is that, even if subject to change, an "ideology of style" inherited from ancient rhetorics and reformulated in humanist treatises taught that one's writing and speech were the ineffable and highly *personal* result of deploying conventional expressive techniques. As Hoskyns put it, "There be . . . sentences particular to some men."[35] Or as Joseph Brinsley asserted in his pedagogical guidebook, students were to work at double translations in order to "attaine to the phrase, stile and composition of any Author which they use to reade oft over, and . . . make it their own."[36]

There are many ways to interpret this kind of injunction and the effects it might have had on students working to attain such style.[37] My interest here is to underscore the pervasiveness of an early modern attitude to style which linked it to notions of personal ownership. I do so not to settle definitively the question of what constituted the Renaissance individual and his possessions but to resituate questions about collaborative writing in the context of vexed and multifarious debates about the relation of style and self. For as the Poetomachia makes clear, such a relation was a pressing issue for the professional stage. Insofar as style was both a measure of personal identity and a means of professional and economic viability, it was both a potentially powerful and potentially vulnerable "commodity." Crispinus' style, for instance, simultaneously distinguishes him and makes him susceptible to attack. It is precisely this capacity of style—the capacity to identify and betray—that informs my approach to collaborative work for the stage. Collaborative drama, *writing with another*, makes specific demands—sometimes precarious, sometimes stabilizing—on its practitioners. So even if joint writing, as we are now coming to acknowledge, was a common practice, its prevalence does not at all guarantee that it was always a comfortable, easy, reassuring undertaking. Indeed, as I suggest in the next chapter, even if it was designed or pursued to be easy or reassuring, it might not end up being so. Collaborative writing at a time when language was understood to "most show a man" would always have involved an orchestration of self and style that had potentially rewarding as well as potentially threatening effects.[38] In the case studies that follow, even as I attempt to consider how collaborative playwriting was shaped by material conditions, I continue to assume that joint work will bear some of the impressions of having been forged in an institutional environment in which the dramatists' identities were one of the things at stake.

TWO

"Work upon that now":
Collaborative Labor and Loss in the *Hoe* Plays

The *Hoe* "trilogy"—*Westward Hoe, Eastward Hoe,* and *Northward Hoe* (performed, respectively, 1604, 1605, 1606)—is a kaleidoscope of collaborative activity: five different authors contributing to three different but related stories for two different theaters. Such activity is unique to the plays' venues, authors, and genres, allowing us to isolate the enterprise as an identifiably conscious moment in the history of collaboration, a moment when joint composition can be read as a deliberate dramatic and commercial strategy as well as a means of interpersonal expression. In this chapter, I show how the plays represent a perspicacious instance of joint work by writers attempting to accommodate the professional competition and hostility bred by the unstable theatrical climate in the period immediately following the succession of James I.[1] In *Eastward Hoe,* by George Chapman, Ben Jonson, and John Marston, the collaborative enterprise was a form of aggressive parody *avant la lettre,* or parody at the level not only of representation but also of production. That is, their joint effort was a snub at Dekker and Webster. That it was so—that the play can be seen as an aggressive gesture toward the collaborative effort behind *Westward Hoe*—means that *Eastward,* usually interpreted as the transcendent melding of three distinct dramatic voices into a congenial tissue of commonplaces,[2] instead needs to be read as a malicious mockery, a confrontation with and dismissal of the collaborative enterprise which ultimately bleed into the play itself. In the historical elaboration and reading that follow, I address the competitive, territorial instinct that sparked the *Eastward Hoe* authors' response to the production of *Westward Hoe* and explore how this aggressivity rebounded back onto the *Eastward* dramatists themselves, making their collaboration a potentially contentious affair that they deflected through particular rhetorical strategies. My somewhat counterintuitive claim is that competition among the *Eastward Hoe* playwrights emerges in their parodic play as stylistic coherence.

This coherence or "seamlessness"—an integrity of plot, tone, and diction—has been explained by earlier as well as more recent critics as the result of cooperative collaboration among well-disposed equals. F. E. Schelling, in his 1903 edition of the play, is the most eloquent spokesman for a point reinforced in most subsequent considerations of the comedy. He writes: "When the three poets joined in the writing . . . their relations must have been the most cordial. That three dramatists should achieve in union a success . . . is in itself a remarkable circumstance; for there is a geniality of spirit in *Eastward* foreign to Marston, a definition of character . . . above Chapman, and a fluidity of movement . . . not always to a similar degree Jonson's."[3] In a more contemporary discussion of city comedy, Theodore Leinwand attributes the "successful collaboration of three playwrights on one wonderfully homogeneous play" to their ability to "agree upon a style . . . and [to] know that the formulae with which they had agreed to work could lead in only one direction."[4]

Such views, which intimate a kind of amiable softening of personalities as the dramatists worked agreeably together, ignore the difficulties and implications of collaborative work in a professional environment in which dramatists were both known and compensated for their particular ways of writing. Renaissance rhetorical theory, as we have seen, explicitly equated speech with self. As John Hoskyns, in a typical gesture, wrote in *Directions for Speech and Style*: "How shall he be thought wise whose penning is thin and shallow? How shall you look for wit from him whose leisure and whose head, assisted with the examination of his eyes, could yield you no life in writing?"[5] The equation was only intensified in the world of the professional theater, which, as a market for the exchange of symbolic expression, made linguistic style the specie of both trade and identity. As the dynamics of the Poetomachia or Poets' War make clear, the playwright's style was, quite literally, his substance.

The professional theater, in other words, was part of a cultural economy—what Pierre Bourdieu would call a cultural field—in which identifiable expression was rendered valuable. But insofar as it was valuable, style, like any other commodity, was also rendered vulnerable. It was particularly vulnerable to loss or to theft by unscrupulous others. In *Cynthia's Revels* (1601), for instance, Jonson's character Amorphus suggests to an aspiring courtier that he "wisely mix yourself in rank with such as you know can [speak well]; and as your ears do meet with a new phrase or an acute jest, take it in: a quick nimble memory will lift it away, and, at your next public meal, it is your own."[6] Thomas Dekker makes the same point in *Guls-Hornbook*, in his description of how a gallant should behave at a play: "Hoard vp the finest play-scraps you can get, vpon which your leane wit may most sauourly feede for want of other stuffe, when the *Arcadian* and *Euphuisd* gentlewomen haue their tongues sharpened to set vpon you."[7] These quips express a popular notion that lines from plays, and the "acute jests" they contain, were available to be taken by audience members with a vested interest in making them their own. Jonson and Dekker's satiric stabs signal, at least in part, a writerly preoccupation, whether from a positive or negative perspective, with threats to a work's status and safety. This preoccupation is dramatized in the 1620s play *The Spanish Gipsie* (published 1653), in which two gypsy playwrights accept a newcomer into their midst, a fellow "Mag-py of *Parnassus*," as long as he "will not steale my Plot."[8]

Such preoccupation would have affected, and would have been affected by, the collaborative writing process, a process that, as distinguished even from the handing over of a script to a company of players for perusal and enactment, asked dramatists physically and literally to share or join their compositions with the written work of others. It is of course possible that collaborative enterprises could serve to ameliorate concerns attendant on play production and the stylistic display it involved. As we have seen with Robert Daborne and Cyril Tourneur, collaborating dramatists certainly could share a mutually productive relation, like the one Thomas Gainsford imagines between playwrights and players, who "in trueth . . . are reciprocall helpes to one another; for the one writes for money, and the other plays for money."[9] As I argue, however, on certain occasions joint work could also exacerbate concerns about stylistic exposure, raising anxieties about submitting an individual dramatic voice to a joint text. The narrative and rhetorical structures of *Eastward Hoe* represent responses to—specifically, efforts to blunt—these anxieties. In this play, Chapman, Jonson, and Marston deliberately eliminate the stylistic self-expression that in other venues they champion. They do so by saturating their play with commonplaces, a stylistic maneuver I see as an effort to preempt perceived threats to their personal and professional status.[10] In an inversion of the usual formula for Renaissance subjectivity, the rhetorical program that informs the play is one of *anti*–self-fashioning.

COLLABORATION FOR THE BOYS

The story of this rhetorical program really begins with *Westward Hoe*, performed in 1604 by the Children of Paul's, one of London's children's companies which performed in private (that is, indoor) theaters. A double-plot
comedy concerned primarily with jealous merchant husbands and their con-
spiratorial but chaste wives, *Westward* was an early contribution to a species of
drama that was to flourish rapidly at the private theaters, the "compact sub-
genre" of city comedy that mediated the internal contradictions of the rapidly
changing socioeconomic structure of London.[11] It also initiated what Harry
Levin calls a "seamy trilogy," the sequence of *Westward, Eastward*, and finally
Northward Hoe, written, again, by Dekker and Webster in response to Chapman, Jonson, and Marston's previous play.[12] Levin's obvious distaste for the
plays is shared by the *Eastward* authors, but not for the same reasons. Levin,
comparing the plays to Shakespeare's major tragedies of the human condition—
King Lear, Macbeth, Othello—condemns all three comedies for their mercantile
plots. Unencumbered by Levin's canonical perspective, Chapman, Jonson, and
Marston were not so critical of theatrical interest in city life. But, as R. W.
Van Fossen suggests, they do indeed seem resistant to what has been deemed
the "bourgeois" tone and convictions of *Westward*.[13] Even more, I will argue,
they were antagonistic toward *Westward*'s collaborative composition. For in
writing a joint play for a children's company, Dekker and Webster were importing into the private theater milieu a form of play production associated
almost exclusively with the public amphitheaters.

Theater historians continue to reassess the status of the public playhouses
and their adult actors in relation to the private playhouses and their boy actors.
And while recent studies support significant continuities between the plays
and audiences at both the amphitheaters and indoor houses, nevertheless critics
confirm important distinctions between the two venues in terms of atmosphere
and repertory.[14] In the late 1580s, before their closure in 1590 in the wake of
the Marprelate controversy, John Lyly distinguished the two by price of ticket:
"If he be shewed at Paules it will cost you four-pence: at the Theatre twopence:
at Sainct Thomas a Watrings, nothing."[15] During the second run of the children's theaters, Ben Jonson would have characters in his *Cynthia's Revels* make
the distinctions. In the play's induction, a child player who appears as a gallant
shuffles away two other boys: "Away, wag; what, wouldst thou make an imple-
ment of me? 'Slid the boy takes me for a piece of perspective (I hold my life)
or some silk curtain come to hang the stage here! Sir crack, I am none of your
fresh pictures that use to beautify the decayed dead arras, *in a public theatre*."[16]

The title page to Dekker's *Satiromastix* (1602) indicates that the play was presented "publicly" by the Chamberlain's Men and "privately" by Paul's Boys. And in more recent scholarship, Keith Sturgess notes that at the public theater "the spectators form a crowd," whereas at the private theater "they form an audience":

> At the [public theater], the spectators assist in a community celebration which takes the form of a traditional, city entertainment. Here, the performer demands attention by the force of his personality and the bravura of his performance—his glamour—but the spectators consistently alter the content of the play-in-performance by their overt participation. At [the private theater], the play is less ritual and more art. The performers . . . are now less important than their material and the audience, a group of value-sharing individuals [who] validate the performance. Its participation is less obtrusive . . . but more pervasive in that an awareness of its critical acumen is built into the play and its production. . . . [T]he private theatres favoured wit in the dialogue, poetry in the passion and artful plotting.[17]

Insofar as there were differences between the public stages with their adult actors and the private stages with their child players—and insofar as these differences were noticed by contemporaries, as Dekker's title page suggests— the two venues could generate distinct approaches to or notions of authorship.

As I have suggested, for a variety of reasons—including but not limited to production efficiency—the Elizabethan adult companies performing at public amphitheaters seem to have embraced collaborative activity. *Henslowe's Diary* shows Philip Henslowe, the owner of the Rose and then the Fortune theaters, paying various playwrights for their services between 1593 and 1604. According to G. E. Bentley, Henslowe himself paid for collaborative plays 50 to 60 percent of the time.[18] Between 1590 and 1610, over 37 percent of the plays written for adult companies were composed collaboratively.[19]

This was not the writerly spirit of the children's troupes, which promoted a different authorial sensibility. They were perceived by writers as more prestigious: they offered a more intimate setting for performances, and their audiences, though hardly uniform, tended to come from the young, educated, often brash members of the Inns of Court, who were trained to recognize particular linguistic idiosyncrasies and preferences.[20] The private theaters were a forum that acknowledged and rewarded individual style and speech in particular ways. During the first run of the Children of Paul's, between 1576 and 1590, which included joint performances with the Chapel Children, the company's repertory had been written almost exclusively by the solo figure John Lyly. And after 1599, Paul's Boys' plays were dominated by singular productions by George Chapman, John Marston, and Thomas Middleton, while Ben Jonson during this second period was the "premiere" poet for the Blackfriars Boys.[21]

Indeed, between 1599 and 1608, the dates of the two children's troupes' revival after their shutdown in the 1590s, only eight out of forty-four, or 18 percent, of their plays are known or documented as collaborative.[22] From 1599 to 1606/7, the time when Beaumont and Fletcher started what would become their regular teamsmanship and when adult companies came to inhabit private theaters, the numbers are even more striking. Just three of thirty plays for children's companies are documented as collaborative—and these three were the members of the *Hoe* trilogy.[23] After the reopening in 1599, that is, Dekker and Webster's *Westward Hoe* was the first joint play written for and performed by one of the city's two boy companies at a private theater. A collaborative play for the adult companies at this time, by contrast, would have been one of a majority.

That Dekker and Webster should work on a project together is not in itself surprising. Dekker was a veteran collaborator for the Admiral's Company; Webster had worked with him twice before in larger groups of five, for the first part of *Lady Jane* (1602, lost) and *Christmas Comes but Once a Year* (1602, lost).[24] Charles Forker suggests that the two were friends; he cites Henry Chettle, who called Dekker "Anti-Horace" and Webster "his [Dekker's] friend Moelibee," one-half of the pastoral genre's famous pair.[25] What *is* surprising, however, is that they brought their collaborative work into the private theaters. As far as we know, there was no precedent for this sort of venture. The venture was most likely the product of a variety of professional and personal motives; it may have triggered many kinds of responses from fellow writers and theater men, including no response at all. Here I focus on the reaction to the Dekker-Webster collaboration by Chapman, Jonson, and Marston. The premiere soloists for the boy companies at this time, they may have seen Dekker and Webster's move as an incursion into private theater space, an encroachment of primarily public theater dramatists into the realm of the indoor houses, as well as an encroachment of the collaborative mode into the very arena that had seemed an enclave of a particular kind of individual rhetorical expression. The collaborative effort of *Eastward Hoe* was a response to this incursion, and an aggressive one at that.

HOE, HOE, HOE

The authors signal an aggressive posture in a number of ways. One of the first is their manipulation of *Westward*'s title. Their turning of "westward" to "eastward" is an intertextual maneuver of the sort Gérard Genette calls "paratextual," a result of the way titles, as "distinctive, well-known, brief utterances," are "natural and easy prey to parody."[26] Genette's sense of text as "prey" is helpful here, as *Eastward* does indeed capitalize on *Westward* in a particularly calculated way. For even as the title seems to announce the play's deliberate affinities with the other, in particular, to claim itself as a potential sequel to *Westward* breaches all early modern dramatic custom for multipart plays.

Multi-play series or sequences with shared titles were standard fare on Elizabethan stages; they filled theatrical companies' repertories in a rich collision of commercial and ideological production strategies.[27] Shakespeare's history plays are only the best-known examples of the different kinds of consecutive plays recorded in *Henslowe's Diary* as "i pte," "ii pte," and "iii pte." Although many sequels or prequels were unpremeditated, contingent reactions to the success of a given play, there is evidence that dramatists may have formulated or written plays with an eye to future work. Henslowe's records show that the Admiral's Men commissioned sequels even before predecessor plays had been completed or performed, suggesting that the company was always alert to the possibility of the multipart play, to potential stories whose temporal as well as topical logic the company could exploit.[28] For obvious commercial reasons, the majority of these prequels and sequels were produced within a year—often within months—of each other.

During their proliferation during the 1590s, serialized efforts were reserved for, or cornered by, a single company and its playwrights or playhouse; that is, multi-play series were usually written for the same company, produced at the same theater, and, as I discussed in my introduction, composed by the same playwrights. G. K. Hunter assumes this kind of continuity when he describes the "repetition of shape and design" in sequences such as Christopher Marlowe's *1* and *2 Tamburlaine* and Shakespeare's Plantagenet tetralogies.[29] Indeed, although *contending* companies and playhouses certainly did share dramatic subjects, canonical as well as less well known or lost works such as *The Civil Wars of France*, *Robin Hood*, *Black Batman of the North*, *The Blind Beggar of Bednall Green*, and *The Black Dog of Newgate* were composed by the same writer or writers for the same company working at the same theater. The implicit, assumed protocol here seems to have served as an early modern version of "copyright."[30] When a different company sought to capitalize on or respond to another company's play, it did so not with a "second part" but with a separate, discrete version. The Admiral's Men, for instance, are known for having responded to the Chamberlain's *Henry V* with their own *Oldcastle*.[31]

Chapman, Jonson, and Marston, then, picking up on *Westward's* title, seem to be writing a sequel. But it is a sequel that violates serial decorum. First of all, their play was produced and performed by a different boy company at a competing private theater. *Westward* had been written for and performed by Paul's Boys at their private theater near the cathedral. *Eastward*, however, was written for and performed by the other major boy company, the Blackfriars Boys, who performed at Blackfriars, and who, at least after 1599, were in competition with the children of Paul's.[32] Second, the concept of the sequel was anomalous at the private playhouses—perhaps intentionally so. Play lists from the private houses suggest that children's troupes experimented far less with such sequences than the public theaters. Private theaters certainly displayed identifiable and sustained generic performance or thematic interests— the courtliness of Lyly's *Sappho and Phao* (1584) and *Endymion* (1588), for instance, or the bitter insouciance of turn-of-the-century satires such as *Cynthia's Revels* (1601) and *The Gentleman Usher* (1602). But they did not offer calculated continuations with the frequency of the public stages. Because they featured performances only once a week, the private theaters at this time did not need the expanded repertories that necessitated the amphitheaters' sequels and prequels. After Marston's romance *Antonio and Mellida* (1599) turned tragic in *Antonio's Revenge* (1600), serials at the private theaters remained rare. The complicated production history of *Bussy D'Ambois*, first performed circa 1604, and its "mate" *The Revenge of Bussy D'Ambois*, first performed some six or more years later, only emphasizes the point.[33]

Furthermore, *Eastward* does not share characters, plots, or historical trajectories with the earlier play the way other sequences did. Marlowe's two *Tamburlaine* plays, for instance, despite differences in stylistic and thematic emphasis, are joined by the central character's tyrannical feats; Marston's *Antonio* plays share a court milieu and progress from the comic to the tragic; Shakespeare's tetralogies repeat historical circumstances and details. There are no such connections between *Eastward* and *Westward*. So while *Eastward* seems to announce itself as a successor to *Westward*, serial links between the plays are belied by *Eastward's* content and its venue. And finally *Eastward* has no authors in common with *Westward*. Unlike almost all of the serial plays recorded in Henslowe's *Diary, Eastward* offers an entirely new set of writers; there is no conservation of creativity. All these divergences from normative sequel production suggest, then, that while *Eastward's* writers *seem* to follow Dekker and Webster's title and play, what they really do is steal them.

Such stealth is the work, I believe, of authors threatened or angered by a collaborative incursion into a theatrical zone customarily reserved for the single playwright. And insofar as stealth underwrites the relation of these two plays at the level of representation, it should also be seen as part of the relation between these plays at the level of production. Stealth, that is, is an aspect or element of the collaborative effort behind *Eastward*. Chapman, Jonson, and Marston's joint work should be seen, like their use of the title, as a "theft" of Dekker and Webster's mode of writing. Their collaboration, then, should appear not only as a commercially efficacious ploy but also as a complicated form of irony or parody. Such a move, and the play that results, could be perceived as an essentially good-natured maneuver, a mimicry of *Westward* that signals the *Eastward* authors' respect for the other play even as it registers a "difference between texts [that] depends on audiences or readers to recognize the signaled historical or formal distance between works of art."[34] I see the parody, however, as exceptionally aggressive, more spontaneous and combustible than this kind of calculated, almost circumspect distancing. For while Dekker and Webster endorsed a transfer of a collaborative model of writing from the public to the private theater, the *Eastward* authors were threatened or angered by this collaborative incursion into a theatrical zone customarily reserved for the solo playwright. They banded together in an imitation of their predecessors which, in its distortion and violation of several implicit protocols of the early modern theater, marks it as a counter and rebuff to *Westward*'s collaborative approach. It was an aggressively imitative gesture meant to admonish the writing *of*, as well as the writing *in*, the play. At its most vindictive, *Eastward* is an attempt to banish *Westward*'s joint writers from the domain of the private stage by exposing their work and its premises not only to the ridicule of parody but to scenarios of linguistic theft as well. Such exposure, however, only recoils on the *Eastward* writers themselves.

"WORK UPON THAT NOW"

Eastward is organized around scenes of pilfering.[35] These scenarios begin with the prologue, in which the authors recognize their engagement with the other play by denying it:

> Not out of *envy*, for there's no effect
> Where there's no cause; nor out of imitation,
> For we have evermore bin imitated;
> Nor out of contention to do better
> Than that which is opposed to ours in title,
> For that was good, and better cannot be;
> And for the title, if it seem affected,

We might as well have called it, "God you good even":
Only *that* eastward westward still exceeds.[36]

Although every line of this prologue seems to compliment *Westward*, the subordinate clauses undercut the first ones, confusing or revoking the praise so that the seemingly generous claim not to write out of envy quickly becomes disparaging, implying that *Westward Hoe* is not worth jealousy. The rhetorical structure climaxes in "Only that east-ward west-ward still excedes," where the equivocal syntax makes it impossible to tell which direction—or which play— the *Eastward* writers believe is better. The prologue is self-definition through negation: the playwrights define their play and themselves by what they are not rather than what they are. The prologue constructs the play's "self" by simultaneously invoking and then denigrating *Westward Hoe*, by maligning the other on which it depends.

This denigration, like the earlier theft of title, is part of a fact and phenomenon of linguistic exchange: the possibility that the sharing of language can become the stealing of it. Such theft in *Eastward Hoe* is supplemented and dramatized in the play's multiple plots of financial and personal loss. The play is organized around two failed trips, one by a prodigal daughter attempting an illusory progress to a nonexistent country castle and the other by a prodigal apprentice casting off for Virginia but wrecked by the capsizing of his ship on the Thames, which thus become hoes to nowhere. Incorporated within these doomed adventures are the tales of a jealous usurer and his wife, a pair of puritanical newlyweds, and a proto-bourgeois patriarch, Touchstone, a goldsmith and the central character of the play. These scenarios are, of course, ironic inversions of Dekker and Webster's plot of citizen cooperation that results in a trip west to Brentford and the happy reconciliation of nervous husbands with their wives. But they are also scenes dedicated to loss. That is, robbing Dekker and Webster's play means making *Eastward* about loss as well—the loss of money, possessions, identities—which coalesces with loss of linguistic or stylistic display.

Plots of loss take various forms, including the story of Security, whose tale is lifted from a sixteenth-century Italian novella designed to condemn money-lending. Frightened of forfeiting his savings and his wife, Security refuses to leave the city and journeys only vicariously by financing others' trips. As he says, "We that trade nothing but money are free from all." Thus he agrees to fund the fabulous adventure to Virginia, thinking that this is precisely the way to protect his money and his mate:

QUICK. Ay, dad, thou mayst well be called Security, for thou takest the safest course.

SECURITY. Faith, the quieter, and the more contented, and, out of doubt the more godly. For merchants in their courses are never pleased, but ever repining against heaven: one prays for a westerly wind to carry his ship forth; another for an easterly to bring his ship home; and at every shaking of a leaf he falls into an agony, to think what danger his ship is in on. . . . Where we that trade nothing but money are free from all this, we are pleased with all weathers: let it rain or hold up, be calm or windy, let the season be whatsoever, let trade go how it will, we take all in good part. (2.2. 126–38)

But by participating in the transatlantic trip even in this limited, seemingly protected way, Security unwittingly scripts for himself the very role he wants to avoid. Delighted to believe he is tricking someone else—the lawyer Bramble, whose wife he plans to send to sea with the gallant Sir Petronel Flash—Security unwittingly gives over his own wife, a disguised Mistress Security, to Petronel. In his elaborate plots to get rich and to protect himself by outsmarting others, he becomes an agent in his own cuckolding; the very desire to preserve his belongings, including his wife, is the condition of their loss. His wife's adulterous liaison exposes Security to the hazards of material as well as creative ownership: his very plot or plan of trickery is taken from him. Such an experience is deeply antithetical to that of the husbands of *Westward Hoe*, in which the plot-making strategies of both men and women are rewarded with marital fidelity. Here, by contrast, the attempt to construct fictions to trick others recoils, becomes an exercise in self-deception.

A similar dynamic is at work in the "travel" plots, one of which includes Gertrude, the petulant and greedy daughter whose name is an aggressive poach on the leading female character of *Hamlet*. The *Eastward* authors may take Shakespeare's name, but their character is herself taken: she forgoes her dowry, her husband, and almost her entire family in her bid for a landed estate that turns out to be a grand illusion. More significant is the apprentice Quicksilver, who launches the fortune-seeking expedition to Virginia. A storm immediately interrupts the journey and scatters Quicksilver and his sailors on the shores of the Thames, where they are caught by city authorities and taken to jail. The ill-fated adventure, stopped in its tracks while the participants are headed in the exact opposite direction of their intended destination, is certainly a satiric critique of England's nascent imperialist project. But by underscoring the individual rapacity (the participants are out to get rich quick in the colonies) that motivates such fantastic voyages, the misadventure also calls attention to more local and symbolic commerce: personal and social investments and sacrifices manifested in the humiliation and loss of status of being washed ashore in ignominiously iconic places and carted to prison.[37]

Such symbolic commerce is figured specifically in terms of language. Many of the figures in *Eastward* are associated with the different slogans they voice, and they deploy these quips either to assert their own or to coopt others' identities. Touchstone's very being is bound up and expressed in his mantra, "Work upon that now!" which he pronounces throughout the play to assert control and authority over his apprentices. Juliet Fleming sees Touchstone's terms precisely as a "possession":

> In the beginning of the seventeenth century, proverbs are perhaps coming into conflict with new notions of subjectivity, originality, and authenticity in writing; and the emphatic redundancy of Touchstone's "wholesome thrifty sentences" . . . seems designed to reflect criticism both on the practice of reducing philosophy to a set of personalized truisms, and on a generation and a class for whom moralizing is . . . fast becoming a signature effect. Read as the engrossing of common to particular interests, the humanist intellectual practice of textual "gathering" now appears emblematic of a mercantile success predicated on an otherwise unlocatable lack of generosity.[38]

But insofar as it is a possession that carries with it a "signature effect," it is susceptible to thefts that will necessarily involve a loss of "signature," status, or self. Indeed, from the start there are challenges to the power of this kind of speech. Touchstone uses "his" phrase so often that he makes it available to others:

> TOUCH. Sirrah, I tell thee, I am thy master William Touchstone, goldsmith, and thou my prentice, Francis Quicksilver, and I will see whither you are running. Work upon that now!
> QUICK. Why, sir, I hope a man may use his recreation with his master's profit.
> TOUCH. Prentices' recreations are seldom with their masters' profit. Work upon that now. You shall give up your cloak though you be no alderman. [*Touchstone uncloaks Quicksilver*]
> QUICK. Work upon that now!   (1.1.12–23)

Taking the words from Touchstone's mouth, even as Touchstone takes his cloak to find him dressed for an evening out, Quicksilver effectively "takes" Touchstone. The latter immediately understands such a move as a threat to the established (and already fragile) master-apprentice hierarchy: "Thou shameless varlet, dost thou jest at thy lawful master contrary to thy indentures?" he demands (1.1.24–25). Touchstone thus sees, rightly, this "taking" not only as a verbal ploy but also as a threat to his status and thus, ultimately, to his "self." In this way the scene becomes the signature moment of the play's verbal self-construction and de-construction: it portrays a verbal theft possible because of the assumption—not only by Touchstone but by Quicksilver and the other characters as well—of linguistic style as a possession and a marker of personal identity. That the 1605 quarto italicizes the line only reinforces the point.

Touchstone's linguistic plight is representative of one of the paradoxes of stylistic ownership: possession always heralds its own loss. His plight also adumbrates a related paradox—the paradox of speech as the expression of self or the scene of the expression of others. The climactic symptom of this paradox can be seen in the character Slitgut, a butcher's apprentice whose job it is to place a set of horns on the famed tree planted at Cuckold's Haven on the shores of the Thames. From his perch in the tree he gets a panoramic view of the shipwreck, and he relates the scene for the audience as the sailors wash up on the bank, arriving at various symbolic locales along the river: Security at the haven itself; his wife at St. Katherine's, where there is a hospital for prostitutes; and the gallants at the Isle of Dogs, where the royal hounds are kenneled. From his tree Slitgut reports the wreck in a description that is a sophisticated display of multiple perspectives (other characters' cries are interspersed with his) as well as a recognizable remnant of medieval moral allegory (he narrates the characters' landings as they assume places appropriate to their "crimes"). Slitgut offers a broad survey of the scene before focusing on individual characters and their fates. But as he describes the characters, he surrenders the situation to them, stopping his monologue to allow the others' conversations to be heard or to join them. So although he seems distinct, distant from the figures he observes, he also becomes like them, even to the point where he is affected by the same storm that capsizes the sailors. "Up then, heaven and Saint Luke bless me, that I be not blown into the Thames as I climb, with this furious tempest," he exclaims. He then goes on:

> And now let me discover from this lofty prospect what pranks the rude
> Thames plays in her desperate lunacy. O me, here's a boat has been cast
> away hard by. Alas, alas, see one of her passengers, labouring for his life to
> land at this haven here; pray heaven he may recover it. His next land is
> even just under me. Hold out yet a little; whatsoever thou art, pray, and
> take a good heart to thee. 'Tis a man; take a man's heart to thee. Yet a little
> further, get up o' thy legs, man; now 'tis shallow enough. (4.1.9–32)

Meanwhile, Security comes ashore and begins to mutter to himself and then to converse with Slitgut:

> SEC. Heaven, I beseech thee, how have I offended thee! Where am I cast ashore now, that I may go a righter way home by land? Let me see. O, I am scarce able to look about me! Where is there any sea-mark that I am acquainted withal?
>
> SLIT. Look up, father; are you acquainted with this mark?   (4.1.37–43)

The apprentice occupies a semi-divine, semi-debased position—literally above Security and safe from his woes, and yet figuratively beneath him as his son and an apprentice. The position simultaneously allies him with the human display he observes as it detaches him from it. Later in the scene he will duck out of conversations even as he introduces them; he "conducts" the action by noting the wrecked characters and then cedes the stage to them. He notices Quicksilver, for instance:

> See, see, see! I hold my life, there's some other a-taking up at Wapping now! Look, what a sort of people cluster about the gallows there! In good troth, it is so. O me, a fine young gentleman! What, and taken up at the gallows? Heaven grant he be not one day taken down there. O' my life, it is ominous. Well, he is delivered for the time. I see the people all have left him; yet will I keep my prospect a while, to see if any more have been shipwrecked.   (4.1.125–34)

Quicksilver then arrives and breaks into his own monologue, which is followed by appearances by Sir Petronel as well as Winifred. Finally Slitgut closes off the scene with a "farewell" moralizing speech:

> Now will I descend my honourable prospect, the farthest-seeing-sea-mark of the world; no marvel, then, if I could see two miles about me. I hope the red tempest's anger be now overblown, which sure I think heaven sent as a punishment, for profaning Saint Luke's memory, with so ridiculous a custom. Thou dishonest satire, farewell to honest married men. Farewell to all sorts and degrees of thee, farewell, thou horn of hunger that call'st th' inns o' court men to their manger.   (4.1.315–25)

Slitgut's performance here, his speech and his scene, seems both his own and someone else's.

Insofar as Slitgut works in this way, narrating the shipwreck while interspersing his own description with the voices of others, he represents for the play a figure of collaborative endeavor. Reading Slitgut allegorically is not novel; editors such as Van Fossen discuss the entire scene against its collaborative backdrop, assessing its depiction of Slitgut as the serendipitous conjunction of three dramatists working together. But Slitgut's representation of collaborative work is far more ambiguous, just as he is a much more ambiguous "figure" of speech. He speaks from neither the land nor the sea; he speaks neither fully in dialogue nor fully alone; he speaks in connection with and yet separated from the people he describes; he speaks in moralizing tones that are sympathetic to the usual objects of satire. Stuck on top of a tree in a storm while he narrates the spectacle, he is a compromise between air and land, between moral convention and theatrical innovation, between author, audience, and character. He heralds the emergence of a single authorial voice even as he continues to represent the piecemeal process of joint playwriting. And he disappears afterward completely.

As an apprentice, one of the most liminal positions or stations in the early modern urban social spectrum, Slitgut thus functions as an enigmatic or ambivalent representation of the collaborative encounter. And if Slitgut's liminal, fragile status measures the possible peril of particular kinds of collaboration, so too do the other scenes or scenarios of characterological loss. Touchstone's personal quips are subject to theft; Security's best-laid plans foil him. The vulnerability of personal expression—the possibility that it begins in or will entail the sacrifice of station, speech, or self—represents a serious challenge to the idea of collaborative writing as collegial and mutually productive verbal exchange. And this challenge or problem is at the heart of *Eastward*. That is, while joint work in *Eastward* may have been a parodic response to Dekker and Webster, the play's collaborative basis turns into a threat to its own authors.

Chapman, Jonson, and Marston, in other words, attempt to mock the *Westward* playwrights by "stealing" their form and making it over as their own. They band together, and they do so to write a play that ironically, denies the possibility of the amiable, cooperative interaction Dekker and Webster depict. Such a move may have begun as a gesture of their own collegiality. But the lesson their play insists on is that both stealth and ownership always recoil on its practitioners, particularly when their objects include strategies of verbal expression that are both possessions and persona.[39] So as long as they were sharing language with one another while demonstrating their ability to filch it from the others, they were subject to the very risks they "worked upon" Dekker and Webster—risks Jean-Christophe Agnew describes as the theatrical pressure of "presumptive loss."[40] In threatening Dekker and Webster, the three collaborators call attention to the vulnerability of verbal selfhood, including their own. Such vulnerability, even in the best and friendliest of circumstances, jeopardizes the writer's financial as well as social and psychological economy. So even if the writers began their work in a harmonious spirit (there is retro-

spective testimony in *Conversations with Drummond* to Jonson's respect for
Chapman as well as Chapman's for Jonson in his commendatory poem on
Sejanus in the 1616 *Workes*), they could not have unequivocally shared the
"most cordial relations," at least not during the composition of their play.
Indeed, only a couple of years earlier Jonson and Marston were maligning each
other in the Poetomachia; Jonson would later claim to Drummond that he
"beat Marston, and took his pistol from him."[41] During the writing of this
play, that is, the trio had to have been at least partly suspicious and protective
of their words and their work. And such attitudes, I believe, are observable in
the withholding—rather than the contribution—of either their personal or a
collective style from *Eastward*. Instead, the dramatists saturate the play with
what Jonson might call "undigested" plots, proverbs, and slogans.

According to Van Fossen, the "prevasiveness [of allusion] is hard to over-
state . . . The play incorporates an astonishing number of proverbs and allusions to proverbs—possibly more than any other play of the period . . . They
are, in their folksiness, their didacticism, and their touch of cliché, one of the
stylistic features that contribute heavily to the total effect of the play."[42] In
addition to the internal repetition or stealing of epithets, these clichés include
multiple invocations of *Westward*, as in Quicksilver's departing exclamation,
"Looke not westward to the fall of Don Phoebus, but to the east—Eastward
Hoe"; repeated references to *Hamlet*, of which Gertrude is only the most obvious as well as most abrasive (there is in fact a character named Hamlet in the
play, who serves as Gertrude's footman); and wholesale use of other fictions, as
in the plot of Security, which is based on an Italian novella. The play relies on
popular ballads and books as well as a patchwork of more sophisticated sources,
including observations from Hakluyt, More, and Rabelais; songs by Campion
and Dowland; lines from *Tamburlaine, The Spanish Tragedy, Henry IV*, and
Richard III.[43]

For Van Fossen, these references give the play its "wit and originality" and
help provide "sophisticated social commentary."[44] This is an accurate assessment of the wit as well as the significance of the play, but there may be an
alternative inspiration for such excessive borrowing. The motives and effects
of the "homogeneous" story are not, as Van Fossen suggests, the transparent
recasting of the playwrights' congeniality. Rather, the play is a seamless blend
of references and allusions that perform an apotropaic function: the authors fill
their work with *others'* language in order to prevent the loss of their *own*.
Thomas Greene has explained—and idealized—literary borrowing as a way
for authors to incorporate themselves in a literary tradition which they then

extend and expand. In *Eastward*, such imitation is part of the broader program of negation seen in the prologue, so that reliance on commonplaces works to submerge rather than enhance individual voice.

This kind of excess borrowing and the stylistic erasure it effects is evident in the play in a number of ways. One is the simple fact that allusions are placed in the mouths of characters who render the *sententiae* ironic. It is Touchstone, for instance, a caricature of the thrifty merchant, who stands most explicitly for sententious wisdom. Early in the play he scolds his apprentice: "I hired me a little shop, bought low, took small gain, kept no debt book, garnished my shop, for want of plate, with good wholesome thrifty sentences" (1.1.54–57). Touchstone's self-congratulation does not endorse the moral or literary value of proverbs here; his "thrifty sentences" are designed to save him money.

But the final scene is both the climactic as well as most instructive moment of the collaborative authors' defensive strategy. By the end of the play, Quick-silver and his friends have been thrown in the Counter prison, and much to the surprise of characters and audience, they undertake a program of ritual repentance. They memorize sequences from Foxe's *Book of Martyrs* and quote *The Sick Man's Salve*, a compendium of penitential commonplaces. Their con-versations are formulaic but at the same time efficacious and even moving; they manage to convert other prisoners and earn the respect of Wolf, one of the prison officers. When the characters consider their penitential practice in meta-critical terms, they think of it as either metaphor or lie:

> FRIEND. Admirable, sir, and excellently *conceited*.
> QUICK. Alas, sir.
> TOUCH. Son Golding and Master Wolf I thank you: the *deceit* is welcome.
> (5.5.109–12)

Rhetorical conceit or practical deceit? The two are inextricable here: the meta-phor is a lie and the lie is a metaphor. When the apprentices-turned-sailors process out of prison in front of onlooking neighbors, it is impossible for the stage or real audience to tell whether or not they are sincerely contrite. The prison scene is thus the playwrights' final brittle homage to combative anti-style: it invokes the symbolic rituals of repentance and forgiveness only to negate their own independent voices and challenge regulatory authority. This self-effacement through *sententiae* is a metadramatic parallel to the playwrights' collaborative performance, and it marks the dramatists' most aggressive turn against Dekker and Webster as well as one another. The scene's comic conven-tionality represents the final dissolution of recognizable as well as reliable individual voice. The play thus does away not just with the persona of the writer but with the idea of authorial voice altogether.

Renaissance "self-fashioners," as Stephen Greenblatt has shown, leave their indelible marks, no matter how conflicted, on their works. But these three playwrights remove their signatures from the play altogether. The play's internal consistency exists in spite of, or perhaps because of, its deep ambivalence toward and denial of an "agreed upon style." In fact, it eschews style. This is a strategy Jonson invoked later to defend himself when he and Chapman were imprisoned for three weeks following the September performance of the play. Supposedly Sir James Murray, a Scottish courtier, was outraged by the play's satiric jabs at his countrymen, and he reported the play to the king. In a letter to William Herbert, earl of Pembroke, asking for release from prison, Jonson insists that the jibes were not his fault, and that in *Eastward* he deliberately "attempred my stile."[45] This tempering of style, then, is the play's rhetorical character; if there is a style here, it is an *anti-style*.

This anti-style has been celebrated as the source of the play's "wonderful homogeneity," a feature critics invoke only to attempt to determine who wrote what.[46] Ironically, this is precisely the endeavor the playwrights are trying to forestall; they do not want their audiences to "decompose" their text. Their resistance, however, is not in the service of a magnanimous collective spirit, the kind that motivates the old wives' tales at the end of *Westward*. Nor is it the kind that critics see in various forms of anonymous or multi-authored texts.[47] Rather it is an element of a vicious, deliberate caricature and a rejection of the collaborative process that can be seen even in their parody of *Westward*'s narrative of citizen cooperation—of a writing teacher with mercantile roots who assists a group of women in a general celebration of urban married life. The first target of their scorn is Dekker and Webster, whose joint work on *Westward* represented a collaborative encroachment on private theater space. But the final object is the playwrights themselves, the impossible "we onely" of the prologue, the paradoxical singular collective, the divided group. As the play demonstrates, having a style means making yourself vulnerable to having your style stolen, and by the very people with whom you work. The dramatists' coherence is designed to limit their own investments in this play and to protect their interests in the private theater enterprise.

But the coherence has broader implications as well. Although it is championed today by scholars who find the presence of authorial order and control in uniformity of design, in the early modern theater *Eastward* would have represented a rhetorical and philosophical program that obfuscated not just the concept of authorship but that of authority itself. A deliberate denial of style and self would challenge any number of structures of power in Renaissance England—be they commercial, familial, religious, or monarchical hierarchies. For authorities that govern these various orders depend on both the stable identity of their subjects and their acknowledgment of their degrees and positions. Stylistic effacement eliminates such recognizable individuals, leaving potential figures of power unable to locate subjects to "work upon." This is parody's most radical, as well as its most reactionary, potential.

POST-SCRIPT

Dekker and Webster were undeterred by such implications; they found and continued to work upon the other authors. They replied to *Eastward* with *Northward Hoe*, another comedy of urban travel that not only capitalizes on "the success, not to say the scandal, occasioned by [*Eastward*]" but also deliberately subverts the other play's rhetorical strategies by bringing the self-effacing trio on stage in the figure of Bellamont.[48] Bellamont is both poet and playwright whose "profession as dramatist spills over into nearly every episode."[49] He is at the center of both of the play's plots, facilitating a comic revenge against two gallants who try to snare his best friend's wife and ensuring his son's escape from a local bawd who is eroding his savings. As the director of the escapades that guide the characters to a denouement in the northern suburb of Ware, Bellamont participates in collaborative performances that both blunt and reinforce his authorial identity. The comic and ultimately celebratory fate of Bellamont, then, may be seen as Dekker and Webster's parodic response to the authorial dimensions of the *Eastward* writers' play.

In a move that deflates any romanticized view of the writer, Bellamont as well as the other characters recognize that his literary powers conspicuously fulfill motives and designs far from idealized poetic inspiration. At times Bellamont presents himself as a deferential seeker of court patronage:

> I will have this Tragedy presented in the French Court, by French Gallants.
> . . . It shalbe sir at the marriages of the Duke of *Orleans*, and *Chatilion* the admiral of *France* . . . and while tis acted, my self wil stand behind the Duke of *Biron*, or some other cheefe minion or so,—who shall, I they shall take some occasion about the musick of the fourth Act, to step to the French King, and say, *Sire, voyla, il et votre treshumble seruiteur, le plu sage è diuine espirit, monsieur Bellamont.*[50]

But he also admits that his subject matter can come from as common a scene as the marketplace of Sturbridge with its bawds and cuckolds. "I could make an excellent discription of it," he says at the beginning of the play, "in a Comedy" (1.1.55). And, indeed, the comedy he is to invent in the course of *Northward* is a tale of adultery. When two gallants, Greenshield and Feather-stone, feign an affair with Bellamont's friend Mayberry's wife, torturing May-berry with the prospect of his wife's infidelity, Mayberry asks his friend's help in a way that displays the rather blighted patronage of the poet figure: "You are a Poet Maister *Bellamont*, I will bestow a piece of Plate upon you to bring my wife upon the Stage" (1.3.30–33). Bellamont maintains a dignity here, however, as he does elsewhere in the play, in the face of this exposure of his compromised poetic source. He encourages Mayberry to trust and listen to his wife, and by the end of the first act the characters have dispensed with tradi-tional cuckoldry intrigue in favor of a festive form of revenge on the gallants, a cooperative scene and scheme of public shaming and rehabilitation for the two gallants that appeals to both a civic and a Christian ethic of a plot for a plot rather than an eye for an eye.

Bellamont, assisted by the other characters, orchestrates a journey north-ward to Ware. Along the way his poetic practices will be both invoked and called into question. His authorial supremacy is challenged by Dorothy, or Doll, the bawd who has seduced his son as well as an international clientele, and who is also headed to Ware in search of better business. Doll reveals Bellamont's ambiguous literary status when she hires him to write sonnets for her and promptly falls in love with him. Her solicitation includes a description of his practice as variegated and mercenary: "Goe to him, and say such a Lady sends for him, about a sonnet or an epitaph for her child that died at nurse, or for some deuice about a maske or so" (2.1.269–72).

Doll is not the only character who calls attention to the social interests at stake in Bellamont's work. Even his friends recognize the competing motives that ground Bellamont's writing, perceiving it as the effect not of ambition but of madness. In the play's central spectacle they trick Bellamont, who has suggested that on their way to Ware the characters all practice jokes on one another in a comic version of the Chaucerian journey: "For mirth on the high way, will make vs rid ground faster then if theeues were at our tayles, what say yee to this, lets all practise iests one against another, and hee that has the best iest throwne vpon him, and is most gald, betweene our riding foorth and comming in, shall beare the charge of the whole iourney" (4.3.13–18). In a streak of aesthetic justice, the travelers visit Bedlam and convince the master that Bellamont is crazy and requires hospitalization.

Although Bellamont protests at first, he quickly and graciously accepts his defeat, acknowledging that his fellow travelers can also be witty plotters. "My comrades have put this fooles cap vpon thy head: to gull me" he tells the Bedlam warden (4.3.171–72). Indeed, the possibility of multiple devisers emerges from the start of the play. Doll is a plotter of sorts, instructing her man Hornet in a performance designed to net her new customers, "Play my Father, take heed you be not out of your part, and shame your adopted Daughter" (2.1.28–29). Her directorial strategies do not merely suggest that Bellamont has to share authorial space; they also create a structural affinity between the bawd and the poet. And Bellamont also shares authorial space with Mayberry, who takes an active part in shaping the revenge plot, at one point explaining plans to the bewildered Bellamont. "The plot lies in *Ware*," he has to remind him. "Maister poet there you misse the plot" (4.1.213–14, 247). Even as he orchestrates the melding of plots and plans into a final revenge, Bellamont recognizes the input of others. He relies on Mayberry to act: "You shall see my reuenge will haue a more neate and unexpected conueyance. . . . [M]y counsaile is onely this, when [Greenshield] comes in, faine your selfe very melancholie. . . . And this is your part of the Comedy: the sequell of the iest shall come like money borrowed of a Courtier and paid within the day, a thing strange and vnexpected" (5.1.16–22). Bellamont then uses Greenshield's devices in the latter's duping. It is Greenshield who, unaware it is his wife at stake, proposes to play the pander, and, thinking himself the improviser, ends up playing a role—the cuckold—in Bellamont's more sophisticated play. But Bellamont refuses full credit, admitting that it was Greenshield's "unfortunate wit [that has] helpt my lasie inuention" (5.1.102). Bellamont believes his success rests with his fellow travelers: "Gentlemen youle stick to the deuise, and looke to your plot?" (5.1.414), and this knowledge gives him the freedom even to improvise around mistakes. When the travelers end up at the wrong inn at Ware, Bellamont promises a worried Mayberry that "it will fall out farre better, you shall see my reuenge will haue a more neate and unexpected conueyance" (5.1.6–7), submitting to the contingency of cooperative creativity. In Bellamont, then, the *Northward* writers demystify the status of the individual writer while celebrating his reincarnation in the collaborative playwright. They place him in a British literary tradition aligned with Chaucer and formulating his power to train and heal. "I am younger than I was two nights agoe, for this physick," says Mayberry at the end of the play (5.1.453).

Bellamont has been read by critics as an impersonation of Chapman.[51] There are certainly manifold references to Chapman written into the character, including allusions to his docudrama *The Old Joiner of Aldgate* (1603, lost), which brought real citizens onto the stage in a dramatization of local adultery, [52] and jibes at his interest in the French court, which he had displayed in *Bussy D'Ambois* (1604) and which Bellamont manifests in his interest in writing a tragedy for the French king. But it is also necessary to consider the resonances Bellamont's character generates with the figures of Jonson and Marston. In other words, we should consider the ways in which Bellamont is a composite image of aspects of all three of the *Eastward* authors.

Bellamont, for instance, despite his humility, has specific laureate ambitions. He plans to write a tragedy for the French court, and he proclaims that he will be recognized as "the learned old English Gentleman maister *Bellamont*, a very worthie man, to bee one of your priuy Chamber, or Poet Lawreat" (4.1.58–60). Such aspirations certainly gesture to Chapman's motives in his translations of Homer. But they can also be seen in relation to Jonson's claims to literary prestige, which, particularly in the form they took in 1604, when Jonson published his own contributions to King James's Accession Day pageant separately from Dekker's, would have been especially evident to the *Northward* author. [53] In addition, these aspirations are presented in specific connection to the court masque. Although Bellamont speaks of plotting a play, his description of its moment and venue invoke the court revel. It will be performed, Bellamont suggests, for "two seuerall marriages" and will be shown on a "stage hung all with black veluet" (4.1.53). The bawd Doll also describes Bellamont as a masque writer, suggesting that she will lure him to work for her on "some deuice about a maske or so" (2.1.271–72). The work that Bellamont proposes for himself (or others propose for him) resembles Jonson's efforts during this period, when he was writing masques for royal and nuptial occasions: *Blackness* (performed 1605) for Queen Anne and *Hymenaei* (1606) for the infamous marriage between the third earl of Essex and Frances Howard.

Bellamont has a reputation for topical caricature; his own son, for instance, says he will not malign or harm his father "lest his ghost write satires against me" (3.1.80). Chapman, as Allardyce Nicoll has pointed out, was certainly involved in such "personating" activity in plays such as *The Old Joiner*. But this portrayal of Bellamont could also gesture to the other *Eastward* playwrights, all of whom participated in this kind of invective. Indeed, this phrase can be seen as a jibe at *Eastward* itself, which got all three in trouble with Privy Council authorities for precisely this kind of personalized mockery. And Jonson and Marston were associated with topical invective in other ways as well, perhaps first and foremost with the interpersonal exchange of the Poetomachia. In addition, Jonson's lost *Ile of Dogs* (1597) resulted in his imprisonment on account of its scurrility. Even more striking, Marston had been one of several writers whose works were singled out by name in the 1599 Bishops' Ban, and Marston's pieces were, specifically, satires: *The Metamorphosis of Pygmalion's Image and Certain Satires* (1598) and *The Scourge of Villainy* (1598).

The character of the poet-dramatist Bellamont, then, is an amalgamation of all three playwrights, and thus the means by which Dekker and Webster get back, comically, at the *Eastward* trio. For Bellamont performs what the *Eastward* writers most feared: their incorporation. He consolidates Chapman, Jonson, and Marston as a single, unindividuated figure in precisely the way the trio had tried, in their play and with their stylistic refusal, to prevent. This is parody that straddles the levels of production and product. Of course, Bellamont is a representation, a textual character deployed to mock the other writers' literary ambitions and techniques. But he addresses not so much their subject, theme, or form as their attitude toward dramatic composition, their suspicion of collaboration, and their protectiveness of singular authorship. In the character of Bellamont, then, Dekker and Webster offer a rebuttal to the *Eastward* writers that is nevertheless not an attack on playwriting itself: instead, they promote a vision of collaborative authorship and its power both to create and to represent the early modern theatrical experience.[54] Their additional achievement here, in both *Westward* and *Northward*, is to introduce joint authorship into the private theaters, paving the way for the advent of the indoor playhouses' most important collaborators, Beaumont and Fletcher, whose work and motivations, and whose understandings of authorship, are the subject of the next chapter.

THREE

Beaumont, Fletcher, and Shakespeare:
Collaborative Drama, the Stuart Masque, and the Politics of Identification

When *Westward Hoe* appeared at Paul's in 1604, its collaborative origin, as I have suggested, was an anomaly at the private theaters of Paul's and Blackfriars. By the turn of the decade, however, collaborative writing there—or at least at the premiere private theater, Blackfriars—had become the norm. This development could, of course, be related to the occupation of the indoor theater by the King's Men. The adult companies, as we have seen, relied on collaborative work to a far greater extent than the children's companies, and now in 1608 and 1609, the years in which the King's Men regained the indoor hall and resumed playing after the plague, they were simply importing their customary practices into their new venue.[1] Although such an explanation is pragmatically sound, it not only takes for granted the causal transparency of the adults' occupation of Blackfriars, but also fails to specify the stakes and interests fueling playwrights' joint undertakings for this venue. Mary Bly has traced out some of those stakes, particularly in relation to urban sexual gamesmanship, for the largely amateur playwrights working for the King's Revels Boys at Whitefriars in 1608.[2] In this chapter I identify such investments for writers for the King's Men by situating collaborative writing against the increasingly elaborate culture of Jacobean courtly masquing. These investments, in contrast to the ones discussed by Bly, have less to do with the nature and construction of a local audience than with available notions of dramatic authorship in relation to the composition of court masques. I thus situate the collaborative work of Francis Beaumont, John Fletcher, and William Shakespeare as a form of cultural production that speaks to and against emerging forms of court revelry.

Such an argument builds on, while it attempts to move beyond, earlier work by Suzanne Gossett on Beaumont and Fletcher's inset masques and more recent approaches to the Fletcher corpus by Jeffrey Masten and Gordon Mc-Mullan. Bracketing the issue of collaboration, Gossett focuses on the aesthetic function of inset masques in Beaumont and Fletcher's plays, arguing that the dramatists, attuned to the gentrified composition of their Blackfriars audience, rely on the masque form to effect a fashionably tragicomic tone.[3] According to Gossett, professional playwrights incorporated the masque "not just . . . as a form, but [as an] idea and . . . *genre*," and in so doing they made it an integral part of their plays.[4] Masten and McMullan are concerned with the authorial significance of the Beaumont and Fletcher team, Masten with their role in the genealogy of authorship, and McMullan in Fletcher's dramatic work as an extension of his political affiliations. For Masten, the pair manifests early, tentative signs of literary autonomy in the form of "an authorial presenter implicated in a rhetoric of patriarchal absolutism."[5] For McMullan, joint work represents the opposite: he argues that Fletcher's wide-ranging collaborative endeavors serve as a rejection of sovereign agency at the levels of theory and practice. His writing is part of a larger commitment to a "politics of involvement . . . at once collaborative, consensual, and conservative, seeking wider involvement in political processes and rejecting absolutist claims, yet resting on an established hierarchical framework."[6]

In this chapter I blend Gossett's interest in the inset masque with Masten's and McMullan's attention to the joint production of plays by Beaumont, Fletcher, and Shakespeare. But rather than addressing the formal functions of their masques or arguing for the ways their collaborative work allegorizes an ideological position or political conviction, I argue that their joint endeavors represent efforts to engage with the hermeneutic principles organizing the production of the Stuart masque and its forms of interpretive experience.[7] Such an argument suggests that masquing principles affected not only the work of masque writers proper but also, because of established relationships between court and public theatricals, the work of professional dramatists.[8] I thus attempt to respond to Jerzy Limon's call for a "thorough revision" of the "question of masque authorship."[9] Here, though, I focus on that question in order to address the effect of what James Knowles has termed the "masquing culture" of the Stuart court on the work of playwrights writing for the public stage.[10]

THE HERMENEUTICS OF IDENTIFICATION

The cultural milieu of the Jacobean court was characterized by a variety of shifts in aesthetic production and consumption which were partly, though not entirely, the result of the existence of different royal and noble households.[11] My goal is not to offer a comprehensive description and analysis of this environment—indeed, Malcolm Smuts's insistence on the culture's "heterogeneity" suggests that such a description would be impossible—but rather to emphasize from the beginning the mutually constitutive connections between a setting of elite extravagance and expenditure, whether on behalf of a coherent political design or the vagaries of personal gratification, and the development of a culture of court masquing. Such a masquing culture is, I believe, an especially effective backdrop for understanding the dynamics behind the most famous of Renaissance collaborative pairings, that between Beaumont and Fletcher, the "brace of Authors, who like the *Dioscuri, Castor* and *Pollux,* succeeded in Conjunction more happily than any Poets of their own, or this Age," as well as that between Fletcher and Shakespeare.[12]

Masquing culture refers to a broad ensemble of performative and interpretive activities, dramatic and political, nestled in a larger system of patronage relations and organized around the production, consumption, and propagation of the elaborately staged court "devices" or displays which evolved during the reign of James I.[13] Of course, masques and similar revels had been an essential part of English courtly and educational life at least since the early Tudors, and there are significant affinities between these entertainments and the ones performed for Stuart royalty, nobility, and schools.[14] (If links are recognized between masques and tournaments, as Alan Young suggests, the affinities extend to the eleventh century.)[15] But, as scholars have noted, there are also essential differences between Elizabethan revelry and Jacobean masques at court. The differences have been articulated in terms of form, function, or cost. For Stephen Orgel, the shift from Elizabethan to Jacobean masque, which he attributes largely to Ben Jonson, is characterized by the development of narrative integrity, first within the masque itself and later extending to the relation between the masque and the antimasque, the comic and topsy-turvy show that preceded the more formal and graceful dancing of select nobles.[16] James Knowles distinguishes between the "openness" of Elizabethan masked entries and the increasingly exclusive masques under the Stuarts.[17] J. Leeds Barroll's cultural biography of Queen Anne argues for the unique political and social significance of the court masque in the Stuart era, a significance that he attributes to the queen rather than her husband.[18] This significance is given ample testimony by records such as John Finet's *Finetti Philoxenis* (1656) and by foreign and domestic letters that document the importance to courtiers, ambassadors, and rulers of not just attendance but placement at royal masques.[19] Finally, records from the royal Office of Works, from the Treasurer of the Chamber, and from the Inns of Court demonstrate the exorbitant amounts of money spent on James's revels, some of which were funded out of the royal coffers and others by groups (such as the Inns of Court) or individuals or groups, such as Francis Bacon or civic leaders. My intention here is not to determine which account of these differences between Elizabethan and Jacobean revelry is most compelling, but to remark how essential their combination was in establishing a milieu in which lavish masque performances and the interpretive meanings and values they generated took on exceptional importance during James's reign even as they came to be more and more expected or routine. Insofar as masque culture and the public drama were to intersect in new ways under the Stuarts, such interpretive meanings and values can be shown to play a role in shaping collaborative work for the stage.

These meanings and values hinge on a "hermeneutics of identification" implicit in the Jacobean masque. By this I mean the special set of interpretive interests, political as well as aesthetic, guiding the production, reproduction, and effect of court performances so that the masque became a forum for making—for quite literally staging—distinctions or classifications between and among the people performing as well as watching.[20] Making discriminations is the basic purpose of cultural production and consumption, according to Pierre Bourdieu, who says that both "are predisposed, consciously and deliberately or not, to fulfil a social function of legitimating social differences."[21] Bourdieu's notion is that cultural display operates so that its participants, by correctly or incorrectly producing or appreciating a work, become part of—become identified with—a certain class or category of people. Such a dynamic can certainly be seen to be at work in the Stuart masque, but only insofar as the masque subsumed its participants into particular groups—fit them into the elaborate social structures fundamental to the Jacobean court—by *singling them out*. The masque, that is, functioned simultaneously to identify an individual and to align him or her with a broader social class or category. The process of singling out, dramatized at the end of the masque when the masquers "took out" lords or ladies to dance, reinforced a participant's ties to or identification with a social or political class or even, as in the case of foreign ambassadors and guests, a nation. But it also served another kind of identificatory process, an identification not "with" but "of": of a single person, a single

personality. For although Frank Whigham maintains that it was only established aristocrats who wanted to "maintain their privileged position [by] con-
stitut[ing] their own fundamental difference from their ambitious inferiors,"
while those upstarts "who would relocate aimed to make themselves *indistinguishable* from their future peers," I would argue that, in the masque at least,
both groups desired to set themselves apart, if only to "fit in" more surely.[22]
Much contemporary writing around these performances (some of which I consider later in this chapter) bears out the way in which the masque functioned—
indeed, its purpose was—to isolate figures even as it integrated them into a
hierarchical social system or a political message. As Jean MacIntyre writes, the
idea "that a masking costume . . . *must still distinguish the noble wearer and occasion* from the model it was based on, was . . . growing even stronger in the
Jacobean period."[23]

The roots of this hermeneutic system are bound up with the unique relation
between private and public life at the Stuart court, a relation that underwrote
the network of patronage relations that made individual affiliations the driving
force of political and cultural activity. But they are also bound up with theatrical practice, with the institution of masking as a form of entertainment
organized around the deliberate hiding of a "real" person's—that is, not a stage
character's—identity. Enid Welsford has traced the development of the
masque to a variety of early English entertainments: mummings, tourneys,
and barriers, festivities of misrule at court. All of these various forms involved
dancers, jousters, or (mock) rulers who performed for audiences in disguise.[24]
But the disguises of mummings and tournaments were never simply arbitrary;
the ground and the efficacy of the disguise *depended on* an assumed relationship
between it and the identity of the wearer. Such a structure goes beyond basic
topicality; a masker or knight-at-arms assumed a persona that he both believed
and desired himself to be. So the point of the ceremonial disguise was the
adoption of a persona that bore a necessary relation to the masker's real or
desired identity. Indeed, according to Paul E. J. Hammer, the court ceremony
thrived on such identifications and distinctions. Discussing the second earl of
Essex's performance for Queen Elizabeth at the Accession Day festivities of
1595, he notes that "Essex's Accession Day entertainment also included a
number of . . . fleeting references which would have elicited flickers of recognition among the audience."[25] Such references, he explains, are part of the
larger situation of Elizabethan public occasions: "Because they had to pay so
much out of their own pockets, and because the chivalric mode placed so much

stress upon the individual, Elizabethan aristocrats could, and did, manipulate public entertainments for the sovereign to suit their own ambitions."[26]

Hammer further suggests that this kind of dramatic manipulation was reproduced at the Stuart court not in jousts or tourneys, the large-scale public entertainments of Elizabeth's period, but in the masque: "Under James I and Charles I, chivalric endeavour increasingly lost place in royal celebrations to the carefully scripted medium of the masque."[27] The masque, in such an account, becomes the locus in the Stuart period for the theatricalized allegories of identity that once dominated the Elizabethan tournament. These were displays that called attention to, were designed to reinforce, the identity of the performers they seemed to disguise and the patrons they were devised to honor. Masques depended on the audience's ability and desire to know who the masquers were; they depended as well on the audience's ability to recognize the specific auspices (like the "marriage and happy alliance between two such principal persons of the kingdom as are the Earl of Suffolk and the Earl of Somerset" declared by the 1614 *Masque of Flowers*) under which the masque was performed.[28] Jonson assumes this dependence in the published version of his *Masque of Queens* (1609), which he opens by insisting that "the Nobility of the Invention should be answerable to the dignity of they[r] [Queen Anne and her ladies] persons," and which he closes by admitting, "I know no worthyer way of *Epilogue*, then the celebration of Who were the *Celebraters*."[29] He then lists the queen and her ladies, including the countesses of Arundel, Derby, Huntingdon, Bedford, and Essex. In his earlier *Masque of Blackness* (performed 1605, published 1608), he decorated his aristocratic and royal performers with two fans, "in one of which were inscribed their mixt *Names*, in the other a mute *Hieroglyphick*, expressing their mixed quallities. Which manner of *Symbole* I rather chose, then *Imprese*, as well for strangeness, as relishing of antiquity."[30] Much scholarship of the masque has focused on the way it was designed to pay homage to King James or other patrons; what emerges here in Jonson's ending is another purpose of the masque: to orchestrate an elaborate interaction between dancers and audience so that both groups participate in a revelation of numerous identities in addition to the monarch's. At stake in such identifications is the public reinforcement, for both participant and viewer, of social positioning. But because of the unique overlap of the personal and political in Stuart culture, such positioning relied on a moment of individual recognition and distinction. It is this moment, I am suggesting, that characterizes the hermeneutics of identification in which masque-goers would have been trained. As Bourdieu suggests, even "social identity is defined and asserted through difference."[31]

Jonson's "celebration of the Celebraters," his definition through difference and distinction, is part of a published version of the revel. But the strategy should be seen to echo, in one of the only ways available in print, the dynamic of revelation or identification that organized the Stuart masque; here it simply extends the dynamic to a reading audience. Although recent scholarship has cautioned us to be suspicious of Jonson as the only voice representing a theory of the masque, other impressions or accounts of the masques call attention to this interpretive emphasis.[32] In a letter dated December 1614, John Chamberlain reports to Dudley Carleton that "for all this penurious world we fpeake of a mafke this Christmas toward wch the K. geues 1500 £ the principall motiue wherof is thought to be the gracing of younge [George] Villers and to bring him on the stage."[33] Villiers was again the object of attention in 1618, when he appealed to a petulant king during *Pleasure Reconciled to Virtue*. The Venetian ambassador at the time notes:

> After [the cavaliers] had made an obeisance to his Majesty, they began to dance in very good time, preserving for a while the same pyramidical figure, and with a variety of steps. Afterwards they changed places with each other in various ways, but ever ending the jump together. When this was over, each took his lady, the prince pairing with the principal one among those who were ranged in a row ready to dance, and the others doing the like in succession, all making obeisance to his Majesty first and then to each other. They performed every sort of ballet and dance. . . . Last of all they danced the Spanish dance, one at a time, each with his lady, and being well nigh tired they began to lag, whereupon the king, who is naturally choleric, got impatient and shouted aloud: "Why don't they dance? What did they make me come here for? Devil take you all, dance." Upon this, the Marquis of Buckingham, his Majesty's favourite, immediately sprang forward, cutting a score of lofty and very minute capers, with so much grace and agility that he not only appeased the ire of his angry lord, but rendered himself the admiration and delight of everybody.[34]

Other court correspondence notes the role of Charles, duke of York, alongside noble daughters in the 1610 performance of *Oberon* before enumerating the more established performers:

> The next day [after the creation of Henry Prince of Wales] was graced with a most glorious *Maske*, which was double. In the first, came first in the little Duke of *Yorke* between *two great Sea slaves*, the cheefest of *Neptune*'s Servants, attended upon by *twelve little Ladies*, all of them the Daughters of Earls or Barons. . . . These light Skirmishers having done their *devoir*, in came *the Princesses*; first the *Queen*, next the *Lady Elizabeth*'s Grace, then the

Lady *Arabella*, the Countesses of *Arundell, Derby, Essex, Dorset*, and *Mont-gomery*, the Lady *Hadington*, the Lady *Elizabeth Grey*, the Lady *Windsor*, the Lady *Katherine Peter*, the Lady *Elizabeth Guilford*, and the Lady *Mary Win-tour*.[35]

While this letter focuses on the ladies, the Venetian ambassador remarks the prince himself: "On Tuesday the Prince gave his Masque, which was very beautiful throughout, very decorative, but most remarkable for the grace of the Prince's every movement."[36]

Nor was it only Jonsonian masques that capitalized on this principle of distinguishing participants. Campion's *Lord Hay's Masque*, performed in 1607 for the marriage of Lord Hay and Susan de Vere, accounts first for the scene of the masque, and then for the performers: "From thence let us come to the persons. The masquers' names were these, whom both for order and honour I mention in the first place."[37] Campion then lists the lords who danced in the masque. Even "country house" masques, whose politics and political align-ments may have been quite different from those at court, rely on the discrete identities of participants to generate plot and theme.[38] Marston's masque for the earl of Huntingdon, for instance, which begins with a performance before the gate of the estate, calls attention to the guest of honor, the dowager count-ess of Derby, as its motivating principle: she melts the frost of winter that has paralyzed the estate:

> Pace then no further, for vouchsafe to know,
> 'Till her approach here can no comfort grow;
> 'Tis onely one can ther sad bondage breake,
> Whose worth I may admire, not dare speak;
> She's so compleat, that her much honored state,
> Gives Fortune Virtue, makes Virtue fortunate.
> As one in whome three rare mixt virtues set,
> Sene seldom joyned, Fortune, Beauty, Witt;
> To this choice Lady and to her dere State;
> All hearts do open, as alone this gate
> . . . .
> Peace! Stay, it is, it is, it is even shee,
> Hayle happye honours of Nobilitye!"[39]

Once the masque proper begins indoors, an even larger audience—the suppos-edly glamorous and noble women—are regarded as "stars that in yon valley glister."[40] Here the audience, rather than the performer, is called out and distinguished. Of course, this principle operated in earlier revels, usually in the integration of Queen Elizabeth into her ceremonial occasions. Philip Sid-ney's *Lady of May* invited the queen to choose between two suitors at the end of a debate; and the conceit of George Peele's court play *The Arraignment of Paris*, as John Astington notes, "is that in the beauty contest of the goddesses which launched the Trojan War the prize of the golden apple was wrongly awarded, and that in 1584 it should rightly be given to the great queen of England, as indeed it was at the end of the performance. The queen's presence is necessary to make the combined denouement and compliment work, and thus the play as it was published is a court play like no other, especially designed in the writing to connect the performance with the central member of the audience." But it is precisely this mechanism that Astington associates with the Jacobean era: "The staging of [this] play resembles the unique, particular character of the Stuart masques.[41]

Part of what Astington recognizes as distinctly Stuart in the role of the audience is determined not only by our knowledge of Stuart masque texts but also by our knowledge of their contexts: the ambassadorial altercations over masque attendance which testify not simply to the diplomatic status of the masque, but to the importance of the personal recognition of an ambassador— a recognition that established and announced his political significance. As the editors of the collected *Ben Jonson* note in their commentary on the masque, "The competition of foreign ambassadors to secure precedence at these Court exhibitions obtrudes itself into the history of the masque."[42]

If the history of the masque is, in some sense, a history of its behind-the-scenes controversies—and also of its reception or "after-life"—it is essential to note that these controversies involved nice distinctions between ambassadors and between countries that would or would not attend or be placed together at a performance. In particular, the Jacobean court took especial care never to pair the French and Spanish ambassadors. Nicolò Molin, the Venetian ambassador in 1605, thus reports that "at Court they are studying how the Ambassadors can be present at the festival. But as the King declines to make any decision as to precedence between France and Spain, it is held certain that no Ambassador will be invited."[43]

The official way around this dilemma seems to have been to invite ambassadors in their "private," rather than their "public," capacities. But this strategy hardly held up. As Molin records, for the masque celebrating the creation of the duke of York in 1605, the Spanish ambassador appealed for public recognition as soon as he discovered that the French representative was ill:

> The morning of that day, the Chamberlain sent to say that if I cared to see the Queen's masque that evening he would secure a convenient seat for

myself and three or four of my suite. He explained that all the Ambassadors were being invited privately, so as to avoid quarrels for precedence. I said I would gladly attend. Meantime the Spanish Ambassador hearing that the French Ambassador was confined to his bed made vigorous representations at Court to secure for himself a public invitation; and he succeeded. Sir Lowis Lewkener [sic] presently went to visit the French Ambassador, who . . . received Lewkenor very haughtily. Lewkenor said he had come on behalf of his Majesty to enquire how the Ambassador was, and to say how much his Majesty regretted that the Ambassador would be prevented from attending the Queen's masque. The Ambassador burst into a fury and said he knew what was going on and that it was all the work of seven or eight officials, of whom Lewkenor was the chief, whose sole object was to discredit the French and aggrandise the Spanish Ambassador.[44]

Such vying for precedence had real effects on the royal masques: Jonson's 1608 masque for the marriage of Viscount Hadington, for instance, had to be postponed, according to Chamberlain, until Candlemas in order to ensure that the Spanish ambassador would be absent and that the French ambassador, Monsieur de La Boderie, could attend.[45] Indeed, this occasion reached as far as the French king, Henry IV, who "had instructed La Boderie on 23 December 1608 that, if the slight of the previous year was likely to be repeated, he was to leave a secretary in charge of the embassy and quit London."[46] The especially hectic celebrations surrounding the marriage of the Princess Elizabeth and the Count Palatine also involved scuffles that John Finet, master of ceremonies for both James and Charles I, records in *Finetti Philoxenis*. Having invited the ambassador from the Low Countries to the second or third of the three marriage masques, Finet and the Lord Chamberlain he served faced a rejection: "The Invitation hee now had, was in a second place to one [the Venetian ambassador] who was farr from all colour of reason to precede him; that his majesty had herein expressed his affection; that he was sorry he could not be there." Finet's memoirs record further quarreling over place as well as precedence. While the Spanish ambassador, according to Finet, did not object in 1615 to attending a Twelfth Night masque with the States ambassador, he resented the latter's public placement near the king, letting it be known that if Noël Caron "should be togeather with him [the Spanish ambassador] at Supper or in any other place, then in the Kings presence, he would use him with all the respects of civility, but in so honourable a place as that, where the sacred persons of the King, Queene and Prince were to be present, he should never with patience see the Representant of his Masters Vassalls and Rebels (so he called them) hold an equall ranck with him."[47]

The Spanish ambassador's qualms here, like those of the other ambassadors, derive from a brand of political competitiveness that translated into the assigning of precedence to (the distinguishing of) nations by the treatment of their individual representatives at the masque. This treatment might be seen to crystallize *in parvo* the broader interpretive system I have been describing, which relied on an audience's ability or desire to attach a real identity to a staged presence (and the ambassadors, as Finet's account of the Spanish ambassador suggests, did see themselves as being "on stage" when they attended masque performances). For aristocratic performers, the masque was an opportunity for personal display designed, if the performance ran properly, to incorporate them into a status group and simultaneously make their singular identity more visible within that group. They extended this opportunity to their peers when they "took them out" to dance at the end of the performance in a moment that, staged as it was on the dancing space directly in front of the king, offered up members of the audience for special recognition. For ambassadors, the structure of identification was slightly different: their recognition as individuals always involved relating them to their home country. Nevertheless, like the masquers and those they took out to dance (and ambassadors could be among those so taken out), the ambassadors fussed over the masque because they realized it to be an opportunity for being acknowledged, recognized, identified.[48] Such recognition was both an objective and an object of mockery when it took place at the professional theaters. Thomas Dekker, for instance, parodies a gallant who insists on sitting on the stage at Paul's so that he can be noticed by others, suggesting both the commonness of the practice and his particular contempt for it: "By spreading your body on the stage, and by being a Justice in examining of plaies, you shall put your selfe into such true Scaenicall authority that some Poet shall not dare to present his Muse rudely vpon your eyes, without hauing first vnmaskt her, rifled her, and discouered all her bare and most mysticall parts before you at a Tauerne."[49] But, as accounts of the ambassadors' wrangling suggest, earning such notice—being recognized, being distinguished—was precisely the point of the masque.

HERMENEUTICS OF AUTHORSHIP

This hermeneutic ground should be seen as part of the context influencing not only the form and content of the masque, but also ideas about and practices of its authorship. Such ideas and practices have been the focus of recent critical concern. Drawing from literary theory as well as the remarks of Elizabethan and Stuart contemporaries, scholars have suggested that the fundamentally participatory nature of the masque—the way it involved, as Timothy Raylor sums up, "designers, poets, painters, choreographers, musicians, and performers"—as well as the relatively insignificant place of written or spoken text in comparison to scenic, musical, and costume display, should challenge any priority granted to the writer of the masque text.[50] As Paul Hammer asks in reference to the 1595 Accession Day shows, "Who, as it were, 'owned' such occasions as this? Whose agenda was being pursued—the author's or that of the aristocrat who employed the author, or both? Indeed, what does authorship actually mean in this context?"[51] Such a line of questioning is validated by contemporary commentary, which often pays more attention to the financiers than the writers of the masques. John Chamberlain, for instance, calls Sir Francis Bacon, who financed *The Masque of the Inner Temple and Gray's Inn* (1613), the show's "chief contriver" rather than the person who formulated the script, Francis Beaumont.[52]

But if writers of Jacobean court masques—a group consisting, during James's reign, primarily of Jonson, Daniel, Campion, and occasionally Chapman and Beaumont—were not the "chief contrivers" of the pieces, and if Inn and university revels were customarily the work of multiple hands, the position of Jacobean court masque writer should not be assumed to be immune to the pervasive notions of distinction and precedence characterizing the masque culture in which it functioned.[53] Indeed, the fact that masque writers were often specifically commissioned by an aristocratic or royal patron, as Daniel's and Jonson's dedications attest, seems to accord masque writing a particular mark of distinction.[54] Patronage of the masque writer, a cog in the wheel of the larger system of patronage that undergirded the masque's hermeneutic investments in personal recognition, sustained a notion of the individual and identifiable writer, even if that individual was ultimately identifiable by only a small set of people. Ideas of masque authorship, whether of the "masque-in-performance" or the resultant published text, were oriented by this larger set of hermeneutic principles that insisted on the *singularity*, if not the *priority*, of the writer.[55] Indeed, strategies of identification mark masque texts and commentary so that they work to single out masque writers even if, or as, they accord greater significance to architects, musicians, or performers. The fact that the published version of Beaumont's *Masque of the Inner Temple and Gray's Inn* issued a cancel to eliminate his name from the title page calls attention to a conscious effort not to be part of such strategies.[56]

Ben Jonson's productions make this case most clearly. The opening to his account of *Masque of Blackness*, for instance, pays homage to Queen Anne for devising the pageant's conceit: "Hence (because it was her Maiesties will, to haue them *Black-mores* at first) the inuention was deriued by me, & presented thus," Jonson writes. Having explained "the bodily part," he attributes it to "Maister Ynigo Jones his design, and act." He repeats such gestures in other masque accounts. In the published version of *The Masque of Queens* he mentions that "The device of their attire was Mr. Jones's with the invention and architecture of the whole scene and machine," and submits that "the author [of the dancing] was Mr. Thomas Giles" and that the lyrics to the last song of the masque "were the work and honor of my excellent friend Alfonso Ferrabosco."[57]

These references are part of a particularly Jonsonian model of self-fashioning, what critics have long considered Jonson's unique agenda for molding himself into a laureate: he champions himself by associating with a royal patron; he credits himself by giving credit to others.[58] But these strategies, reiterated as they are by other writers as well as viewers, are also part of the ambience of the masque, a genre that recognizes individual claims even as it privileges some over others. Thus, Jacobean letter writers note court approval of distinct persons associated with particular masques and measure participants against one another. John Chamberlain, for instance, writes to Dudley Carleton of *Time Vindicated* (1623): "They fay yt was performed reafonablie well both for the deuice, and for the handfome conueyance and varietie of the fcene whereof Innigo Jones hath the whole commendation. Ben Johnfon they fay is like to heare of yt on both fides of the head for perfonating George Withers a poet or poetaster as he termes him." And John Pory can address Sir John Cotton with news about *Hymenaei*: "I haue seen both the mask on Sunday and the barriers on Munday night. The bridegroom carried himself as grauely and gracefully as if he were of his fathers age. . . . But to returne to the maske; both Inigo, Ben, and the actors men and women did their partes wth great comendation. The conceipt or soule of the mask was Hymen bringing in a bride and Juno pronubas priest a bridegroome, proclaiming that those two should be sacrificed to Nuptial Union: and here the poet made an apostrophe to the union of kingdomes. But before the sacrifice could be performed, Ben Jonson burned the globe of the erth standing behind the altar."[59] Such comparisons of select participants is echoed at a broader level in comments that evaluate one performance against another, reinforcing the fundamentally competitive sensibility of the masque. Sir Edward Phelips, for instance, judged among the three masques presented for Princess Elizabeth's wedding, noting that "the Masques of the Middle Temple and Lincoln's Inn were praised above all others."[60] Phelips does not mention the writer (George Chapman) of the Middle Temple and Lincoln's Inn masque, but his thinking demonstrates the way masques prompted from their audiences activities of judging, comparing, distinguishing.

So when Samuel Daniel, for instance, is circumspect about the limitations of masque authorship, deliberately minimizing his own role in *Tethys' Festival* and attributing the show to Inigo Jones ("in these things wherein the only life consists in show, the art and invention of the architect gives the greatest grace, and is of most importance, ours the least part and of least note in the time of the performance thereof; and therefore I have interserted the description of the artificial part, which only speaks Master Inigo Jones"), his circumspection works to reinforce categories and modes of distinction.[61] The only difference here is that he distinguishes Jones, rather than himself, for notice. Such distinctions may have been anathema to Daniel, who rails against "singularity" in his *Defence of Ryme*: "Next to this deformitie [self-love] stands our affectation, wherein we always bewray our selues to be both vnkinde, and vnnaturall to our owne natiue language, in disguising or forging strange or vnvsuall wordes, as if it were to make our verse seeme an other kind of speach out of the course of our vsuall practise, displacing our wordes, or inuesting new, onely vpon a singularitie."[62] But they are part of an interpretive sensibility associated with the masque, and they made the position of masque writer, if not the originary fount of the show's invention, a distinct type of undertaking. George Chapman, for instance, defines his undertaking in terms of the occasionality of his *Memorable Masque*:

> To answer certain insolent objections made against the length of my speeches and narrations: being, for the probability of all accidents rising from the invention of this masque, and their application to the persons and places for whom and by whom it was presented, not convenient, but necessary, I am enforced to affirm this: that, as there is no poem nor oration so general but hath his one particular proposition . . . so all these courtly and honouring inventions . . . should expressively arise out of the places and persons for and by whom they are presented.[63]

Campion's message to the reader at the close of the printed version of *The Lord Hay's Masque* also considers the experience of writing for masque performance, particularly its relation to a female audience and its limited generic scope:

> Neither buskin now, nor bays
> Challenge I; a lady's praise
> Shall content my proudest hope;

> Their applause was all my scope,
> And to their shrines properly
> Revels dedicated be:
> Whose soft ears none ought to pierce
> But with smooth and gentle verse.
> Let the tragic poem swell
> Raising raging fiends from hell,
> And let epic dactyls range,
> Swelling seas and countries strange.
> Little room small things contains,
> Easy praise quites easy pains.
> Suffer them whose brows do sweat
> To gain honour by the great;
> It's enough if men me name
> A retailer of such fame.[64]

Campion's address was not part of the performance, but it voices, if after the fact, an understanding of the humble but individualized position of the masque writer, an understanding that precedes the text.

The behavior of the Merchant Taylors, when they were to host the royal family (in the end, only king and prince attended) at their hall in 1608, can serve as a final testimony to the position of the masque writer at this time. The company consciously chose and asked Ben Jonson to devise a performance for the special occasion rather than leaving it to volunteers already associated with the eponymous grammar school. Minutes record that

> whereas the Company are informed that the King's most excellent Majesty, with our gratious Queen and the noble Prince, and divers honourable Lords and others, determyne to dine at our hall on th'elecc'on of M'r and Wardens; therefore this meeting was appointed to advise and consult howe every thinge may be performed for the reputac'on and creditt of the Company, and to give his Majesty best lykeing and contentment, &c. &c. And Sir John Swynnerton is entreated to conferr with Beniamyn Johnson, the Poet, about a Speech to be made to welcome his Majesty, and for Musique and other inventions, which may give liking and delight to his Majesty; by reason that the Company doubt that their Scholemaster and Schollers be not acquainted with suche kind of Entertagnements.[65]

The Merchant Taylors, in competition for royal attention with the Clothworkers' Company, which had recently feasted the king and prince, want to duplicate as closely as possible the scene of the court, and they imagine that they can do this by hiring "the Poet" with whom they associate the genre.[66] Of course they hired others to assist in the various elements of the lavish performance, and of course their striving was in the service of company recognition before the king. But the point here is that as far as contemporaries were concerned, masque or revels writing was a distinct position occupied by particular and identifiable individuals.

Like the other examples, then, the Merchant Taylors' employment of Jonson suggests that the position of masque writer occupied a distinct or distinguished, if not what is considered today "authoritative," status; it was recognized for its role in offering a unique and structuring element to the performance. This may help explain why masques were rarely composed by more than one writer. There is relatively little manuscript or published evidence of joint work between multiple writers on masques.[67] There is the *Masque of Flowers*, whose dedicatory letter to Sir Francis Bacon is signed with the initials I.G., W.D., and T.B. (initials that may simply reflect the men in charge of publication, not necessarily writers), and Thomas Middleton and William Rowley's 1620 *Courtly Masque: The Device Called the World Tossed at Tennis* (which was never actually performed as a masque at court). But in general, collaborative writing, though certainly not "collaborative production" broadly construed, for a court masque was at the very least an anomaly. I would suggest that this fact of masque authorship is so not only because masques were usually brief, but also because masques operated within a culture of privileged identification, a culture that recognized distinct contributors among its range of designers: the musicians, the architect, the dancers themselves. Preserving the singularity of the writer, no matter how much the writing would have been subordinated to other concerns, seems to have been an assumption of most, if not all, masque creation in the Stuart period. There exists evidence from guild records that during James's reign, professional dramatists competed to write the yearly Lord Mayor pageants, but there was no sharing of scripts for these festive displays.[68] Writers of masques, the recipients of royal or aristocratic patronage, may not have "competed" with one another in exactly the same way as pageant writers, but their reliance on a sponsor is part of a similar principle of picking and choosing. Even if the masque writer was subjected to the plans of other performers or participants, he was part of an aesthetic agenda devoted to establishing or singling out the individual. John Fletcher acknowledges and mocks this agenda in what Samuel Tannenbaum believes was a poem commissioned from him by the countess of Huntingdon, when he says he won't write of

> whether ytt be true
> Wee shall haue warrs w^th *Spaine*: (I wold wee might:)
> Nor whoe shall daunce I'th *maske; nor whoe shall write*

Those braue things done): nor summe up the Expence;
Nor whether ytt be paid for ten yeere hence.[69]

Such mocking suggests that Fletcher was alert to the potential effects of
masque culture and its emphasis on a particular species of individuation. Indeed, insofar as public playwrights participated in court theatricals as either
writers, performers, or observers, they were regularly exposed not only to the
material demands of masque presentation but also to the competing interests
and investments of theatrical production organized by a specific and highly
regulated set of hermeneutic principles. They interrogate these interests on the
professional stage. In what follows, then, I look at the particular ways in which
Beaumont and Fletcher, the period's most recognized collaborative team, as
well as Fletcher and Shakespeare mount critiques of court drama in their plays'
inset masques. Of course, a variety of plays, including those scripted by single
dramatists, employ inset masques, some of which can also be shown to critique
both the genre itself and the "individualizing" elements I have associated with
it. I am not arguing, therefore, that concern with the politics of the court
masque is limited to collaborating dramatists or is made visible in their plays
alone. I am suggesting only that it is important to see how the collaborative
activities of these particular playwrights, at this particular point in time, respond directly to a prevalent Jacobean aesthetic that affected dramatic writers
whether they were working in groups or on their own. Their response, in other
words, foregrounds a key difference between the production of professional
plays and court masques, and thus demonstrates their awareness not only of
the motives and methods of the court masque but also of its hermeneutic
situation. Writing together may not itself have been an intentional critique of
the court masque on the part of Fletcher, Beaumont, or Shakespeare (although,
as we have seen, Fletcher's letter to the countess certainly suggests that he is
suspicious about the form). But the very fact of joint writing clearly highlights
the kinds of challenges plays such as *The Maid's Tragedy* and *The Two Noble
Kinsmen* level at the individualizing tendencies of masque hermeneutics. In
what follows, I examine the inset masquing in these plays and discuss how
they confront the hermeneutics of identification and the discriminations that
masquing culture demands.

THE MAID'S TRADEGY

Beaumont and Fletcher are perhaps the best-known collaborative team the
English Renaissance produced; indeed, if some of their commenders are to be
believed, they were more a pair than they were individuals. Many of the

opening tributes to them in the 1647 folio anthology of their (previously unpublished) works attest to a mutually close relationship whose emotional valence is inextricable from its professional one. In his stationer's address to the reader, Humphrey Moseley remarks that he chose to publish all their works, and not just Fletcher's alone, because, since they were "never parted while they lived, I conceived it not equitable to seperate their ashes."[70] Jasper Mayne notes that "you are / In fame, as well as Writings, both so knit, / That no man knowes where to divide your wit, / Much lesse your praise."[71] Perhaps the most famous account is John Aubrey's, from his *Brief Lives*, which offers a glimpse into the duo's domestic as well as writing arrangements: "There was a wonderfull consimility of phansey between [Beaumont] and Mr. John Fletcher, which caused that dearnesse of friendship between them. . . . They lived together on the Banke side, not far from the Play-house, both batchelors; lay together, had one Wench in the house between them, which they did so admire; the same cloathes and cloake, &c.; betweene them."[72]

Although a number of scholars have assessed this kind of collaborative work, offering reasons for the pair to join forces—their antipathy to the court or their shared experiences of dramatic failure and success[73]—Jeffrey Masten is the most thorough reader of the Beaumont and Fletcher pair and the implications of their relationship, particularly the way these writers may be seen to represent the homosocial energies driving and complicating dramatic and print production in the early modern period. Masten emphasizes the existence and shape of their friendship—in writing, housekeeping, dressing—even as he remains careful to note the contradictory models of authority and authorship such friendship generated. For Masten, as we have seen, the Beaumont and Fletcher pair represents a manifestation of joint writing that, ironically, signals the advent of proprietary authorship. My reading of the Beaumont and Fletcher collaboration contextualizes Masten's interest in their "proprietariness" by focusing on their joint work in relation to the politics and aesthetics of the masque. I focus on *The Maid's Tragedy*, whose full and fully integrated inset masque demonstrates the writers' shared interest in the form and its relationship to drama more generally.[74]

The Maid's Tragedy was the third in a series of theatrical successes by Beaumont and Fletcher for the King's Men.[75] The play owes its emotional and rhetorical effects to the compelling frisson of sex and absolutist politics colliding in a debate about the validity of regicide. It takes place in the court of Rhodes, where the king, to protect a liaison with the court lady Evadne, has arranged for her to marry Amintor, who is already betrothed to Aspatia, the daughter of a lord named Calianax. All four of these characters are dead by the play's close, and theirs as well as others' assorted deaths at the end of the play set *The Maid's Tragedy* against the playwrights' other comedies and tragicomedies.[76] But the significance of the play lies also in the way it integrates an elaborate wedding masque into the opening act. A number of critics have suggested that the imagery of this initial masque is consonant with, or prophetic of, the tragic trajectory of the play.[77] Most critics, like T. W. Craik in his introduction to the 1988 Revels edition of the play, have explained this prophetic effect as an aspect of dramatic irony, of the playwrights' ability to set their characters up to believe in their good fortune, only to have them haunted or destroyed by the very situations they believed would yield their success. I want to stress that certain elements of this irony are due specifically to the characters' inability to distinguish or discriminate—or, rather, to discriminate *correctly*—between the people and the circumstances with which they come in contact. This inability, observable specifically in characters' responses to masque situations, can be viewed as a dramatic impeachment of a culture or cultural form that operates according to interpretive strategies that rely on principles of distinction and identification.

A more general demystification of court revels begins at the outset of the play. The very first scene of the play thrusts us into masque preparations, as the Rhodesian courtiers discuss, with a mixture of skepticism and contempt, the future masque:

LYSIPPUS. Strato, thou hast some skill in poetry.
What thinkst thou of a masque, will it be well?

STRATO. As well as masques can be.

LYSIPPUS. As masques can be?

STRATO. Yes, they must commend their king, and speak in praise of the assembly, bless the bride and bridegroom in the person of some god: they're tied to rules of flattery.[78]

Strato's reading sees right through contemporary claims like Jonson's that the masque's "riches and magnificence in the outward celebration or show" also provided "high and hearty inventions to furnish the inward parts, and those grounded upon antiquity and solid learnings."[79] The point of the masque, he makes clear, is simply flattery. Strato's comment here goes by without remark; his view seems already apparent to the other characters. But even their knowledge of the crass purpose of the masque does not prevent or protect them from misinterpreting it. Indeed, the king, who understands the entertainments specifically along Strato's mercenary lines, is still foiled by the form.

It is the king who orders the revels for the evening of Amintor's wedding to Evadne, as the playwrights are careful to note: "The King my brother did it [married Amintor and Evadne] / To honour you," Lyssipus tells Melantius, "and these solemnities / Are at his charge" (1.1.78–80). And it is the king who steps in to resolve disputes about seating for the masque which arise because Calianax, who functions as a kind of master of ceremonies, is so upset about the betrayal of his daughter that he insults the favored soldier, Melantius. Calianax argues with Melantius over the placement of the latter's (female) guest. In short, the father of the scorned daughter attacks Melantius, the brother of the chosen bride: "Who placed the lady there, so near the presence of the King? . . . My lord, she must not sit there. . . . The place is kept for women of more worth" (1.2.66–69). The quarrel continues until the king himself intervenes. He is concerned not with discovering the motives or meanings of the debate but with reconciling the parties so that decorum can be observed and the festivities can proceed. "Melantius, thou art welcome, and my love is with thee still; but this is not a place to brabble in. Calianax, join hands," he tells them, adding quickly, "Begin the masque" (1.2.105–7). Such attention to patronage is part of the play's fidelity to the conditions of masque production and its function as homage and gift. But it also allows the dramatists to set up a scenario to show how little control the patron has over the entertainment he has ordered. In his eagerness to see a masque and to preserve its decorum, the king does not recognize the hostility brewing between Melantius and Calianax. Here the contexts of the masque exceed the interpretive capacities of its patron.

At this point the inset masque itself begins. Dominated by the characters Night and Cynthia, who order the release of the winds and sea gods to honor the married couple with songs and dance, the masque has been read by critics as an ironic "foil" to the rest of the play. Celebrating the wedding night, it both satirizes and foreshadows the doomed union of Amintor and Evadne. As Suzanne Gossett explains, "The masque by its very formality establishes a background contrast to the increasingly frenzied play."[80] But even the seeming thematic integrity of the masque in contrast to the "frenzied" play is undermined by the decline of poetic transcendence into personal dispute. Masque mythos is mocked, for instance, in the exchange between Cynthia and Night, when Night suggests that the moon

> shine at full, fair queen, and by the power
> Produce a birth, to crown this happy hour,
> Of nymphs and shepherds; let their songs discover,

Easy and sweet, who is a happy lover;
Or if thou woo't then call thine own Endymion
From the sweet flow'ry bed he lies upon,
On Latmos' top, thy pale beams drawn away,
And of his long night let him make this day.   (1.2.150–57)

Cynthia scolds in return:

Thou dream'st, dark queen; that fair boy was not mine,
Nor went I down to kiss him. Ease and wine
Have bred these bold tales; poets when they rage
Turn gods to men, and make an hour an age.
But I will give a greater state and glory,
And raise to time a nobler memory
Of what these lovers are.   (1.2.158–64)

Cynthia's suggestion that mythology is the drunken work of poets satirizes the elaborate iconography undergirding masque conceits and the authors who construct them. (Beaumont uses the same satiric ploy in his 1613 masque when he has Mercury and Iris quarrel with each other over their antimasque designs, and this scenario suggests that Beaumont may have taken these earlier suspicions articulated in his plays with him into the production of a real masque.)[81] In the masque of *The Maid's Tragedy*, the critique is extended when the masque's patron contradicts the explanation given by the show for the epithalamion. The sea deities sing three songs, all of which celebrate the nuptial night, calling for day to delay to give the wedded lovers more time in bed. The second song is the most explicit:

Hold back thy hours, dark Night, till we have done;
The Day will come too soon.
Young maids will curse thee if thou steal'st away,
And leav'st their blushes open to the day.
Stay, stay, and hide
The blushes of the bride.
Stay, gentle Night, and with thy darkness cover
The kisses of her lover.
Stay and confound her tears and her shrill cryings,
Her weak denials, vows, and often-dyings;
Stay and hide all,
But help not though she call.   (1.2.223–34)

The deities' epithalamic conceit, a variation on the purpose of the epithalamion outlined in Puttenham's *Arte of English Poesie*, is that the song prolongs the evening on behalf of the coupling couple (although this coupling sounds decisively uncomfortable and even violent).[82] But as soon as the masque closes, the king eagerly calls for "lights there; ladies, get the bride to bed" (1.2.283). His order suggests that the masque songs have actually been hindering, rather than helping, the bedding of bride and groom. The king, who claims the same interests as the masque does in helping the new couple to bed, betrays the fact that the two are really at cross-purposes. The supreme irony, revealed to the audience in the next scene, is that the king sends the couple off to bed with the full expectation that they will not sleep together. There will be no consummation of their marriage, for, as Evadne tells Amintor, she is the king's mistress, and she "sooner will find out the beds of snakes, / And with my youthful blood warm their cold flesh, / Letting them curl themselves about my limbs, / Than sleep one night with thee" (2.1.204–9).

By offering competing approaches to the epithalamion—one in the voice of the masque and the other in the voice of its patron, the king—the drama calls attention to the limitations on both play and ruler to determine absolutely the meaning of courtly display. Such competing approaches can be understood as the exposure of the frailties of masque distinction and distinguishing. The play continues to expose these frailties in a series of scenes that emphasize activities of differentiating or "singling out" associated with the masque.[83] These scenes are usually deeply ironic. Amintor, for instance, is told by the king and Evadne that he was chosen to serve as her cuckolded-before-the-fact husband because he is "honest" and "valiant." Here the playwrights mock any principle of courtly recognition: although receiving credit for virtuous qualities is usually desirable, here it only leads directly to Amintor's humiliation. And not only his humiliation but Aspatia's as well, as she spends the bulk of the play grieving for her lost love.

But the most important scene of royal failure to discriminate comes at the close of the play, when Evadne goes into the king's bedroom. For the better part of the play, Evadne has shown no remorse over her manipulation of Amintor and its consequences. Unlike her brother, Melantius, she is not disgusted by her role as the king's mistress; unlike Amintor, she is not horrified by her status as an adulteress. And she demonstrates no sympathy for the plight of Aspatia, the woman whose place she has taken as Amintor's bride. She is changed, however, by Melantius, who in the fourth act condemns her for spoiling her chastity and their good name. As Herbert Blau suggests is common in Fletcher's fictions, the play supplies no psychic drama to account for the recriminations that seize Evadne and precipitate her confession of guilt.[84] But the effects of her contrition are plain. They involve Evadne's repudiation of the king ("O, hear me gently! It was the King" [4.1.125]) and a concomitant estrangement from herself ("Mine own remembrance is a misery / Too mighty for me" [4.1.115–116])—which eventually lead her to beg for Amintor's forgiveness and to pledge to kill the king.

The justifications for regicide offered by Evadne and her brother are commonplace, compatible with various Stuart political theories in favor of political resistance even against a monarch.[85] But the strategy for it is stunning, and not only because Evadne may be the one woman in Renaissance drama who is actually witnessed stabbing a man (let alone a king). While the other rebels of Rhodes are occupying forts and battlements on the edges of the town, Evadne moves to a much more intimate battlefield, the king's bedroom. She pauses and renews her spirit before crossing the threshold, her thoughts turning bloodier than Hamlet's over Claudius:

> I must kill him,
> And I will do't bravely: the mere joy
> Tells me I merit in it. Yet I must not
> Thus tamely do it as he sleeps: that were
> To rock him to another world; my vengeance
> Shall take him waking, and then lay before him
> The number of his wrongs and punishments.
> I'll shape his sins like Furies till I waken
> His evil angel, his sick conscience
> And then I'll strike him dead.   (5.1.26–35)

The allusion to *Hamlet* is clear here.[86] What makes it especially interesting is the absence of a "mousetrap" scene to precipitate these thoughts. Evadne is not interested in a public demonstration staged by outside players to "catch the conscience" of the king. This may be simply because she already knows—she has been part of—the king's guilt, but it may also be because she herself executes a "mousetrap" at this juncture. I read her approach to and treatment of the king as just such a performance for the monarch, a "masque element" that dupes this king far better than Hamlet's duped Claudius. For the king of Rhodes misinterprets—cannot distinguish correctly—the implications of her exhibition. When he wakes to Evadne "t[ying] his arms to the bed," he takes the ropes as a sexual come-on that conforms to a mythical plot line:

> What pretty new device is this, Evadne?
> What, do you tie me to you? By my love,
> This is a quaint one. Come, my dear, and kiss me.
> I'll be thy Mars; to bed, my Queen of Love,
> Let us be caught together, that the gods may see
> And envy our embraces.   (5.1.47–52)

The king's term here, "pretty new device," paired with his allusion to Mars and Venus, suggests that he sees Evadne's antics as, among other things, a *masque*. The term "device" had multiple meanings in the Renaissance, from a scheme, plot, or ploy to a desire, will, or intention. It also had aesthetic definitions: it could be "a fancifully conceived design or figure" or "an emblematic figure or design, [especially] one borne or adopted by a particular person, family, etc., as a heraldic bearing, a cognizance," or "a fanciful, ingenious, or witty writing or expression, a 'conceit'" (*OED*). And finally, a device could be "something devised or fancifully invented for dramatic representation; 'a mask played by private persons,' or the like." The *OED* quotes Shakespeare's *Love's Labor's Lost* for this last meaning: "But I will forward with my deuice," says Armado (5.2.669). Stuart contemporaries seem to have used the term to refer both to the masque in its entirety, as Armado does (however ironically), and to its individual inventions or components. John Chamberlain invokes the latter connotation when he reports to Dudley Carleton that Jonson's *Golden Age Restored* "was so well liked and applauded that the king had yt represented again the sonday night after, in the very same manner, though neither in deuise nor shew was there any thing extraordinarie but only excellent dauncing."[87] This is J. Leeds Barroll's sense of the term when he explains that "early modern masques were visually organized according to a central motif that determined the scenery, costume, and even the figuration of the dances, this motif being termed the 'device.'"[88]

Whether the king in *The Maid's Tragedy* invokes the term to refer to a whole masque performance or to its organizing conceit, he makes clear here that he understands Evadne's approach as simultaneously a sexual game and a courtly show. Indeed, Evadne capitalizes on the proximity of masque display and erotic possibility.[89] The king, though, fails to identify the implications of Evadne's display. Although she insists on her murderous intent, she can convince the king of her radical purpose only after multiple testimonies:

> EVADNE. I know you have a surfeited foul body,
> And you must bleed.
> KING. Bleed!
> EVADNE. Ay, you shall bleed. Lie still, and if the devil
> Your lust will give you leave, repent. This steel
> Comes to redeem the honour that you stole,
> King, my fair name, which nothing but thy death
> Can answer to the world.
> KING. Thou dost not mean this, 'tis impossible;
> Thou art too sweet and gentle.

EVADNE. No, I am not,
I am as foul as thou art, and can number
As many such hells here.

. . . .

I am come to kill thee.   (5.1.57–83)

With almost comic blindness, the king continues to protest through several more cycles of debate, eventually invoking the divinity of kingship he has asserted at multiple points through the play. This time his claim has no effect:

KING. Hear, Evadne,
Thou soul of sweetness, hear! I am thy King.
EVADNE. Thou art my shame. Lie still; there's none about you
Within your cries; all promises of safety
Are but deluding dreams.
KING. Hold, Evadne!
I do command thee, hold!   (5.1.97–103)

It is at this point that Evadne topples the king's royal decree ("I do command thee"), and she does so by adopting the king's own language, the language of the device. She tells him: "I do not mean, sir, / To part so fairly with you; we must change / More of these love-tricks yet" (5.1.104–6). Evadne's use here of "love-tricks," her blending of sado-masochistic artifice with plans for murder, is part of a performance that is tied not to the rules of flattery but to the belief that the king will (mis)interpret it *as if it were*. Evadne capitalizes on the king's failure to determine or distinguish her behavior properly; she thus turns against the king the kind of display that earlier had enhanced his sovereignty.

Evadne further undermines the identificatory logic of her performance in the scene's climax, when she justifies each stab with which she assaults the king. She names Amintor and her brother Melantius as she delivers the first two stabs, but the third she claims for "the most wronged of women!" (5.1.111). In this last moment she confuses—or, more accurately, *refuses*—the precise identity of the third of the king's victims. She thus makes the end of the "performance" for the king, usually the most overdetermined moment in a masque or device, a moment of uncertainty.[90] Who is the "most wronged of women?" Of course, Evadne is doubtless thinking of herself, but it seems likely that the playwrights are gesturing equally to Aspatia, who was treated cruelly by the king and Amintor as well as Evadne. That Aspatia, disguised in the next scene as a soldier, is not recognized by her former lover Amintor, who eventually slays her in a duel, only emphasizes the uncertain status of the "most wronged of women." This final scene is a rewriting of Sidney's story of

Parthenia and Amphialus, and its divergences from the original are telling. In Sidney's story, the concealed Parthenia is killed by the murderer of her lover, Argalus; in *The Maid's Tragedy*, Aspatia is killed by her lover himself. Amintor's embodiment here of both love and destruction is more than a literalization of the Renaissance conceit joining sex and death; here it exacerbates again the play's emphasis on the failed distinctions on which court display relies.

THE TWO NOBLE KINSMEN

A similar version of failed identification is at the heart of another Fletcher collaboration, this time one with Shakespeare. Although authorial ascription for *The Two Noble Kinsman* has been the subject of some debate, there is now what Philip Finkelpearl calls "much corroboration" for taking as accurate the 1634 quarto edition that names both Fletcher and Shakespeare the authors of the play.[91] In my reading I follow Jonathan Hope's findings in *The Authorship of Shakespeare's Plays* as well as the assessments of Lois Potter in her introduction to the Arden edition, assuming with them, as with the publishers of the earliest quarto edition, that there are stylistic and thematic reasons for believing this play to have been the work of both Shakespeare and Fletcher.[92] Such reasons have also been linked to specific professional concerns. Some scholars, for instance, have suggested that Shakespeare, having retired to Stratford, was called on to join or "train" the younger Fletcher to take up his mantle as chief playwright of the King's Men, precisely when the company was sustaining financial hardships connected with the burning of the Globe.[93] I too am interested in the dramatists' professional concerns, but I base my reading of their collaboration and the resultant play on their engagement with the politics and poetics of the court masque. *The Two Noble Kinsmen*, I will show, works to subvert the notions of identification and distinction so essential to masque writing and interpreting. And the playwrights' joint work, whether or not demanded by financial exigencies, echoes and augments such a position.

The connection between *The Two Noble Kinsmen* and the masque has a specific topical basis: the 1613 marriage of Princess Elizabeth to the Elector Palatine. An event that generated a wide variety of ceremonial festivity, even against the melancholy backdrop of the recent death of Prince Henry, the wedding celebration included among other displays three different masques: Campion's *Lords' Masque*, Chapman's *Memorable Masque* (performed by members of Lincoln's Inn and the Middle Temple), and Beaumont's *Masque of the Inner Temple and Gray's Inn*.[94] Such designations and measures were essential to the three wedding masques with which the play associates itself. These masques certainly used typical ploys of singling out performers or audience members. Chapman, for instance, defended the length of the speeches as "rising from the invention of this masque, *and their application to the persons and places for whom and by whom it was presented*, not convenient, but necessary, I am enforced to affirm this: that, as there is no poem nor oration so general but hath his one particular proposition . . . *so all these courtly and honouring inventions . . . should expressively arise out of the places and persons for and by whom they are presented*."[95] But they were also involved—and understood by their audiences and benefactors to have been involved—in competing with one another for distinction in front of King James. John Chamberlain observed that the masque presented by the Middle Temple and Lincoln's Inn

> made fuch a gallant and glorious fhew that yt is highly commended. . . . [T]he twelue Mafkers wᵗʰ theyre torch-bearers and pages rode likewife vpon horfes exceedingly well trapped and furnished, befides a roufen litle boyes dreſt like babones that ferued for an antimafke (and they fay performed yt exceedingly well when they came to yt), and three open chariots drawn wᵗʰ foure horfes apeece that caried theyre muficians and other perfonages that had parts to fpeake, all wᶜʰ together wᵗʰ theyre trumpetters and other attendants were fo well fet out, that yt is generally held for the best fhew that hath been feen many a day. . . . [t]hemfelues and theyre deuifes (wᶜʰ fay were excellent) made fuch a glittering fhew that the king and all the companie were excedingly pleafed and fpecially wᵗʰ theyre dauncing, wᶜʰ was beyond all that hath been yet.[96]

Sir Edward Phelips, as we have seen, confirmed the evaluation when he said that "the Masques of the Middle Temple and Lincoln's Inn were praised above all others."[97] Francis Bacon, when the masque he had funded was postponed because James was too exhausted for more entertainment, complained that the decision would both ruin him and prevent the reception the men of Gray's Inn and the Inner Temple deserved. Chamberlain wrote to Carleton that the masquers, arriving by boat on the third day after the wedding,

> were receued at the priuie stayres: and great expectation theyre was that they shold euery way exceed theyre competitors that went before them both in deuife daintines of apparell and above all in dauncing (wherein they are held excellent) and esteemed far the properer men: but by what yll planet yt fell out I know not, they came home as they went wᵗʰ out doing anything. . . . [W]orst of all was that the king was fo wearied and fleepie wᵗʰ fitting vp almost two whole nights before that he had no edge to yt, whereupon Sʳ Fra: Bacon aduentured to interest his maiestie that by this disgrace he wold not as yt were bury them quicke and I heare the king fhold aunfwer that then they must burie him quicke. [98]

In *The Two Noble Kinsmen*, efforts at the kinds of preeminence that characterized the wedding masques only recoil on themselves (not unlike Bacon's).
Indeed, each masque element, as well as the trajectory of the play as a whole,
simultaneously effects and unravels precise designations of people or precise
measures of achievement. Donald Hedrick has discussed this phenomenon as
part of the play's presentation of "a spectacle of collaboration" between the two
kinsmen, Palamon and Arcite, whose paradoxically contentious friendship results in the dissolution of their sense of difference. Noting that their shared
rivalry, and their shared techniques for pursuing this rivalry, make them seem
more and more alike, Hedrick suggests that "the play reduces the consequen-
tiality of any differences" between the two.[99] In what follows, I trace first the
kinsmen's insistence on maintaining their differences and then the way their
"reduction" admits to a *meaninglessness* at the core of ceremonial distinction.

This dynamic of assertion and denial of distinction begins in the play's
second scene, when Palamon and Arcite appear on the outskirts of Thebes,
both anxious to leave behind the potentially corrupting effects of the city. The
scene introduces the audience to a world of tremulous differentiation. Discussing the city's threat to their nobility, Arcite notes:

> This is virtue
> Of no respect in Thebes. I spake of Thebes—
> How dangerous, if we will keep our honours,
> It is for our residing, where every evil
> Hath a good colour; where every seeming good's
> A certain evil.[100]

This confusion of good and evil, one that is not so much a conflict between
appearance and reality—a staple conundrum for the Renaissance stage—but a
conflict of dangerously interchangeable value systems, sets the tone for the rest
of the play. Called away to battle, Palamon and Arcite appear the next time on
hearses in Athens, where Theseus and others cannot determine whether they
are alive or dead ("Theseus: They are not dead?/Herald: Nor in a state of life"
[1.4.24–25]). From this moment on, Palamon and Arcite, although they do
prove themselves to be "in a state of life," inhabit liminal realms—prison,
woods, jousting arena—which give a local habitation to the characters' indistinction. For in these places they cannot help but mirror each other in various
desires: to escape (or not) from prison, to meet and have Emilia. Finkelpearl
notes that critics fault Fletcher for "failing to differentiate the protagonists,"
but that, he says, "is the point."[101]

For Finkelpearl, the point is a critique of an antiquated honor code that

turns these men into undifferentiable "automatons." But this is not the kinsmen's critique: they are devoted to a faith in their identifiable singularity. The
play goes to great lengths to dramatize this faith. Even before they go to fight,
Palamon asserts his uniqueness:

> What need I
> Affect another's gait, which is not catching
> Where there is faith, or to be fond upon
> Another's way of speech when by mine own
> I may be reasonably conceived, saved too,
> Speaking it truly?   (1.2.44–49).

Once in prison, of course, the two kinsmen plead for their closeness, emphasizing a mutuality which recent critics explain as an essential part of the courtly
homosocial dynamic. Resigning themselves to a future deprived of opportunities for military and amorous achievement, they take comfort in their relationship:

> Let's think this prison holy sanctuary,
> To keep us from corruption of worse men.
> We are young and yet desire the ways of honour,
> That liberty and common conversation,
> The poison of pure spirits, might, like women,
> Woo us to wander from. What worthy blessing
> Can be but our imaginations
> May make it ours? And here being this together,
> We are an endless mine to one another;
> We are one another's wife, ever begetting
> New births of love; we are father, friends, acquaintance.
> We are, in one another, families;
> I am your heir and you are mine.   (2.2.71–83)

The rhetoric here can be understood idealistically or ironically: as the epitome
of male closeness or as the exaggerated assertion of a relation that cannot
possibly exist; as the playwrights' endorsement of a male bonding vulnerable
only to the demands of marriage or as their exposure of a hyperbole that takes
only the appearance of Emilia to disrupt. Either way, the play demonstrates
that even this moment of "twinning" relies on the kinsmen's assertion of
personal recognition. Palamon responds to Arcite's hymn to their camaraderie
by simultaneously reinforcing it—"is there record of any two that loved /
Better than we do, Arcite?" (2.2.112–13), a claim to uniqueness even if it is
shared—and by asserting his *own* understanding of the speech:

> *I* find the court here—
> *I* am sure, a more content; and all those pleasures

> That woo the wills of men to vanity,
> *I* see through now and am sufficient
> To tell the world 'tis but a gaudy shadow
> ....
> Shall *I* say more? (2.2.99–111; emphasis added)

To which Arcite replies, finishing his cousin's line, "I would hear you still." The "I" here is not necessarily more primal or originary than their relationship; rather, the two categories reinforce each other. Both Palamon and Arcite are more themselves—more "I"—precisely because of their kinship.

The same dynamic is repeated when they first glimpse and claim Emilia, who has been wandering in the garden below their window. Palamon claims that he, having seen her first, deserves her, while Arcite insists on his right to love her because

> I will not as you do, to worship her
> As she is heavenly and a blessed goddess.
> I love her as a woman, to enjoy her:
> So both may love. (2.2.163–66)

Arcite suggests that because they love her differently, they are both entitled to her, a perfectly impossible solution. So although Arcite will suggest that he loves Emilia because Palamon loves Emilia, their verbal argument becomes a duel, a contest of proprietary rights:

> Yes, I love her
> And, if the lives of all my name lay on it,
> I must do so; I love her with my soul:
> If that will lose ye, farewell, Palamon.
> I say again,
> I love her and in loving her maintain
> I am as worthy and as free a lover,
> And have as just a title to her beauty
> As any Palamon. (2.2.176–84)

The introduction of Emilia thus forces Palamon and Arcite to assert their singularity ("I . . . I . . . I") in ways that, unlike in the earlier scene, undermine rather than reinforce the connection between kinship attachments and individual personality.

The repetition of this dynamic continues. Just as Arcite finishes this speech, for instance, a messenger arrives with an order from the king that will work to differentiate the two kinsmen: Theseus has decided to set Arcite free and banish him while he keeps Palamon in prison. Palamon and Arcite reinforce this effort at differentiation. Both men call attention to their dissimilarity when they envy the other (Palamon worries that Arcite will find a way to get back to Emilia; Arcite worries that Palamon remains close to her). Arcite even uses his new freedom as an opportunity to distinguish himself before Theseus' court. Concealed in a "poor disguise," he returns to the Athenian wedding games to wrestle:

> who knows
> Whether my brows may not be girt with garlands
> And happiness prefer me to a place,
> Where I may ever dwell in sight of her?   (2.3.81–85)

Arcite articulates the very point of noble display: to gain recognition through outstanding performance. The costume only enhances this accomplishment: whether Arcite's weeds match his recent emotional impoverishment or model the inverse of his noble birth, they only reinforce the singularity of his achievement—an achievement that is rewarded, in true ceremonial fashion, with the trophy of a woman. Indeed, the result—the awarding of recognition—rather than the wrestling event is portrayed here. Afterward, Arcite enters into Emilia's service, and both she and Pirithous, Theseus' dear friend, offer him a horse to ride in the afternoon.

Arcite's triumph here seems to reinforce the distinction that both he and Palamon have been vying for. They succeed in maintaining it even through the arming scene in the woods. Arcite meets the chained Palamon, who has been freed by the jailer's daughter, and he decorously agrees to feed and free his cousin before battling him. Palamon works to distinguish between them: he simultaneously insists that Emilia is his and complains that Arcite is made stronger for battle by his proximity to her; he also scoffs at Arcite's displays of nobility and military prowess. "The whole week's not fair," he tells Arcite, "If any day it rain" (3.1.65–66). In the jousting scene they compete to be maximally deferential: each checks to make sure the other is comfortable, and they offer to give up the best sword. As they arm each other in this intimate scene of courtly manners, they renew the former sense of personal assertion within communal bonds. Palamon tells Arcite: "Thou art mine aunt's son / And that blood we desire to shed is mutual, / In me thine and in thee mine" (3.6.94–96). They rely on this dynamic even when Theseus arrives and blasts both as "ignorant and mad malicious traitors" (3.6.133). Both Palamon and Arcite assert themselves in contrast to the other. Palamon speaks first:

> We are certainly both traitors, both despisers
> Of thee and of thy goodness. I am Palamon
> That cannot love thee, he that broke thy prison—

> Think well what he deserves—and this is Arcite:
> A bolder traitor never trod thy ground;
> A falser ne'er seemed friend. This is the man
> Was begged and banished.   (3.6.137–43)

Arcite answers similarly, emphasizing his unique status with superlatives:

> Where this man calls me traitor,
> Let me say thus much: if in love be treason,
> In service of so excellent a beauty,
> As I love most, and in that faith will perish,
> As I have brought my life here to confirm it,
> As I have served her truest, worthiest,
> As I dare kill this cousin that denies it,
> So let me be most traitor and yet please me.   (3.6.160–67)

This need for recognition is fully realized in the play's most telling requests, when Palamon asks Theseus that they both be killed, only Arcite first: "Let's die together, at one instant, Duke. / Only a little let him fall before me, / That I may tell my soul, he shall not have her" (3.6.177–79). There is something deeply moving as well as utterly ridiculous about this demand to die with someone but a little after, and it represents an emotional impact consonant with what the play's last two acts will demonstrate as the ultimate meaninglessness of the urge for distinction.

This demonstration depends on both Emilia's inability to choose between the two kinsmen and the fundamentally ambiguous manifestation of the will of the gods. After Hippolyta and Emilia plead for Theseus to spare the men, Theseus asks Emilia to decide which man can live. Emilia refuses: "I cannot sir; they are both too excellent" (3.6.286). Palamon and Arcite may have spent the better part of the play vying to distinguish their different interests in Emilia, but at this critical moment she *cannot choose*. It is not that she does not recognize their differences or that she does not recognize her options, however. In the next act Emilia appears alone, contemplating two pictures, and in her soliloquy she enumerates precisely the "difference of men." I quote at length:

> What a sweet face has Arcite! If wise Nature,
> With all her best endowments, all those beauties
> She sows into the births of noble bodies,
> Were here a mortal woman and had in her
> The coy denials of young maids, yet, doubtless,
> She would run mad for this man . . .
> . . . Palamon
> Is but his foil; to him, a mere dull shadow.
> . . . .

I am a fool, my reason is lost in me,
I have no choice, and I have lied so lewdly
That women ought to beat me. On my knees,
I ask thy pardon, Palamon: thou art alone
And only beautiful . . .
. . . .
I am sotted,
Utterly lost. My virgin's faith has fled me.
For if my brother but even now had asked me
Whether I loved, I had run mad for Arcite;
Now, if my sister, more for Palamon.
. . . .
What a mere child is Fancy,
That, having two fair gauds of equal sweetness,
Cannot distinguish, but must cry for both!
                              (4.2.7–54; emphasis added)

As Emilia says, although she can identify each character—she notices Arcite's liveliness, Palamon's melancholy—she cannot distinguish between them. Insofar as impressing Emilia, their primary audience, is *the* object of the men's ceremonial performances, their displays are rendered meaningless. It does not matter how much they have established unique personae; it does not matter how well Emilia can identify them and their different characteristics. It doesn't matter that she is being offered a choice. Their difference makes no difference.

If Emilia cannot choose between Palamon and Arcite, neither can the gods, to whom both she and the men appeal in the concluding scenes. Theseus has arranged an elaborate joust for the kinsmen, one modeled with medieval resonances but departing enough from Chaucer's original—which says that the winner either kills his opponent or drives him out of the lists—to signal its topical interest.[102] Theseus decrees that each man return with three compatriots; the teams will battle to see who can force whom to touch a pyramid structure. All members of the losing team will be executed.

In the majestic scene that precedes the battle, Palamon, Arcite, and Emilia make obeisance at the altar of the Greek god that matches each one's demeanor. The three appeals, all rhetorically voluptuous, mark a highly ritualized moment that again works to discriminate among the characters. Arcite's appeal to Mars smacks of his militancy; Palamon's to Venus reinforces his role as hopeless lover; and Emilia's to Diana, goddess of chastity, once again establishes her reluctance to choose between the men which may be part of a larger reluctance to marry. But despite the difference in their gods and their entreaties, all three characters finish their sacrifice by asking for the same thing: a sign that their prayers will be answered. All three receive it. That Palamon and Arcite both do is most important, because their prayers are mutually exclusive: both want to win the joust, both want to marry Emilia. They can't both receive signs foretelling victory. Nevertheless, Arcite hears the "clanging of armour, with a short thunder" (5.1.61), and Palamon is treated to music and fluttering doves, so each believes that he will be triumphant. The prayer scene thus renders the distinction even of winner and loser incoherent.

The play's outcome bears out the paradoxical oracle, proving them both simultaneously right and wrong. The unperformed joust, the offstage cries for which make it hard to tell who is winning, see-saws between the combatants. The audience is treated to a few moments of thinking Palamon the winner, but Arcite emerges the eventual conqueror. The military signal given him at the altar, in other words, is fulfilled. But in a miraculous turn of events, Palamon's sign is also, however impossibly, realized. During his triumphal parade through the city, which is once again hidden from view, Arcite's proud horse topples and crushes him. Mortally injured, he lives just long enough to stay the execution of his friend Palamon and bequeath to him his bride-to-be. His naming of Palamon as Emilia's husband is the play's ultimate irony and its ultimate demonstration of a failure of distinction. Despite their competing claims, despite the elaborate ceremony concerning their triumph and defeat, at the end of the day they have both won Emilia. But neither really has her, as her lugubrious final words make clear, since the memory of the dead victor will always compete with his living runner-up: "I'll close thine eyes, Prince; blessed souls be with thee. / Thou art a right good man and, while I love, / This day I give to tears" (5.4.96–98). Theseus closes the play by rationalizing the mutually prohibitive signals:

> The powerful Venus well hath graced her altar
> And given you your love. Our master Mars
> Hath vouched his oracle and to Arcite gave
> The grace of the contention. So the deities
> Have showed due justice.   (5.4.105–9)

Theseus makes sense of the outcome by distinguishing between Arcite's military and Palamon's amorous triumph. But the distinction here, in light of the events surrounding it, seems specious at best. Both Arcite and Palamon wanted both success in battle and Emilia; Arcite's victory makes no sense without her, and Palamon's possession of the latter is hardly valid without the former. Theseus tries here to distinguish between the two kinsmen and their separate victories, but the facts of the ending obscure the meaning of the distinction he draws.

One way of understanding the fulfillment of these contradictory oracles is in terms of what Stephen Orgel sees as the fundamental ambiguity of royal oratory. Looking specifically at *The Winter's Tale*, Orgel argues that playwrights at the time deliberately obfuscated their characters' proclamations in an effort to repeat an opaqueness or obscurity consistent with Jacobean political rhetoric.[103] Here, however, it appears as a continuation of the playwrights' response to the demands of a masque hermeneutic based on identification. Although there are mythological precedents for the realization of conflicting divine injunctions (Juno may rob Tiresias of sight, for example, but Jove rewards him with prophetic "foresight"), in *The Two Noble Kinsmen*, the fact that both Mars' and Venus' signs are fulfilled represents the final achievement of the meaninglessness of distinction. The gods also cannot choose. Indeed, the play suggests that those who do choose—like the jailer's daughter, who knows "the difference of men" between Palamon and Arcite and becomes crazy as a result—are plagued by this ability. The fact that she is cured only when her lover pretends to be someone else (a blurring of discrete personality) suggests that to make and be aware of distinctions, to notice and reward differences, is to go mad.

DIVIDED AND DISTINGUISHED WORLDS

The jailer's daughter, of course, is neither a typical masque watcher nor performer, and I do not want to suggest that the playwrights equate courtly masquing and the distinctions its interpretive principles reinforce with madness. But Beaumont, Fletcher, and Shakespeare are nevertheless concerned by what they observe in masquing culture, and we can observe their concern in these plays not only in the dramatic content but also in the collaborative condition of their dramatic writing. In other words, collaborative writing, in this particular instance, can be assessed in relation to the masque's interpretive demands and protocols.

The masque both depended on and served principles of rigid identification between persons on stage and their positions or value in a social world (even if those positions, as Frank Whigham makes clear, were somewhat elastic), a hermeneutic system that reflected and affected ways of thinking about all the elements of the performance. Renaissance public drama, by contrast, was committed to precisely the opposite assumption: the notion or belief that there was no absolute connection between characters on the stage and actual persons in the world. This is not to say that strategies of recognition and identification did not play an essential role in public or professional drama, nor is it to neglect the fact that some theater actors clearly exerted the force of their unique personalities both on and off stage.[104] And it is not to minimize the fact that Renaissance plays are saturated with topical references and allusions to "real" events and people, from historical kings to local craftsman to the playwrights or actors themselves. It is, however, to remind us that such kinds of topicality in the theater are necessarily contained by and maintained as theatrical illusion. As John Earle comments in *Micro-cosmographie* (1628), the player "pleases, the better hee counterfeits."[105] There was no such counterfeiting in masque display: at the level of moral identity, Queen Anne really *is*, or is asked to be thought of, as Juno. The mythic masque is intended to reveal and proclaim an aspect of the masquers' real or desired-to-be-real characters.

The important difference between the public drama and the court masque, then, registers at the level of their fictional status. Jean MacIntyre, for instance, points out that "unlike players, whose personal identities were normally replaced by the roles they played . . . maskers concealed personal individuality just enough to express the 'idea' they for the time embodied," and she adds that "because the resolution of masque conflict was asserted to depend on the 'divinity' of the king, and that same 'divinity' gave him his power in his actual kingdom, masques could not end with an epilogue to remind the audience that the masque was a theatrical illusion."[106] Although I have been downplaying the priority of the king in determining the reality of the masque, MacIntyre's point is relevant insofar as it suggests that the masque provided an allegorized "slice of life," a space for the stylized performance of political aspirations and designs. The popular stage insulated its fictions from these sorts of commitments. Its fictions remain fictions even when they glance, beneath the censor's gaze, at political matters.

This is precisely the notion of drama that Paul Yachnin believes rendered the early modern stage "powerless" (a powerlessness he sees as sometimes, ironically, enabling).[107] Powerless or not, it seems to be the notion of theater that Beaumont, Fletcher, and Shakespeare show themselves committed to, over and against the masque, in these particular collaborative enterprises. This commitment, and its materialization in their collaborative efforts, may or may not have been *intentional*, and I do not want to suggest that this was so in any strict sense. But I do want to conclude that they were *institutional*. This commitment and its collaborative effects represent responses to the growing institutional proximity, despite the hermeneutic divergence, of the professional theater and the Jacobean court masque around the time when the King's Men moved to their indoor theater. During this period specifically, the masque's formal development came to involve the employment of professional playwrights and players (in the antimasques); its social development involved the evolution, through the publication of masque accounts as well as through a variety of public displays that could precede exclusive performances, of an audience not restricted to a narrow court circle and familiar with a hermeneutic system at odds with the conditions of public theatricals.[108] At the same time, the King's Men inherited a clientele at the Blackfriars that, as Gossett has shown, were more intimate with alternative dramatic and interpretive schemes. How this situation was perceived by the dramatists, either consciously or unconsciously, will always remain just beyond our powers to reconstruct with absolute certainty. But it is impossible simply to accept, as Gossett, Lee Bliss, and others do, that the situation was understood only as an opportunity for the aesthetic experimentation involved in incorporating masques into the repertoire. The skepticism of the masque in plays like but not limited to *The Maid's Tragedy* and *The Two Noble Kinsmen* suggests otherwise. My reading of these plays' presentation of the court masque implies that dramatists may have harbored doubts and concerns about not only the interpretive engagements of the masque, but also the viability of professional drama alongside it—insofar as "alongside" has both geographic and hermeneutic connotations. It is the environmental closeness of the professional drama and the court masque, in the face of their interpretive incongruity, that underwrites the activity of Beaumont, Fletcher, and Shakespeare in these collaborative plays.

FOUR

The Changeling and the Perversion of Fellowship

In the previous chapter I considered ways of understanding the various meanings of collaborative work by Beaumont, Fletcher, and Shakespeare. My specifically institutional focus on the implications for the playwrights of the court masque differed from the tendency among critics to discuss these dramatists' joint efforts, particularly those of Beaumont and Fletcher, in relation to their purported friendship, measured in terms of the pair's domestic arrangements, political affiliations, or shared social status.

The ideas and ideals of friendship these critics present, however, are central to thinking about collaborative work for the stage. In this chapter I consider the possibilities for playwright friendships as they are embodied in the joint work of Thomas Middleton and William Rowley. I identify in these two playwrights' patterns of collaborative activity a species of friendship, and discuss how their relationship, because of its affinities with professional *fellowship*, may have differed from the typically "gentlemanly" one posed for Beaumont and Fletcher. I begin with a discussion of the theatrical environment, and the concept of fellowship it supported, which was the context for Middleton and Rowley's joint work, and continue by examining their relationship in terms of its affinities (and differences) with early modern discourses of friendship. These affinities and differences point to a special relation which, though unavailable in some form of "transparent" documentation, can be understood to manifest itself in a striking ability to share language. Finally, I read the playwrights' most masterly work, *The Changeling* (1622), in terms of this relation, using it to illuminate the verbal dynamics of the play.

These verbal dynamics have, of course, been a source of fascination for a variety of scholars who have noted how the play translates into a vocabulary of sexual and social transgression several religio-political anxieties linked to the political frictions of the early 1620s.[1] In his essay "Hidden Malady," for instance, Michael Neill discusses the play's "abolition of social distinction" and "collapsing of differences," which in turn reveal the "formlessness of human identity" and the "bestial chaos" of sexual desire.[2] Writing from a different perspective, Annabel Patterson has suggested that *The Changeling* is a "toxic brew of domestic violence, sexual obsession, and madness" in which Middleton and Rowley deliberately "disrupt evaluative reflexes."[3]

I suggest the play's verbal as well as socio-psychological power, its ability to serve as a critique not only of the way people behave but also of the way they think, in light of its collaborative production. By considering the play's composition by two writers working together as friends, I show how Middleton and Rowley depict in *The Changeling* the impossibility of friendship at court through the *inversion* of friendship values for both different and same-sex couples, and how this inversion is represented as the *perversion* of linguistic exchange from the amicable sharing of texts and self into the malignant inhabiting of minds and consciences. At the play's most frightening, some of its characters, rather than respecting the mysterious mutuality of friendship ideology's idealized experience of "one soul in bodies twain," seek to inhabit one another's wills, to control and direct one another's pleasure.

The success of this program is expressed in the density of the play's verbal innuendo, the way the play, as Christopher Ricks has explained, capitalized on "a group of words each of which has two meanings, one of them sexual; at the beginning of the play, the two meanings are distinct; by its end, they have become inextricable."[4] Such a trajectory of punning represents a special brand of dramatic irony: the *characters'* experience of interpersonal misprision is the exact opposite the *playwrights'* experience of ideal verbal exchange.

A CRY OF PLAYERS

Middleton and Rowley's verbal exchange begins in a larger theatrical context. The theater environment that the dramatists inhabited at the time of their collaborations—approximately the latter half of James's reign—saw its fair share of contention: the brawls between Philip Henslowe and Lady Elizabeth's company testify to the prickliness and competitiveness of the industry, and the attack by apprentices on the Cockpit on Shrove Tuesday, 1617, testifies to the emotional intensities and attachments associated with the public theater. But it was also a milieu that was experiencing a period of stability in spite of company realignments.[5] By the second decade of the 1600s, according to Andrew Gurr, "the companies were developing a settled way of life" that contributed to the "stability and financial security that investment in playhouses . . . clearly offered"; playwriting, playacting, and playgoing at this time had become "standard daily activities and were slowly becoming more socially respectable."[6]

It is this environment that T. W. Baldwin may have been invoking long ago when he compared the theater community with those of the early modern London livery companies: "It was of course a natural thing for these actors to be . . . closely connected with each other. The guild system emphasized and fostered the clan spirit . . . This business was founded, especially in Shakespeare's day, both in theory and in practice on a closely knit, self-propagating society of friends, whose whole aim in life was to make their mystery a success."[7] Baldwin's transparent notion of the "friendliness" fostered by the "clan spirit" (whether for the theater or for guilds more generally) today seems naïve, especially given what is known of volatile feuding over the very "business" elements that Baldwin considers the basis of positive emotional bonds.[8] Rather, the contours of such professional relationships would have been multiple and contradictory, involving conflict and hostility as well as a "clan spirit." More nuanced sociological treatments of London business circles, including the theater community as well as different guilds, have emphasized these diverse contours.[9] These contours are also observable in the language of the playwrights and players themselves, a language or terminology not given substantial consideration in various histories of Renaissance drama, including the exceptionally precise introduction to the theater community in E. J. Honigmann and Susan Brock's *Playhouse Wills.*[10] The terminology is that of "fellowship," the term "fellow" being the designation by which members of the dramatic community recognized one another and were recognized by those familiar with but outside of the public theater.

Instances of the use of "fellow" to refer to writers as well as players proliferate in dedications, will, and fictional representations of the theater community. John Heminges and Henry Condell call Shakespeare "so worthy a Friend, & Fellow" in their dedication to the 1623 Shakespeare folio; Thomas Heywood addresses his "own quality" as "my good friends and fellowes the citty-actors" in the opening of his *Apology for Actors* (1612). In his will (proven 1616), Shakespeare left "to my fellows John Hemynnges Richard Burbage & Henry Cundell" money to buy rings for his funeral. And John Underwood, in giving to his children all his estate and goods, leaves to them "all the right title or interest part or share that I have and enjoy att this present by lease or otherwise or ought to have, possesse, or enjoy in any manner or kinde att this present, or heerafter within the Blackfryers London or in the Companie of his Majesties Servantes my loving and kinde fellows in theire house there or att the Globe on the Bankside."[11]

These moments invoke the term with a degree of solemnity and dignity. By contrast, it is mocked in the induction to Beaumont and Fletcher's *Knight of the Burning Pestle* (1606) when a citizen calls for Bankside players in these terms: "Let's have the wits of Southwark. They are as rare fellows as any are in England; and that will fetch them all o'er the water with a vengeance, as if they were mad."[12] In the Inns of Court play *Lingua* (1607), a character uses the term "fellow" specifically in reference to writers: "Heuresis, this Inuention, is the proudest Iack-a-napes . . . conceited Boy that euer breath'd, because for-sooth some odde Poet, or some such Phantastique fellowes, make much on him."[13] Ben Jonson complained to William Drummond that the writer and dramatist Gervase Markham "was a base fellow." [14] Verses that mocked the Dutton brothers (Laurence and John) for switching companies applied the term to actors: "The Duttons and theyr fellow-players forsayking the Erle of Warwycke theyr mayster, became followers of the Erle of Oxford, and wrot themselves his COMOEDIANS, which certaune Gentlemen altered and made CAMOELIONS."[15] William Rowley, however, celebrates the term and its conno-tations in *A Cure for a Cuckold*, written jointly with John Webster.[16] In the play, the comic figure Compass compares his rights to his wife's illegitimate child (fathered by a local gentleman while Compass was four years at sea) to the bonds between players. He praises the latter for a cooperative spirit char-acterized by a willingness to share the wealth:

> WIFE. Pursu'd by gifts and promises, I yielded: consider, husband, I am a woman, neither the first not last of such offenders, 'Tis true I have a child.
> COMPASS. Ha' you? And what shall I have then, I pray? Will not you la-bour for me, as I shall do for you? Because I was out o' th' way when twas gotten, shall I lose my store? *There's better law amongst the players yet, for a fellow shall have his share, tho he do not play that day.* If you look for any part of my four years' wages, I would have half the boy.[17]

Even as this exchange, like the play as a whole, mocks Compass's prioritization of his finances over his wife's fidelity and gestures to the gendered stakes of a fellowship that exists exclusively among men and in contrast to relations with women, it endorses a charmed view of players as supportive and loyal companions who observe an ethic that can be legal, equitable, and cooperative. And perhaps no other use of "fellow" to refer to the theater community is better known than when Hamlet wonders whether he will be able to get himself "a fellowship in a cry of players."[18]

More striking is the use of the term in payments to playing companies by officers *outside* the theatrical community. Payments in the Treasurer's *Declared Accounts* testify to the recognition of players as a band of "fellows." In 1571, "Lawrence Dutton and his fellowes" are paid "for presentinge a plaie before her highnes uppon St Johns daie." In 1617–18, the Lord Treasurer pays close to £20 "to Ellis Worth the Queenes Maties Servaunte in the behalfe of himselfe and his fellowes for presentinge twoe severall plaues before his Ma^ty." John Heminges is paid on behalf of "the rest of his fellowes the kinges Maties Players for presenting fifteene plaues before his Ma^ty and the Princes highnes." In 1620–21, John Newton is paid "in the behalfe of himselfe and his fellowes the Princes Players."[19] Such references to theater men proliferate in the account books, while other payees, like musicians, officers of the Jewelhouse, keepers of the bears, Yeomen of the Guard, and watermen, are not denoted by such terms, even by the same hand that registered the players' payments.[20] Often these payments were to a distinct person rather than a group that person represented; nevertheless, what is seen here is the formulaic recognition, by people and institutions *outside* the stage, of a special name—and therefore a special relation—among company men. One player is invoked on behalf of the others, and these others are, in turn, called his fellows. Philip Massinger dramatizes this kind of outside recognition in his especially metatheatrical play *The Roman Actor* (1629) when he has Caesar's mistress, Domitia, critique a court performance except for a single actor: "the fellow / That played the doctor did it well."[21]

Of course, the term "fellow," and the particular relations that it implies, were widely used in different contexts both during and before the rise of the London theater. According to the *OED*, the term had from the eleventh century been understood as meaning a partner or colleague, a comrade at professional as well as personal levels. In addition, the term has been understood from the sixteenth century as denoting one part of a duo: a "fellow" is the "complementary individual of a pair, the mate." But the term also has a distinctly plural sensibility; a fellow is not simply the match of a mate but "one of a company or party whose interests are common." A fellow is, therefore, not so much a companion or comrade for one person but for a group; he is "one of a company or party whose interests are common." To "be playing the good fellow," the *OED* explains, is "to be enjoying oneself in gay *company*" (emphasis added). Part of this plural sense, then, is the definition of "fellow" as "belonging to the same class," an equal "in position or rank." Likewise, the meaning of "fellowship" maintains this same connotation of multiplicity: fellowships are not restricted to two people (though they can be); rather, from the thirteenth century, fellowship means "companionship, company, society"; "a body of fellows or equals." So, unlike the more restricted terminology of friendship, which classical and Renaissance definitions limit to a relation between two people, fellowship connotes not only the intertwining of personal and professional comradeship but also a leveling pluralism: fellows are of the same station or class; they can be one or more than one. This seems to be a distinction implicit in John Taylor's descriptions of the "The Good-Fellow-Ship," "The "Fellow-Ship," and "The Friend-ship" in his satire *An Armado* (1627). The "Good-Fellow-Ship," he notes, "is very old, and much out of reparations," and he relates it to a wide range of mercantile adventurers:

> Wine merchants, vintners, brewers, and victuallers, have thrust themselves into the whole Lordships, by the often returns, lading and unlading of this ship, yet now she is so weather-beaten, with the storms of time, and so wind-shaken with too much use, that through want she is not able to bear half the sail which she formerly hath done.

"The Friend-ship," by contrast, is limited to famous, usually royal or noble, pairs:

> [It] was a vessel of great account and estimation, David and Jonathan, Damon and Pythias, Pleiades and Orestes, Alexander and Lodowick, Scipio and Laelius, did lovingly and unfeignedly sail in her: indeed she was ever free for all comers of what country, sex, age, or state soever, for the word friend imports free end, which is as much as the end and intention of *Friend-ship* is free.[22]

In the early modern period there would have been a number of immediately available referents for the term "fellow": a student at the universities or Inns of Court, a knight at King Arthur's court or a member of the Order of the Garter, a pilgrim on a Chaucerian journey. Such referents may have reinforced the term's relation to more "ideal" worlds: those of scholarship, of chivalry, of religious calling. "Fellowship" is also used in more worldly senses, however. It can be invoked to refer to more suspicious characters, as it is by Middleton and Dekker in *The Roaring Girl*, in which Moll warns the gallants Dapper and Noland of the approach of a cutpurse: "This brave fellow is no better than a foist."[23] But the term does not have to be pejorative; Rowley uses it in his dedication to the readers of his 1609 pamphlet *A Search for Money*, in which he addresses a group of associates bonded together as "fellows" owing to their lack of finances: "Yee are indeed the onelie *Maecenasses* and *Patrons* of *Poesie*, for to your weake purses there are alwaies ioyned willing hearts. . . . I ioye (*most respected benefactors*) in your fellowshippe, for from me yee are like to receiue nothing but good words."[24] As the *OED* makes clear, fellowship in the early modern period referred to "a guild, corporation, company"; a "fellow" was a member of such a corporation. Middleton invokes the term to refer to a specific guild in his dedication to *The Triumphs of Truth* (1613), in which he notes that "the Noble Fellowship and Society of Grocers" wait in patient expectation of the performance of their next mayor.[25] In this last instance, fellowship is interchangeable with the brotherhood associated with the city companies; the term trammels up various interpersonal relations that invoke simultaneously emotional and business ties involving loyalty and goodwill as well as potential hostility, competitiveness, even disdain. Such sentiments are invoked in Ben Jonson's use of the term in *Bartholomew Fair*, when the Book-holder tells the crowd, "The author hath writ it [the play] just to his meridian, and the scale of the grounded judgements here, his play-fellows in wit."[26] Here the term expresses disdain for a particular class of writers and theatergoers even as it accords them, however ungraciously, a measure of communal spirit. The complicated sensibilities that accrue around the term "fellowship" describe particularly well the relations within the early modern theater milieu, where companionship and collegiality were inflected with a distinctly commercial flavor.

Given the milieu, *friendships* among theater men would have occupied a special relation to this category of *fellowship*. That is, theater friendships may be understood as heightened or intensified versions of fellowships; such friendships would both exceed the emotional and political commitment and restrict the plurality of fellowships while at the same time remaining rooted in the latter's professional, communal sensibility. The terms, in other words, overlap, but with a difference. Often the overlap is deployed for particular persuasive effects, as when representatives from Prince Charles's company negotiated with Edward Alleyn and referred to their group as friends. Their letter apologizes for having left Alleyn's theater (the Curtain) on the Bankside, and then asks him for money:

> Lest wee make a second fruitlesse paines, and as wee purpose to dedicate all ou[r] paines, powers, and frends all referent to yo[r] vses: so wee entreate you,

in the meane time, to look toward o' necessityes, leaving you ever a certaine forme of satisfaction. Wee haue neede of some monie (indeed urdgent necessitie,) wch wee rather wish you did heare in conference then by report in writing, wee haue to receiue from the court (wch after shrovetide wee meane to pursue wth best speede) a great summe of monie; meane while, if you'le but furnish vs wth the least halfe, wch will be fourtie pounds, it shall be all confirm'd to you till your satisfaction.

The group sign themselves "In your emploimentes, frendes to their best powers, Robert Palent, William Rowley, Joseph Taylor, etc."[27] In this contractual scenario, fellows become friends out of a shared interest in a particular legal suit.

Of course, the term "fellow" was widely available to describe many groups of people; the rhetoric of formulaic documents like requests and contracts was not the monopoly of professional theater men. But their use of the terms "fellowship" and "friendship" is concerted and consistent. Such use pervades the wills of and dedications to theater men. There can be a strong class element in such use; for instance, in his will (proven 1578), Richard Tarlton distinguishes his gentlemen neighbors, whom he calls "very loving and trustie friendes," from his "fellowe William Johnson also of the Groomes of her majesties chamber."[28] Thomas Heywood, in his letter to the reader affixed to John Cooke's 1614 *Greenes Tu Quoque*, distinguishes writer and actor in terms of friend and fellow: "To gratulate the loue and memory of my worthy friend the Author, and my entirely beloued fellow, the Actor, I could not chuse . . . but to prefixe some token of my affection."[29] But Heywood, Heminges, and Condell call the actors their fellows *and* friends. And Underwood distinguishes between fellows who are just fellows and fellows who are fellows as well as friends. Having referred, as we saw earlier, to his "loving and kinde fellows in theire house there or att the Globe," Underwood "does nominate and appoynte my loving freindes. . . . Henry Cundley Thomas Sanford and Thomas Smyth gentlemen my Executors. . . . And doe[s] intreate my loving freindes Mr John Hemynges and John Lowyn my fellows overseers."[30] By the close of the will, that is, Underwood's fellows have become his friends. And when they do so, they should be understood as participating in the conventions of friendship predicted by early modern friendship theory.

Such participation is especially charged, because purveyors of this theory seem to restrict the experience of friendship to members of, or aspirants to, nobility. But the persistent critiques of aristocratic partnerships in plays as well as the equally consistent overlap of friendship and fellowship in their daily language and deportment suggest that the terms of friendship were available to and being revised by both titled and untitled men of the London theater.[31] So while it might be argued that some dramatists, players, and shareholders were emulating noble ideals in their pursuits or depictions of theatrical friendships, such pursuits or depictions, even as they share with friendship theory a set of conventional principles, could be put to alternative uses. In what follows, I explore one of those principles, that of language exchange between friends, and the uses to which it is put by a set of collaborating dramatists and actor-dramatists, Thomas Middleton and William Rowley. My goal is to describe a standard of friendly communication against which to understand both the work and the product of the Middleton-Rowley pair. In so doing, I suggest that while friendship theory might have held out such verbal sharing as a means of gentle identification, Middleton and Rowley's dramatic sharing of a text marks another kind of exercise and commitment.

SEMBLABLE CONCURRENCE

Renaissance friendship literature, and the classical models from which it derived, idealized friendship as an expression of, as well as a means to, the good and virtuous life.[32] Friendship was celebrated for a number of its aspects and effects: for the constancy, durability, mutuality, and equality it simultaneously demanded of and promised its pairs; for the selflessness—even unto and after death—that it encouraged, which was rewarded, paradoxically, by the reinforcement of the submerged or abandoned ego. Montaigne is perhaps the most eloquent spokesman for this paradox as he describes the terms of a male-male intimacy in which ideal companions dissolve into each other only in order to emerge as better selves:

> The amitie I speake of . . . was not to bee modelled or directed by the pattern of regular and remisse friendship. . . . [T]his [one] hath no other *Idea* than of it selfe, and can have no reference but to it selfe. It is not one especiall consideration. . . . It is I wot not what kinde of quintessence of all this commixture, which having seized all my will, induced the same to plunge and loose it selfe in his, which likewise having seized all his will, brought it to loose and plunge it selfe in mine, with a mutuall greedinesse, and with a semblable concurrence. I may truely say, loose, reserving nothing unto us, that might properly be called our owne, not that was either his, or mine. . . . It is not in the power of the worldes discourse to remove me from the certaintie I have of his intentions and judgements of mine: no one of its actions might be presented unto me, under what shape soever, but I woulde presently find the spring and the motion of it. Our mindes have jumped so unitedly together, they have with so fervent an affection considered of each other, and with like affection so discovered and sounded,

even unto the very bottome of each others hearts and entrails, that I did, not onely know his, as well as mine owne, but I would rather have trusted him concerning any matter of mine than myselfe.[33]

Montaigne's description of friendship is nothing less than a complete sharing of wills and minds. Such sharing depends on a series of recognitions: of the self, of the other, of the self in relation to the other, and finally of the self and the other's desire or will. In the friendly exchange of bodies and minds Montaigne depicts, a friend is the readiest path to one's own good and vice versa; in knowing each other, friends know themselves so completely that they know that their own best interests are better known by the other.

In this, its richest Renaissance formulation, friendship discourse articulates the possibility of self-knowledge through sustained and constant closeness or intimacy with an other. The height of such intimacy, furthermore, is a form of idealized communication in which friends both understand and honor a concrete verbal exchange. According to early modern tracts such as Walter Dorke's *Tipe or Figure of Friendship* (1589), there is no greater comfort to a "penciue mind, than to power out the plaints thereof into the secret bosome of a sincere friend, by whose sweete communication is receaued a sodaine delight, and soveraigne consolation."[34] Dorke's image is simultaneously a linguistic and a bodily one in which the connection between friends is in part made possible by a conversation that begins in the mind and ends in the flesh. Furthermore, it depends on an assumption that this conversation is a very particular kind, that it is built on the sharing of secrets. Both the requirement and the reward of a good friend is an ability to shelter and honor privileged information. Thomas Breme in *A Mirrour of Friendship* (1584) insists that "to be a true and assured friend, a man may discouer the secrets of his hearte, and recounte to him all his griefes, trust him with things touching his honour and deliuer him to keep his goods and treasures." Breme recommends that in choosing a friend, one find someone who is "aboue all, faythfull and constant . . . in keping thy secretes."[35] Sir Francis Bacon's elucidation of this principle in "On Friendship" is similar: "A principal fruit of friendship is the ease and discharge of the fullness and swellings of the heart, which passions of all kinds do cause and induce. . . . But one thing is most admirable . . . which is, that this communicating of a man's self to his friend works two contrary effects, for it redoubleth joys, and cutteth griefs in half. For there is no man that imparteth his joys to his friend, but he joyeth the more; and no man that imparteth his griefs to his friend, but he grieveth the less."[36] For Thomas Churchyard, the secrets of friends take the form of mystery: friendship is characterized as a "true love knot" of which the "mysterie and maner of the working is so great" that it is difficult to know "how the mixture is made."[37]

Jeffrey Masten has emphasized the "remarkable homoeroticism" of this language, whose ideals of shared conversation and mutuality represent an "erotics of similitude" that provides a discursive context within which to understand late-sixteenth- and early-seventeenth-century dramatic writing.[38] For Masten, this discourse is class inflected: even as it authorizes sameness or "self-reproducibility," it is in the service of social hierarchy. Friendship "figures importantly in the construction and reproduction of the entitled English gentleman," thus providing one set of terms and conventions for aspirants to nobility. But Masten's stress on friendship as a specifically aristocratic privilege denies it the possibility of providing alternative models of social or political interaction. In my reading of Middleton and Rowley, I argue that the playwrights' friendship, rather than participating in "bonds . . . among those who were, or desired to be, English gentlemen," instead marked a resistance or critique of aristocratic relations.[39] Such a reading draws from the work of Laurie Shannon, who offers a corrective to Masten's model by arguing for the politically productive aspects of friendship as a brake on both absolute monarchy specifically and hierarchical stratification more generally. "If friendship's other-self logics serve widely to maximize the private subject's affective and personal powers," Shannon writes, "friendship's link to counselorship here begins to traverse the divide between this elsewhere of affective sovereignty and real political culture."[40] Shannon's point here is not simply that personal relations are always already political; rather, she is suggesting that friendships, built as they are around mutual communication, provide men in office a model of effective counsel.

Theater men were not men in office, but their theatrical friendships might be seen both to participate in and to be productive of a particular kind of "counsel." I do not intend to read such theater counsel as the voicing of a political position or conviction, although, as Renaissance criticism has shown, the early drama was intensely involved in offering such positions and convictions. Rather, "counsel" can be seen as the more intimate, circumscribed performance of a linguistic theory that describes a model of joint writing as the "discouer[y of] the secrets of [the] hearte."[41] In what follows, I argue that Middleton and Rowley enjoyed this kind of communicative interaction of friends, that *The Changeling* can be interpreted as its modified expression, and that this expression, at the level of production as well as content, is both implicitly and explicitly critical of aristocratic aspiration. In other words, following the interpretive program of John Najemy in his analysis of the Niccolò Machiavelli–Francesco Vettori letters, I suggest that the collaborative text of Middleton and Rowley is an effect, though not necessarily an allegory, of friendship conventions in which Middleton and Rowley participated.[42] From this perspective, then, the dynamic punning in *The Changeling* can be seen as a perversion of the language of friends into the excruciating appropriations and misinterpretations of words.

PLAYING FRIENDS

A friendship between Middleton and Rowley is often assumed (Nigel Bawcutt, for instance, refers to their "unusual closeness") but rarely substantiated by scholars commenting on their collaborative enterprises.[43] My account involves a more precise institutional history of their writerly associations in order to document this closeness. For *The Changeling* was not Middleton and Rowley's first joint undertaking. While work on the Middleton corpus for the Oxford edition continues to offer new information and theories about Middleton's single and joint work, external records and the efforts of a variety of attribution studies suggest that *The Changeling* was the pair's fourth dramatic text devised in six consecutive years of writing together. They had collaborated earlier on two other plays, including *A Fair Quarrel* (1617) and *The Old Law* (1618), and a masque, *The World Tossed at Tennis* (1620). And they may have been collaborating even earlier: MacD. Jackson, for instance, has suggested that *Wit at Several Weapons*, which is enrolled in the first Beaumont and Fletcher folio, belongs to Middleton and Rowley, with a performance date circa 1613–15.[44] Their relationship extended beyond writing: Middleton seems to have designed parts for Rowley in his works, including Plum-Porridge in the *Inner Temple Masque* (1619), and they both must have agreed on his performance as Simple in their joint *World Tossed*, whose dedication, to Lord and Lady Charles Howard, Middleton signed in his own name and whose dedication to the reader Rowley signed as "Simplicitie" himself. And the association continued after *The Changeling*. Although there is scholarly doubt as to whether the two wrote *The Spanish Gypsy*, first published and assigned to them in 1653, Middleton seems to have designed for Rowley the role of the Fat Bishop in his blockbuster *Game at Chess* (1624).[45] As Joost Daalder comments, "According to the evidence of modern scholarship there was no dramatist with whom Middleton collaborated so extensively and intensively as Rowley; their collaboration lasted for several years and resulted in the co-authorship of five dramatic works" (Daalder counts *The Spanish Gypsy* as theirs).[46]

I consider in more detail Daalder's summary of the writing team by attending to the pair's institutional setting. The Middleton and Rowley corpus, with its range of generic interests, can certainly be seen to attest to the writers' ability to adapt to the shifting dramatic trends and demands that characterized theater production in the last decade of James's reign. More significant, however, is that this corpus—or, more accurately, the production details behind the corpus—embodies characteristics unique to the Middleton and Rowley pair. And these characteristics, when viewed in comparison to other joint writing ventures we have seen, testify to a particular deliberateness in their working relationship.

The first salient aspect of the Middleton and Rowley pairing is that their joint efforts, even if dated as early as 1613 with the composition of *Wit*, were undertaken when the two were established professionals in the theater with various and broad attachments to city life. At the time of the production of even their earliest collaborative enterprises, Rowley was a veteran sharer—meaning an actor and shareholder as well as a writer—with Prince Charles's Men and had held that position since 1609 (he would remain a sharer until 1623). He had already been writing for the theater since at least 1607, when he collaborated on *The Travels of Three English Brothers* for Queen Anne's Men. In 1615, he represented Charles's troupe at a meeting of the professional companies called before the Privy Council, and he represented his company, along with other sharers, in negotiations with Henslowe and Alleyn.[47]

Middleton was neither an actor nor a sharer, but he was a thoroughly civic professional. In addition to writing for the public stage, his jobs included that of city pageant writer, a competitive position on which he held a virtual monopoly from 1616 to 1622, the period of his most concerted writing with Rowley, as well as that of city chronologer, which made him responsible for documenting city affairs in some capacity. He was awarded the position in 1620, and it earned him gifts from £6 to £20 yearly. G. E. Bentley remarks on his long-term "association with prominent members of the liveried companies."[48] By the time Middleton began writing with Rowley, he had enjoyed several years of writing plays both alone and collaboratively: first for the Admiral's Men with other writers such Dekker, Drayton, Munday, and Webster, and then for the boys' companies, especially Paul's. Since leaving his work for that troupe around 1606, he had maintained what Brian Corrigan calls a "protean relationship" with the theater companies, writing for various ones. "Evidence from Middleton's later career, 1610–1624," Corrigan adds, "lends credence to the suggestion that Middleton wrote for companies freelance."[49]

But there are patterns to this "freelancing": it appears that when writing alone during this period, Middleton supplied the majority of his work to the King's Men, the reigning city company, at least to judge on the basis of performances at court. Between 1613 and 1621, before *The Changeling*, he had written at least five plays for them, including *Anything for a Quiet Life, The Mayor of Quinborough, More Dissemblers Besides Women, The Widow*, and *The Witch*.[50] His infamous *Game at Chess* (1624) was also a King's Men's play. His only other solo play before *The Changeling, A Chaste Maid in Cheapside*, is linked to Elizabeth's Men in its 1630 quarto publication.

As the playwrights' vitae suggest, the two men were associated with different acting troupes. This means that in their multiple collaborative enterprises, Middleton and Rowley ignored the boundaries of company affiliations to work together. This cross-company connection contrasts with the majority of other Jacobean writing pairs who wrote together with some consistency. The teams of Francis Beaumont and John Fletcher or Fletcher and Philip Massinger, while they maintained a kind of aristocratic distance from involvement as company sharers, were associated with the same company (largely the King's Men) during the period of their joint writing.[51] In contrast to the practices of these regular pairs, Middleton and Rowley were variously associated with different civic enterprises and seem to have collaborated across company bounds and loyalties.

Of course, in the fluid world of the early Elizabethan theater, collaborating playwrights often breached strict company allegiances. As Neil Carson has demonstrated, professional playwrights worked in "syndicates," some of whose members might be tied to Worcester's Men while others were linked to the Admiral's Men.[52] But Middleton and Rowley remain distinct in comparison to these syndicates. The Elizabethan groups could number up to five writers, and even though they might be prolific in their output, their ties did not last more than a year or two. Also, writers such as Thomas Heywood wrote for multiple companies and with a changing array of collaborators. Middleton and Rowley, by contrast, worked largely as a duo, and they continued their association for several consecutive years. Furthermore, they demonstrated a commitment specifically to each other that they do not show to other peers at that time. Although both writers collaborated with other playwrights during the 1610s and 1620s, including Thomas Dekker, John Ford, and John Webster, each wrote with these others only one or two plays, as opposed to their mutual four-plus endeavors.[53]

So while we may rely on the testimony of commendatory poems or late-

seventeenth-century histories of the stage to surmise the close relations between playwrights such as Beaumont and Fletcher, for Middleton and Rowley
we need to look instead at the patterns of their writing practices and at those
patterns in comparison to those of other writing teams. Their collaborative
work, which joined Middleton and Rowley across company lines and multiple
civic and professional roles at a time when they were established in the business, suggests that writing with each other was for them a deliberate undertaking. I have already suggested that the collaborative work of Chapman, Jonson,
and Marston as well as Beaumont, Fletcher, and Shakespeare was also "deliberate"—that for these other groups, working together was an intentional effort
that responded to specific institutional pressures. Here, however, I read such
deliberateness as a sign of a desire to work together, as an indication of a
friendship. It is a friendship that, as I have already suggested, has as its backdrop their connections as professional fellows, as writers and actors who make
clear in their writings their specific civic ties. As Walter Dorke suggests as he
evaluates its benefits, friendship can be related to particular locales: his rhetoric
differentiates friendship on the basis of place, saying that it "is so conuenient
for the Court, and so fit for the Countrey; it is such a treasure abroad in the
warres, and such an ornament to the citie in time of peace."[54] What I am
suggesting, then, is that we look at Middleton and Rowley as friends who
both emerge from a particular institutional scene of fellowship at the same
time that they enjoy a relationship which conforms to the paradigms, particularly of linguistic exchange, articulated by Renaissance friendship treatises.

Of course, positioning Middleton and Rowley in this way must be qualified
and cautious. The playwrights themselves are suspicious of these paradigms.
In *A Fair Quarrel*, for instance, Middleton and Rowley show friendship falling
victim to narcissistic and class interests when the protagonist, Captain Ager,
who proclaims at one moment that " 'twixt friend and friend / There is so even
and level a degree / It will admit of no superlative," finds himself challenging
an esteemed colonel to a duel over pedigree.[55] And Rowley mocks the abuse of
the term "friend" when it is deployed by merchants scheming for money in *A
New Wonder, A Woman Never Vext* (1632): "As evenly we will lay our bosomes
as our bottomes / With love as merchandise."[56] But such critiques do not
mean that the playwrights were immune to, or entirely cynical about, the
potential of and for friendship. Indeed, it is possible that the existence of their
friendship *enabled* them to note moments and places of its failure elsewhere.
One place of failure is the court of Alicante in *The Changeling*. In their play,
Middleton and Rowley translate the dynamics of collaboration predicted by

friendship treatises, the textualized exchanges of secrets and self, into their precise *opposite*. *The Changeling* inverts the characteristics and rewards of friendship in a particularly meaningful way, namely by perverting friendly communication, by betraying its characters to moments of verbal *méconaissance* that parade as scenes of linguistic intimacy. If the language of friends, according to friendship treatises, was one of immediate and mutual apprehension (Montaigne's "semblable concurrence" of thought and feeling), language in *The Changeling* is entirely opaque: it sounds the same to its characters but means very differently to each of them. As Lois Bueler points out, "As each character picks up an other's language, the referents shift."[57] Although scholars who have given considerable attention to the language of the play consider this opacity a measure of the writers' (and audience's) punning ability, it is for the characters dangerous, distressing, and eventually fatal. What happens in *The Changeling*, then, is yet another form of "change": the lucid and satisfying conversation of friendly writers changes into the "frightful pleasures" of its characters.

FRIGHTFUL PLEASURES

These pleasures are spread across two plots. The focus of the main plot is Beatrice Joanna, the daughter of Vermandero, the governor of the Spanish harbor city of Alicante, who has been engaged to the titled Alonzo de Piracquo and who, after falling in love with a visiting nobleman, Alsemero, hires a courtier whom she despises to murder her betrothed so she can marry Alsemero. The hireling, De Flores, does indeed kill Alonzo, for which he demands Beatrice's sexual favors as his recompense, thus embroiling her, ironically, in a relation more odious and doomed than the first. This plot is shadowed by a subplot set in a madhouse on the outskirts of Alicante, where two courtier "changelings" have gone in disguise to woo Isabella, the wife of the asylum's doctor, Alibius—to get Isabella, that is, to "change" her affections to them. Though often demeaned as a less sophisticated, too "literal" exploration of the main plot's central issue of human sexual and social transformation, the subplot, in a vocabulary that echoes that of the main plot, is actually a subtle and witty commentary, a clear demonstration of the playwrights' ability to weave story lines and themes together. Both plots explore the moral consequences of human metamorphosis; and both do so in scenes in which the characters, as they echo or steal one another's language, end up *missing*, whether deliberately or inadvertently, the multiple meanings of the same words.[58]

Such scenes feature various pairs of characters who, despite their status as companions, conduct conversations that are always asymmetrical. Alsemero and Jasperino, his "friend" (so named in the dramatis personae and so called by Alsemero), forfeit the former transparency of their communication when Alsemero falls in love with Beatrice at the play's start. Although together both apprehend that Alsemero has "some hidden malady / Within me," the knowledge only separates them. Alsemero is now a stranger to himself and to Jasperino: "I never knew / Your inclinations to travels at a pause, / With any cause to hinder it, till now."[59] They remain at odds, particularly when Jasperino questions Beatrice's chastity, till the very end of the play, when Jasperino can actually prove, rather than merely repeat a rumor of, Beatrice's infidelity. A similar dynamic severs the fraternal pair of Tomazo and Alonzo de Piracquo, where again the cause is Beatrice. Tomazo tries to convince his brother that Beatrice, who doesn't love him, is a danger. Alonzo shrugs off the warning, but in terms that simultaneously insist on a friendship whose very premise is at that moment denied:

> Preserve your friendship and your counsel, brother,
> For times of more distress; I should depart
> An enemy, a dangerous, deadly one
> To any but thyself that should but think
> She knew the meaning of inconstancy,
> Much less the use and practice. Yet w'are friends.   (2.1.144–49)

Unfortunately for Alonzo, Tomazo is exactly right, and the break in communication here—a break also in trust and belief—results in their literal separation when Beatrice has her fiancé murdered. Even more striking are the scenes between the men in Alibius's madhouse, in which male comrades cheat and lie to each other in their pursuit of Isabella. Lollio, servant to the jealous doctor Alibius, promises his master that he will help guard the chastity of Isabella, Alibius's wife, from the noble hospital visitors and then proceeds to woo her himself. And in order to do this he quite literally takes words from someone he has befriended, Antonio, a rich courtier who has disguised himself as a fool to gain access to Isabella. Antonio approaches Isabella with the sentiments and tropes of a sonneteer, telling her:

> What should I fear,
> Having all joys about me? Do you [but] smile,
> And love shall play the wanton on your lip,
> Meet and retire, retire and meet again;
> Look you but cheerfully, and in your eyes
> I shall behold mine own deformity,
> And dress myself up fairer.   (3.3.182–88)

A moment later Lollio cities his friend word for word, adding, "I could follow now as t'other fool did: / 'What should I fear, / having all joys about me'" (3.3.227–29). Lollio's strategy here is a debauched form of language sharing: it is not between friends themselves but rather involves taking a colleague's language in an effort to spoil or defeat his desires, foolish or not.

It would be easy to see these scenarios of "broken" conversation among friends as the result of female intrusion into male homosocial relations. Or vice versa: it would also be possible to see the collapse of the relation between Beatrice and her waiting woman Diaphanta—who was once her "lad[y]'s cabinet"—as the effect of Alsemero's presence (2.2.6). But as Lisa Jardine has explained in her useful essay on the play, the concept of male friendship in the Renaissance was under ideological pressure, which she attributes to disruptions in older ideals of service and patronage by newer forms of bureaucratic intimacy, and it was thus at the heart of what she calls an emerging "dynastic anxiety." Also at the heart of this anxiety were developing standards of, and developing concerns about, companionate marriage. Jardine thus argues that the crisis in friendship that *The Changeling* portrays is analogous to, rather than the effect of, Beatrice's romantic intentions and the threat to patriarchal and dynastic prerogative her marriage plans represent:

> The source of anxiety is less the instrumentality of women themselves than the way the new marriage model is in contest with traditional social organisation. I shall suggest that the *frisson* caused by the prospect that emotional closeness might prove socially effective charges the relationship erotically—it is intense, secret and powerful. In the same way, the close relations between men of similar social standing which emerges in the late sixteenth and early seventeenth centuries as the model for household service gains an erotic charge from the way it manages to intervene in family matters.[60]

Jardine's argument suggests that homosocial friendship and heterosexual marital relations operated according to common, rather than oppositional, rhetorics of intimacy, secrecy, and cooperation.[61] It goes without saying that this very commonality of vocabulary represented a source of ideological tension, and the overlap—as well as the social pressure it engendered—forms the context of Beatrice's interaction with men in this play. Her interactions can thus be seen as variations on, rather than the antithesis of, same-sex relations, including her own friendship with Diaphanta. For Beatrice's associations with Alsemero and DeFlores, courtiers she respectively loves and abhors, involve precisely a rhetoric of friendship applied, with various degrees of contradiction, to both same-sex and heterosexual relationships.[62] They thus also involve the same kinds of asymmetrical conversation that the men's do. But in the case of Beatrice and the men who surround her, verbal asymmetry becomes more extreme, involving the complete misapprehension of words between people who think or pretend they know exactly what the other is saying, and thus ultimately more violent.

Alsemero and Beatrice both profess to speak the same language, one that combines the vocabulary of companionate marriage with the vocabulary of intimate friendship. Alsemero's opening lines foreground the sanctity of their pairing; he insists he loves her "to the holy purpose" and imagines their marriage as a return to Eden, a place that, like the church, will "join us into one" (1.1.6, 11). And Beatrice imagines herself as a companion, both replacing and fulfilling the function of Jasperino. She calls on Jasperino to deliver a note to Alsemero; as he leaves she comments:

> How wise is Alsemero in his friend!
> It is a sign he makes his choice with judgement.
> Then I appear in nothing more approved
> Than making choice of him;
> For 'tis a principle, he that can choose
> That bosom well who of his thoughts partakes,
> Proves most discreet in every choice he makes.
> Methinks I love now with the eyes of judgement,
> And see the way to merit, clearly see it. (2.1.6–14)

Beatrice here measures Alsemero's relation with Jasperino, and now with her, in the most vaunted terms of friendship discourse: choice, judgment, merit, worth, wisdom. Alsemero, after Beatrice praises him, goes so far as to exalt that "W'are so like / In our expressions, lady, that unless I borrow / The same words, I shall never find their equals" (2.2.12–14). Alsemero too speaks friendship's language of shared, even equal, thoughts and diction.

Ironically, however, their speaking and thinking are deeply veiled to each other. Immediately following this little exchange, Alsemero offers to duel Alonzo for Beatrice's hand. Beatrice refuses vehemently:

> Call you that extinguishing of fear
> When 'tis the only way to keep it flaming?
> Are not you ventured in the action,
> That's all my joys and comforts? Pray, no more, sir.
> Say you prevailed, you're danger's and not mine then:
> The law would claim you from me, or obscurity
> Be made the grave to bury you alive.

> I'm glad these thoughts come forth; O keep not one
> Of this condition, sir!
> . . . .
> Blood-guiltiness becomes a fouler visage.   (2.2.29–40).

Beatrice is now thinking of De Flores, and a plan to have him get rid of Alonzo. But she does not share these thoughts with Alsemero, and, despite his earlier protestations of being "so like in our expressions," Alsemero does not hear or sense in Beatrice's last phrase her impending action. What is witnessed here, then, is an absolute failure of the very promise of companionship, both marital and same-sex, for two to be as one, for one individual to know and think as the other. The pregnancy and virginity tests Alsemero keeps locked in his private closet and which he plans to try on Beatrice (and which Beatrice learns to manipulate) can be seen as another pretense to, as well as failure of, the intimacy of friendly secret-sharing.

This failure is dramatized more exceptionally in scenes in which a character mistakes or confuses the meaning of what another says even as he or she uses the interlocutor's words. A stunning example of such a moment involves a disordering of meaning by the same figure as well as between two characters, a disordering that foregrounds the "exchangeability" of the cast. While De Flores is off murdering Alonzo, Vermandero, Beatrice, and Alsemero gather to talk. Vermandero praises Alsemero as though he were Alonzo: "Valencia speaks so nobly of you, sir, / I wish I had a daughter now for you" (3.4.1–2). His seeming generosity fancies a change in son-in-law that earlier he insisted could not happen ("I tell you, sir, the gentleman's complete, / A courtier and a gallant, enrich'd / With many fair and noble ornaments. / I would not *change* him for a son-in-law / For any he in Spain, the proudest he, / And we have great ones, that you know" [1.1.210–14]). Vermandero's compliment involves wishing for an additional daughter to whom he could marry Alsemero; ironically his wish voices for an imaginary child the desire of his living one. It is Alsemero who replies first, capitalizing on the ambiguous implications of Vermandero's gesture and the introduction of the imagined daughter. "The fellow of this creature were a partner / For a King's love" (3.4.3–4), he says, consciously using the father's comment to express in a censored form his own admiration for Beatrice. Vermandero, again ironically, does not hear the comment as praise for either daughter, real or imaginary. Instead he hears Alsemero's comment as praise for himself, the "king." "I had her fellow once, sir," he rejoins, "But heaven has married her to joys eternal; / 'Twere sin to wish her in this vale again" (3.4.4–6).

Vermandero's reply obfuscates completely the referents of its feminine pronouns and demonstrates a confusion of speakerly intentions around the word "fellow" that will escalate in important ways as the play develops. If Vermandero were following the logic of Alsemero's submerged praise for Beatrice, the "fellow" of his own comment would represent Beatrice's imaginary sister, and the "her" of "her fellow" would represent Beatrice. But if Vermandero is following the syntactic logic that allows him to hear himself in Alsemero's invocation of the "king," the "fellow" stands for a lover—presumably his dead wife—and not an imaginary second daughter. It thus makes Beatrice, the "her" of "her fellow," fellows not with a sister but with a woman, presumably her own mother, whom Vermandero has "had." By the end of this brief but central scene, Vermandero has confused three females—daughter, dead wife/mother, and imagined daughter/sister—and his desires of and for them.

The scene thus exposes a proliferation of antagonistic, incommensurate desires and intentions, a confusion made more palpable because it is voiced in the same words. These words, "her fellow," mark a deliberate obfuscation of the favorite words of dramatic mutuality and equality. When the collaborating dramatists depict the term "fellow" applied at court, in other words, they see, irrespective of the genders involved, its signification as theatrical friendship and reciprocity turned into a sign of unstable and potentially incestuous dynastic courtly desire.

This transformation reaches its peak in conversations between Beatrice and the hired hit man De Flores. Their interaction represents the most extreme—the most "pure"—inversion of a discourse of friendship, for their communication actually echoes, while it misconstrues, the terms of companionship between equals and the ideal verbal exchange that should go on between them. At the beginning of the play they are equals only because Beatrice despises De Flores just as much as he is attracted to her. For instance, early in the play, after Beatrice has scorned him for retrieving her dropped glove, De Flores launches into an enthusiastically abject aside:

> Now I know
> She had rather wear my pelt tann'd in a pair
> Of dancing pumps, than I should thrust my fingers
> Into her sockets here. I know she hates me,
> Yet I cannot choose but love her:
> No matter, if but to vex her, I'll haunt her still;
> Though I get nothing else, I'll have my will.   (1.1.231–37)

Starting with imagined violations of her body ("thrust my fingers"), De Flores's plans for Beatrice extend into what he imagines as her emotional core: he intends to "haunt" her, to aggravate her hatred even in—as part of—his at-

tempt to win her love. This performance, which he calls, resonantly, the execution of his will, mimics the structure while it violates the content of the
mutual exchange of desire or will which friendship discourse trumpets: "The
grettest force of frendship [is that] oure willes, studyes, and felynges were all
one," John Tiptoft translates from Cicero's *De Amicitia* (1481).[63] It does so not
only because of its sadistic design—DeFlores knows Beatrice's different desire
but still tries to force it to fit his pleasure—but because it is masochistic as
well: he loves her more for despising him. Friendship's terms purport to afford
the reinforcement, whether accidental or causal, of *both* participants. As Tiptoft
writes, "Ther is no thynge so conuenyent and veryly apte to men eyther in
prosperitie or aduersite [as friendship]."[64] Here, De Flores accepts his own
destruction as well as Beatrice's in the exercise of his will. And if here the
destruction is strictly symbolic and psychic, it will become quite real by the
end of the play.

Beatrice tries to direct her will against De Flores only. Indeed, the prospect
of banishing De Flores is at first one of the few chances Beatrice has for
determining events and outcomes in a world that is determined by others',
particularly men's, agendas. Annoyed by his persistent presence, she suggests
in the second act that "the next good mood I find my father in, / I'll get him
[De Flores] quite discarded" (2.1.92–93). But even in her attempt to get rid
of him (an effort that still depends on her father, of course), Beatrice cannot
help but invoke De Flores, use his terms. She does not know this, of course,
but immediately before her proposal to evict him, De Flores has reiterated the
abject position he assumed in the earlier scene:

> Why, am not I an ass to devise ways
> Thus to be railed at? I must see her still;
> . . . .
> What this may bode I know not. I'll despair the less
> Because there's daily precedent of bad faces
> Beloved beyond all reason. These foul chops
> May come into favour one day 'mongst his fellows.   (2.1.77–85).

As De Flores sneaks off, Beatrice notes, "I never see this fellow, but I think /
Of some harm towards me, danger's in my mind still" (2.1.89–90). Her end-
stopped emphasis on "still" inadvertently echoes his; but whereas De Flores's
"still" represents his desire, in the face of Beatrice's absence, for her permanent—and perhaps quieted—presence, Beatrice's refers to her fear, in the face
of De Flores's presence, of his continuing—and threatening—persistence.
They share the same word for entirely opposite meanings and sentiments. This

dynamic is even more striking in their use of "fellow." Beatrice clearly intends the term to be pejorative, invoking it for its sinister or contemptuous sense of "a person of no esteem or worth" (*OED*), while De Flores uses it to designate the very range of men who might attract Beatrice, as he hopes to "come into favour one day 'mongst his fellows." Indeed, the term here is as unstable as it was in Vermandero's mouth: it could even be used here a label for Beatrice, into whose favor De Flores wishes to project himself. Beatrice, that is, uses "fellow" to distance herself from De Flores; De Flores uses it to imply their (potential) familiarity.

Beatrice's and De Flores's diction, then, their use of the same words to convey different meanings, constitutes a form of punning. Mary Bly has investigated such punning as both a sign and a practice of the collaborative work of the King's Revels Boys at the Whitefriars; puns for playhouse dramatists such as John Sharpham and William Barkstead, she suggests, represent homoerotic intimacy both within and outside the play, as such puns "grow from an appeal to a theatrically canny community that apparently appreciated the homoerotic wit."[65] But between Beatrice and De Flores, as between all the other characters in this play in a less intense fashion, such punning expresses precisely the opposite of mutually reinforcing joint work. It expresses, rather, a kind of "linguistic *méconnaissance*," a form of misrecognition and misinterpretation that distorts entirely the sharing of language—and the reinforcement of self and other—associated with friends. And it characterizes all of Beatrice's exchanges with De Flores.

The punning is most intense in the scenes surrounding the murder of Alonzo, Beatrice's intended. Beatrice hires De Flores to kill Alonzo; and even here her terms betray her to De Flores. She believes that paying De Flores an assassin's salary for the murder will be an opportunity to "rid myself of two inveterate loathings at one time" (2.2.44–45), the two loathings being, of course, for Alonzo and De Flores. De Flores understands the enterprise in the same terms—of ridding oneself of loathings—but with precisely the opposite meaning. The murder will get rid of two inveterate loathings for him as well, but those are his hatred of Alonzo and the loathing that is Beatrice's hatred of *him*. For De Flores has no intention of disappearing with Beatrice's payoff. Instead, he anticipates their future intimacy, her hatred having become, in the aftermath of the murder, pleasure for them both:

> Methinks I feel her in mine arms already,
> Her wanton fingers combing out this beard,
> And being pleased, praising this bad face.

> Hunger and pleasure, they'll commend sometimes
> Slovenly dishes, and feed heartily on 'em,
> Nay, which is stranger, refuse daintier for 'em.
> Some women are odd feeders.   (2.2.147–53)

This is the same vocabulary Beatrice will use to describe her own delight when she learns of Alonzo's death: "My joys start at mine eyes; our sweet'st delights / Are evermore born weeping" (3.4.225–26). Here their feelings are the same, and offered in the same rich argot of sensual pleasure, but connected to different causes and aimed at different objects.

For this reason, Beatrice cannot savor her pleasure for long. Her unraveling begins when De Flores reveals the physical effects of the murder. He shows her a finger he has severed from the dead Alonzo's hand, with the engagement ring still on. She is repulsed, and he mocks her with a question: "Why, is that more / Than killing the whole man? I cut his heart-strings. A greedy hand thrust in a dish at court, / In a mistake hath had as much as this" (3.1.29–31). De Flores's plain, rational query is also a slick rhetorical maneuver, because for Beatrice the answer here is yes, the finger *is* more gruesome than the murder itself. In Beatrice's way of thinking, as De Flores seems to know, the ringed digit represents the return of everything she tried to deny by hiring a hit man: it is a phallic specter reminding her of a ring, a man, a marriage beyond her choice and control. Before that man and marriage was Alonzo. Now, as he hands her the ring and she gives it back to him as "salary," the man and marriage is De Flores.

Beatrice consciously resists the indictment linking her with De Flores, but he insists on a mutual guilt, as well as a mutual blood lust, which binds them as marital and moral equals. Their disagreement represents the precise antithesis of a friendly joining of souls and selves. For in the conversations that follow the murder, De Flores and Beatrice not only participate in moments of punning misrecognition that I have labeled as a special kind of *méconaissance*, but also are catapulted into claiming access to—or distance from—the other's mind. De Flores initiates this conversation when he scoffs at the ring Beatrice offers him as payment for the murder: " 'Twill hardly buy a capcase for one's conscience, / To keep it from the worm," he tells her (3.4.44–45). The pronoun "one" could be applied to either him or her; their consciences have become, as De Flores suggests, indistinguishable. This is a particularly provocative leveling, insofar as it equates the two characters in terms not of acts or class but of personal interior, for the conscience was associated at this time with private, privileged inner space. It was the point of contact between God and man, a special, internal realm insulated from the reaches of secular authority and exercised by the individual. As the influential theologian William Perkins wrote in 1596, conscience was placed in the human mind and "appointed of God to declare and put in execution of his just judgment. . . . [It] determines or gives sentence of things done."[66] Conscience, that is, is an aspect, a "virtual" region, of mind preserved entirely for the private self or, more accurately, the private self in and for communication with God. So De Flores's statement is predatory, invasive; it violates the sensitive personal space understood under the rubric of conscience. And the conversation continues to emphasize both the term and its violation. Frustrated with what he perceives as Beatrice's obtuseness, De Flores literally claims access to her mind. "Look but into your conscience, read me there, / 'Tis a true book, you'll find me there your equal," he tells her (3.4.132–33). The metacritical register is especially telling: De Flores suggests that he has literally inscribed himself in Beatrice's mind. They now share the same space of writing and reading. De Flores has, then, become the frightening spokesperson for the ability to get inside the mind of another— of one who, if unwittingly, has invited the spokesperson in. And rather than the prized, virtuous sharing of souls in friendship, this exchange of conscience involves occupation, possession; it mimics, even as it directly opposes, the ideal soul-sharing of friends.

But the exchange of conscience is possible because, despite all her intentions otherwise, Beatrice's actions have indeed, as De Flores reminds her, "made you one with me" (3.4.139). As he tells her: "settle you / In what the act has made you, y'are no more now; / You must forget your parentage to me" (3.4.134–36). The claim here is extraordinarily chilling because De Flores exploits the language of companionship—of the Ciceronian "second self" and of Pauline marital joining—to discuss the conditions and effects (murder and adultery) of a friendship that is the absolute antithesis of the sensibility that the language is meant to express and preserve. If Beatrice and De Flores have become one, as he suggests, their change into a couple represents the extreme realization of a discourse which, in its extremity, is also that discourse's perversion. That perversion reaches its climax as the two characters not only keep but become each other's secrets. They both must work to keep their connection from the eyes of the court.

Secrecy for Beatrice and De Flores involves, among other things, outwitting Alsemero, to whom she has been happily betrothed, by putting Diaphanta in Beatrice's place, first in his virginity test and then in his bed on the wedding night. Beatrice has Diaphanta taste the potion Alsemero has concocted to prove whether its drinker, based on her reaction of sneezing, gaping, and laughing, is a true virgin. Beatrice, in giving Diaphanta the potion, simultaneously tests Diaphanta's chastity and verifies the symptoms which she can then imitate. Then she tells her maid to sleep with Alsemero on their wedding night. If the move is an obvious instance of the play's theme of change—Diaphanta has been "exchanged" for Beatrice—it is equally suggestive in terms of the possibilities and failures of the two women's supposed closeness. For Beatrice, the substitution is an expression of friendship meant to reinforce both her marriage and her future: Diaphanta will take her place in Alsemero's bed this once in order that Beatrice may enjoy it for the rest of her life. But once in Alsemero's bedroom, Diaphanta refuses to leave it, and Beatrice laments:

> One struck, and yet she lies by't!—Oh my fears!
> This strumpet serves her own ends, 'tis apparent now,
> Devours the pleasure with a greedy appetite,
> And never minds my honour or my peace,
> Makes havoc of my right; but she pays dearly for't:
> No trusting of her life with such a secret,
> That cannot rule her blood to keep her promise.
> . . . .
> Hark, by my horrors,
> Another clock strikes two.   (5.1.1–11)

The repeated "my fears!" and "my horrors!" record Beatrice's betrayal by a friend whose pleasures were supposed to facilitate, not usurp, her own. To get Diaphanta out of her husband's bed—to protect her secret—then, Beatrice must again join with De Flores in a murderous scheme: she allows him to set fire to the castle and prevent the arson from discovery. Beatrice thus finds herself speaking the desire of and for the man she had once despised: "How heartily he serves me! His face loathes one, / But look upon his care, who would not love him?" (5.1.70–71).

As Beatrice confesses a newfound appreciation for De Flores, the conversion or change of the characters into a couple is complete. But their conversion is not limited to the "main plot" alone. Insofar as some scholars maintain that the two authors were responsible for the different plots, it is important to see how Beatrice's and De Flores's fates ultimately intersect with the "subplot" of the madhouse, for the two characters manage literally to replace the masque commissioned from Alibius by Vermandero earlier in the play. It is a commission to which Alibius responded gleefully:

> We have employment, we have task in hand;
> At noble Vermandero's, our castle-captain,

There is a nuptial to be solemnis'd
(Beatrice-Joanna, his fair daughter, bride),
For which the gentleman hath bespoke our pains:
A mixture of our madmen and our fools,
To finish, as it were, and make the fag
Of all the revels, the third night from the first;
Only an unexpected passage over,
To make a frightful pleasure, that is all,
But not the all I aim at; could we so act it,
To teach it in a wild distracted measure,
Though out of form and figure, breaking head,
It were no matter, 'twould be heal'd again
In one age or other, if not in this.   (3.3.250–65)

Alibius promises to bring "frightful pleasures," in the shape of madmen and fools, to the court. But if the bedlamites' performance threatens to bring mayhem in from the outside, the play reveals that such mayhem already inhabits the court's heart.

For while Vermandero has been accusing Antonio, who had run away from court to the madhouse to woo Isabella, of murdering Alonzo, Alsemero has discovered the true killers, De Flores and Beatrice, and in a perversion of the pair's own perversion of secrecy, Alsemero puts the couple in his private study. There he instructs them to "rehearse again / Your scene of lust, that you may be perfect / When you shall come to act it to the black audience / Where howls and gnashings shall be music to you," preparing them to appear both before the court and before the gates of hell (5.3.114–17). His metadramatic directives confirm that Beatrice and De Flores's closet performance is precisely that, a "performance," and thus when they appear before the court, they quite literally replace the madmen's masque. Their act begins offstage, and takes the form of Beatrice's cries of "O! O! O!"—cries that register either pain or pleasure.[67] When their noises are overheard, the couple is brought before the court tribunal already assembled to indict Antonio, with Beatrice fatally wounded by the stabs that matched her cries. Before she collapses, she offers an elaborate confession to Vermandero that acknowledges her intimacy with De Flores as inevitable:

I am that of your blood was taken from you
For your better health; look no more upon't,
But cast it to the ground regardlessly,
Let the common sewer take it from distinction.
Beneath the stars, upon yon meteor
Ever hung my fate, 'mongst things corruptible;
I ne'er could pluck it from him: my loathing

Was prophet to the rest, but ne'er believed;
Mine honour fell with him, and now my life.   (5.3.150–58)

Her speech does not provide the kind of closure usually sought in the staged
confession; for while she admits her wrongdoing, she also reminds Vermandero
of their blood ties, and she refuses to take responsibility for her sins, tacking
them on to "yon meteor" from which dangled her fate. De Flores echoes this
approach when he refuses to repent but instead celebrates his actions: "Yes,
and her honour's prize / Was my reward: I thank life for nothing / But that
pleasure; it was so sweet to me / That I have drunk up all, left none behind for
any man to pledge me" (5.3.167–71). Even here, then, De Flores insists on
their connection. When Vermandero tries to force him into submission by
threatening further tortures, De Flores deprives him of even this exercise of
authority: "No:— / I can prevent you, here's my penknife still. / It is but one
thread more,—and now 'tis cut," he says as he kills himself (5.3.173–75).
Replacing the supposed masque of madmen, then, Beatrice and De Flores turn
both nuptial celebration and trial into a lurid antimasque that challenges
authority even as it kills the two of them.

No masque proper harmonizes the situation. The play closes with punish-
ments, apologies, and exonerations that simply deny the larger structure of the
tragedy revealed in Beatrice's and De Flores's final statements of abjection or
bids for power. Alsemero condemns and rejects Beatrice without shouldering
any responsibility for the tragic events surrounding the murders, repressing
his own involvement in them and his own original inclination to kill Alonzo
at the beginning of the play. Alsemero's refusal to recognize his affinity with
Beatrice is as horrifying as De Flores's gleeful insistence on his own, and it is
likewise a betrayal of the principles of friendship which demand, among other
things, that "amicus certus in re incerta cernitur," a friend is to be "espyed in
a thynge in certayne [uncertain], that is to saye, in aduersitie."[68]

Even more troubling, however, is Vermandero's reinforcement of Alsemero's brand of response: he too denies a connection with his daughter. With
his dynastic plans destroyed, Vermandero embraces Alsemero as a substitute
son-in-law, a replacement for both Beatrice and Alonzo. The exchange is an
ironic realization of what Beatrice died to achieve. Accomplished with a non-
chalance that represses the tragic events precipitating this replacement of heirs,
the trade in sons is the coup de grâce of a play whose very verbal structure
insists that what inhabits the minds and mouths of its characters are the words
of others.

I am proposing that this linguistic *méconnaisance*, in which characters use the same words for entirely different purposes, should be understood as the precise opposite of Middleton and Rowley's friendly joint work and its concomitant sharing of language, thought, and theme. In other words, the experience of the play's central characters, particularly Beatrice and Alsemero, is the perverted result of the experience of its writers, the experience guaranteed friends in conversation or correspondence: pleasure, satisfaction, delight. Their relationship, then, which I have linked to a particular institutional milieu, helped make possible a portrayal of its antithesis. This portrayal echoes even as it inverts the terms and conventions of the writers' friendship. It is thus a non-transparent encoding of its conditions of production, both an allegory and an anti-allegory of the compositional process and its background.

Whether or not such a portrayal was the deliberate intention of the dramatists, it nevertheless should be seen to reflect an awareness, a consciousness, of the multiple possibilities of early modern friendship as a model both for social conduct and of social aspiration. The dynamics of Middleton and Rowley's collaboration, that is, positions a friendship generated among professional fellows against "fellowships" generated at court. Certainly, as Masten suggests, the discourse of aristocratic friendship offered a paradigm according to which players and playwrights as well as the general populace could emulate aristocratic relations and thereby status. But as my account of their partnership suggests, the writing pair of Middleton and Rowley represent a counter to such an approach to friendship. And it is their collaborative relation, in tandem with the punishing critique of their play, that insists on their privileging of a model friendship outside the gentle or noble. So while it has become commonplace to observe that Renaissance drama was capable of articulating oppositional stances to the policies and practices of the elite based almost exclusively on the content of the plays, the Middleton and Rowley collaboration suggests the need to look in additional places to discover the theater's polemical positioning. *The Changeling* certainly offers a critique of court decadence in the behavior of De Flores, Beatrice, Alsemero, and Vermandero. But this critique is embedded in the relation of these characters to the theatrical fellowship that created them. Not only do the linguistic conditions of the playwrights' relationship facilitate and inform the drama's verbal display, but also their friendship itself, emerging as it did from a profession of fellows, stands as an implicit commentary on the failed relations the play depicts.

FIVE

The Late Lancashire Witches and Joint Work across Generations

Thomas Heywood and Richard Brome shared writing responsibilities for *The Late Lancashire Witches* (1634), a "journalistic drama" depicting a contemporaneous witchcraft scare that had begun in Lancashire late in 1633 and by the summer of 1634 had attracted the attention of the Privy Council.[1] Designed to capitalize on London's interest in the affair, *Witches* was written for and performed by the King's Men and subsequently published in a flurry of activity over the brief space of four months.

The need for such speed is often advanced by critics as the impetus for joint work. Kathleen McLuskie, for instance, writes that "the Jacobean dramatists collaborated for the same reason as Hollywood scriptwriters: they were the employees of a booming entertainment industry which demanded a steady output of actable material."[2] In this chapter I provide a case history that posits for Heywood and Brome a different set of motivations for and investments in collaborative work by exploring both the particular features of the writing pair itself and the writers' embeddedness within a Caroline theatrical milieu. I examine first Heywood and Brome's specific, and quite different, professional affiliations at a time when the theater, as Andrew Gurr notes, was experiencing a socioeconomic bifurcation as a result of the "profound influence" of courtly interest in the stage.[3] I then discuss the various creative pressures exerted on dramatists writing a play about contemporaneous events.[4] Working on the Lancashire material, the playwrights had to address a series of political and cultural determinants that cohered in the Lancastrian witchcraft incident: increasing royal regulation of the provinces and increasing royal regulation of popular entertainment. In this chapter I show how, given the writing conditions they faced, the particular pairing of Heywood and Brome allowed them to answer to—even to defend against—the complex institutional and extra-institutional demands on playwriting during this period. Their dramatic response to these demands is a play that inhibits any predetermined or unequivocal reading of their attitude toward witchcraft.

AN ODD COUPLE

A case history of *The Late Lancashire Witches* must begin with the fundamental observation that Heywood and Brome are a unique writing pair. They do not meet, on the surface at least, the standard of basic similarity for collaborative writers assumed by critics who, focusing on the collaborative model of the gentlemanly pair of Francis Beaumont and John Fletcher, suggest that "the most successful collaborations were those among dramatists who shared the same theatrical experience and assumptions."[5] Heywood and Brome, in contrast, differed from each other, on the one hand, precisely in terms of professional longevity and identity as well as aesthetic training and temperament. On the other hand, they shared a faith in the didactic and pleasing potential of the stage as well as the therapeutic role of the professional dramatist, a conviction that bound them together in a unique commitment to the possible effects of the theater. Such distinctions and congruencies illuminate the thematic and ideological implications of their play itself.

Their special distinction is an impressive "generation gap," a nearly thirty-year hiatus between the production of Heywood's first play and that of Brome's. This gap was possible in 1634 in a way that it had not been before, because the professional London theater, by now around seventy years old, could support multiple and distinct, if overlapping and fluid, authorial "generations."[6] Heywood, born in 1573, had been a professional dramatist, poet, and treatise writer since at least the late 1590s; by 1633 he could boast in the dedication to his *English Traveller* of the duration and extent of his career, which involved acting as well as writing for multiple companies. He announces that the *English Traveller* was "one reserved amongst two hundred and twenty, in which I have had either an entire hand, or at the least a maine finger."[7] Brome's writing experience, by contrast, was intense but much briefer and more limited in scope than that of Heywood, who was also a prolific writer of quasi-historical and mythological tracts. Although Brome, born around 1590, was indeed part of the theatrical community by 1614 (he is mentioned in the introduction to Jonson's *Bartholomew Fair*), his first lost play was recorded nearly a decade later, when *A Fault in Friendship* was licensed for Prince Charles's company by Sir Henry Herbert.[8] Heywood was already writing in the last decade of Elizabeth's reign; Brome began his playwriting career just before the succession of Charles I.[9]

Heywood and Brome's cross-generational reach sets them apart from certain other writing groups we have seen: from the Henslowe "syndicates" of the 1590s; from Beaumont and Fletcher, whose first productions were in the early 1600s; and from Middleton and Rowley, whose writing and acting careers intersected at the end of the first decade of the seventeenth century. And Heywood and Brome's particular pairing sets them apart even from other intergenerational groups, for the older Heywood was decidedly *not* Brome's mentor. Critics have described the existence of numerous "mentoring" relationships between playwrights of different levels or years of training: between Shakespeare and John Fletcher, for instance, and then between Fletcher and Philip Massinger.[10] John Ford, whose writing career began with poetry as early as 1606, is said to have been "through a period of Dekker's tutelage"; the two wrote five joint plays together: *The Witch of Edmonton* (1621, with Rowley), *The Sun's Darling* (1623/4), *The Late Murder of the Son upon the Mother* (1624, with Webster and Rowley), *The Fairy Knight* (1624), and *The Bristow Merchant* (1624).[11] But whereas these relationships seem to have followed an almost developmental pattern, so that mentor and novice write together before the advanced student works solo, Heywood and Brome's association observes no such structure. Not only had Brome been writing solo for as many as six years before his collaboration with Heywood in 1634, but also he had another "mentor," Ben Jonson.

Heywood and Brome's theatrical subjects and styles were also markedly different.[12] Heywood favored theatrical spectacle and exaggerated emotional gesture and rhetoric; his oratory is earnest, eager. His episodic plotting was well suited to a fascination with classical mythology and mythic history: he made Virgil and Ovid available for popular consumption in his "epic" *Ages* plays, a cycle moving from the Golden to the Iron eras (performed 1611–13); he based his royally acclaimed *Love's Mistress or the Queen's Masque* (performed 1634) on Apuleius, focusing on Cupid and Psyche. He was equally interested in British and urban history, writing celebrations of London types in plays such as *The Four Prentices of London* (performed 1599) and paying homage to Elizabeth in the two parts of *If You Know Not Me, You Know Nobody* (performed 1604–5). Brome, by contrast, orchestrated tighter, interwoven plot structures reminiscent of Jonson and provided nuanced characters reminiscent of Shakespeare. His dramatic sensibility, in plays such as *The Antipodes* (performed 1638) and *The Covent-Garden Weeded* (performed 1632), is witty, stylized. Limited entirely to comedies (a generic choice Brome himself acknowledges), his plays are smaller in scope than Heywood's epics; they are more symmetrical and contained than the other's celebratory and expansive histories. Where Heywood continued to aspire, even toward the end of his career, to the loftier dramatic genres, amalgamating English and classical history, tragedy, and travelogue, Brome consciously limited himself to urbane, topical comedies, imaginative slices of life and manners: "A little wit, lesse learning, No Poetry / This Play-maker dares boast."[13]

Brome's protest marks other differences between the pair—differences of ethos and of training. Brome here is decidedly modest about his aspirations. In the prologue to *The Damoiselle*, for instance, he protests:

> Our Playmaker (for yet he won't be call'd
> Author, or Poet) nor beg to be install'd
> Sir *Lawreat*) has sent me out t'invite
> Your fancies to a full and cleane delight:
> And bids me tell you, That though he be none
> Of those, whose towring Muses scale the Throne
> Of Kings, yet his familiar mirth's as good,
> When 'tis by you approv'd and understood.[14]

Heywood, by contrast, advertised his productivity and generic breadth. He championed not only the place of the stage in the education of the nation but also his own role in so situating it. A digression in *The Hierarchie of the Blessed Angells* (1635), for instance, offers a brief, biographically based "history" of the theater that, with its use of nicknames, testifies to a familiarity, even camaraderie, with a variety of other playwrights and poets:

> *Greene*, who had in both Academies ta'ne
> Degree of Master, yet could never gaine
> To be call'd more than *Robin*: who had he
> Profest ought save the *Muse*, Serv'd, and been Free
> After a seven yeares Prentiseship; might have
> (With credit too) gone Robert to his grave.
> *Marlo*, renown'd for his rare art and wit,
> Could ne're attaine beyond the name of *Kit*;
> Although his *Hero* and *Leander* did
> Merit addition rather. Famous *Kid*
> Was call'd but *Tom. Tom. Watson*, though he wrote
> Able to make *Apollo's* selfe to dote
> Upon his Muse; for all that he could strive,
> Yet never could to his full name arrive.

> *Tom.Nash* (in his time of no small esteeme)
> Could not a second syllable redeeme.
> Excellent *Bewmont*, in the formost ranke
> Of the rar'st Wits, was never more than *Franck*.
> Mellifluous *Shake-speare*, whose inchanting Quill
> Commanded Mirth or Passion, was but *Will*.
> And famous *Johnson*, though his learned Pen
> Be dipt in *Castaly*, is still but *Ben*.
> *Fletcher* and *Webster*, of that learned packe
> None of the mean'st, yet neither was but *Jacke*.
> *Deckers* but *Tom*, nor *May*, nor *Middleton*.
> And hee's now but *Jacke Foord*, that once were *John*.

The rhyme, part of a larger section insisting on the importance of poetry in guaranteeing immortality, ends as Heywood includes himself among the list:

> Nor speake I this, that any here exprest,
> Should thinke themselves lesse worthy than the rest,
> Whose names have their full syllable and sound;
> Or that *Franck, Kit*, or *Jacke*, are the least wound
> Unto their fame and merit. I for my part
> (Thinke others what they please) accept that heart
> Which courts my love in most familiar phrase;
> And that it takes not from my paines or praise.
> If any one to me so bluntly com,
> I hold he loves me best that calls me *Tom*.[15]

Brome, who ironically does not appear on the list, figures himself not alongside but *under* these very same writers.[16] The prologue to *The Northern Lasse* (1632) describes the playwright as someone who "boasteth not his worth; and doth subscribe / Himselfe an *underservant in their Tribe*."[17] Sincere or not, Brome, in prologues and other prefatory matter, consistently uses a *humilitas* topos, usually deployed by other playwrights to distance themselves from stage or print, to construct his place as a literary successor, an inheritor of at least two generations of previous playwrights. His commendatory epistle to the Beaumont and Fletcher folio of 1647, for instance, asks to be allowed to "retain still my wonted modesty" and "Become a Waiter, in my ragged verse, / As Follower to the *Muses* followers."[18]

Although such writing is part of the widely accepted *humilitas* topos, peers too recognized Brome in a similar way, acknowledging his position as "underservant" by focusing attention on his "apprenticeship" to Ben Jonson. A commendatory epistle to *The Antipodes* (published 1640) opens by exclaiming:

> Jonson's alive! The world admiring stands,
> And to declare his welcome there, shake hands . . .

Therefore repair to him [Jonson's "ghost,"], and praise each line
Of his *Volpone, Sejanus, Catiline.*
But stay, and let me tell you where he is:
He sojourns in his Brome's *Antipodes.*[19]

In a commendatory epistle to *The Jovial Crew* (published 1652), John Hall congratulates Brome on being "by great Jonson . . . made free o' th' trade."[20] The title page to *The Covent Garden Weeded* reads: *"A Posthume* of Richard Brome, / An Ingenious Servant, and Imitator of his / Master, that famously Renowned / Poet *Ben Johnson."*[21] And the depiction of Brome as Jonson's apprentice is recorded most memorably by the so-called master himself, when he refers in *Bartholomew Fair* to "the poet . . . or his man, Master Brome, behind the arras."[22] Later, after scapegoating Brome for the failure of his own play *The New Inn,* Jonson acknowledge Brome as a "fellow" in a commendatory epistle of 1632, tracing Brome's biography in a verse "To my old Faithful *Servant,* and (by his continu'd Vertue) my loving *Friend,* the Author of this Work, Mr. Richard Brome":

> I Had you for a Servant, once, Dick Brome:
> And you perform'd a Servants faithful parts,
> Now, you are got to a nearer room,
> Of Fellowship, professing my old Arts.
> And you do doe them well, with good applause,
> Which you have justly gained from the Stage,
> By observation of those Comick Lawes
> Which I, your Master, first did teach the Age.
> You learn'd it well, and for it serv'd your time
> A Prentice-ship: which few do now adays.
> Now each Court-Hobby-horse will wince in rime;
> Both learned and unlearned, all write Playes."[23]

Such paratexts place Brome in a writerly generation distinct from Heywood, who wrote for and stalked the boards with the very men "under" whom Brome is said to have "served." They also emphasize his steady progression from apprenticeship to fellowship, the very character of which certifies the stage as a business and a brotherhood, a profession.

Heywood recognizes Brome in the latter's role as a trained professional. In *Hierarchie,* Heywood had advocated just such a systematic progression for playwrights, decrying a species of "youngster" that assumed the name of poet and "taske[d] such Artists as have tooke Degree / Before he was a Fresh-man." Heywood wanted "punies" to wait "until their Beards [are] growne, their wits more staid," and then "be admitted Free-men, and so strive / By Industry, how in that way to thrive."[24] Such privileging of the theater as an "industry" marks a point of intersection for the two dramatists. For although Brome's modesty seems at odds with Heywood's positioning of himself as chronicler of and apologist for an ideal, or idealized, theatrical community, the two playwrights share a number of convictions grounded in a shared conception of the professional dramatist—the conception of what Brome, as we have seen, calls the "playmaker."

PLAYMAKERS

Such a concept opposed the influx into the theater in the Caroline period of courtier aspirants and their romance-driven aesthetic—an institutional and aesthetic situation that was the result, Gurr writes, of the "closeness of the court's grip on the companies."[25] The influx fomented what has been called the second "Poets' War" of the early 1630s, a battle of taste between private theaters as well as between "supporters of the new courtier poets and those of the old guard of professional writers," specifically William Davenant and Thomas Carew, on the one hand, and Philip Massinger and James Shirley, on the other.[26] Barbs were exchanged between Davenant and Carew and Massinger and Shirley, but the implications of the aesthetic controversy would not have been lost on other dramatists, like Heywood and Brome, whose professional positions were at stake in the feud. Heywood's castigation of the "punies" in *Hierarchie*, for instance, was directed not only against unschooled balladeers, the usual objects of writers' derision, but also against this new group of courtier-writers emerging at the Blackfriars. And Brome championed a classical, understated style which he linked to the "great Masters of the Stage and Wit," and which was directly opposed to the novelty of courtly romance and pastoral:

> The title of our play, *A Jovial Crew*,
> May seem to promise mirth, which were a new
> And forc'd thing in these sad and tragic days
> For you to find, or we express in plays.
> We wish then you would change that expectation,
> Since jovial mirth is now grown out of fashion.[27]

In *The Court Beggar* (performed 1640), he offered a satiric attack on Davenant as well as Sir John Suckling, another courtier-dramatist. John Freehafer calls Brome's play "one of the chief records of opposition to Davenant's project for bringing courtly innovations into the public theater in 1639."[28]

Later I discuss the way in which what R. J. Kaufmann calls a "resistance to courtier encroachment on the drama" may have been part of Heywood and

Brome's experience of addressing events in Lancashire.[29] Here I focus on how such resistance can be observed in the shared suspicion both playwrights voice of theatrical publication. Although such protestations certainly can be interpreted as disingenuous—disavowals that ironically highlight a real interest in being men in print—the writers clearly wanted to appear skeptical of the printed drama. While the lavish presentation of Heywood's *Gynaikeion: or, Nine Books of Various History. Concerning Women* (1624) or *Hierarchie* testifies to his interest in the textual object, Heywood opposes an ideology of elite publication of the drama, taking stabs at Jonson's 1616 *Works*. In *The English Traveller*'s address to the reader, Heywood proclaims that his plays "are not exposed unto the world in volumes, to bear the title of Workes, (as others)," not only because they have been lost in the shuffle of companies and playhouses but also because "it was never any great ambition in me, to bee in this kind Volumniously read."[30] He is also at pains to make clear that his interest in print, which, as Barbara Baines notes, becomes more acute later in his career, derives from a desire to correct stolen or corrupt editions.[31] The prologue to the version of *If You Know Not Me, You Know Nobody*, printed in the 1637 *Pleasant Dialogues and Dramma's*, says that in it "the Author taxeth the most corrupted copy now imprinted, which was published without his consent."[32] Similar sentiments are echoed in its 1639 quarto publication, where Heywood complains that "some by Stenography, drew / The plot."[33] And Brome, while never directly mocking Jonson, seems similarly wary of or uninterested in publication. Except for *The Antipodes, The Sparagus Garden, The Northern Lasse*, and *Witches*, the bulk of his work was either not published in his lifetime or else lost. He mocks what he sees as courtly pretension in Suckling's printing of *Aglaura* (1638):

> By this large Margent did the Poet mean
> To have a comment writ upon his Scene?
> . . . .
> A Room with one side furnish'd, or a face,
> Painted half-way, is but a faire disgrace.
> This great voluminous Pamphlet may be said
> To be like one that hath more haire than head;
> More excrement than body.[34]

In opposition to the work of the printed play, then, these two dramatists are invested in the work of performed theater. For them such a theater could be powerful. Indeed, both Heywood and Brome are highly conscious of and concerned with the theater as a popular enterprise and endeavor; they both have and share with their audiences coherent notions of the potentially significant, catalyzing role of the stage in the popular imagination.[35] Heywood's *Apology for Actors* (1612) offers a carefully organized presentation of the theater's unique ability to represent real or invented events in an imaginative display so that both nobles and the common man can see that "vertues . . . are extolled, or . . . vices reproved . . . either animating men to noble attempts or attacking consciences of spectators."[36] Brome's terms are quieter and less self-congratulatory, but like Heywood, he believes in the potential of theatrical delight, and he adheres to a theatrical credo that, while concerned with audience approval, remains true to "antient Comick Lawes." The epilogue to *The English Moor* (performed 1637) offers:

> Now let me be a modost undertaker
> For us the players, the play and the play-maker:
> If we have faild in speech or action, we
> Must crave a pardon; If the Commedy
> Either in mirth, or matter be not right,
> As 'twas intended unto your delight,
> The Poet in hope of favour doth submit
> Unto your censure both himself and it,
> You judge but by the ancient Comick Lawes
> Not by their course who in this latter age
> Have sown such pleasing errors on the stage.[37]

And, for all his modest and humble appeals to the audience, Brome provides an extremely broad vision of the playmaker's craft. His plays themselves articulate for the theater a decidedly therapeutic potential; playmakers and plays are, for him, healers, especially healers of the mind. *The Antipodes* is his most developed meditation on this possibility, as it focuses on the antics of the aptly named doctor, Letoy, who stages household revels in order to cure the members of the Joyless family from various psychic preoccupations. The physician's success in curing not only the various Joylesses but himself as well is one of Renaissance drama's most unequivocal endorsements of the value of theater; it dramatizes and extends Heywood's claims in the *Apology*.[38]

For all the important differences between them, then, Heywood and Brome share commitments to the real and imaginary resources of the stage, not only as a site for performance but also as an enterprise with an existence independent of court infiltration. Their work together, I suggest, would have been fueled by these commitments. They would have bound the two disparate playwrights together in their other two collaborations, now lost: *The Life and Death of Sir Martin Skink* and *The Apprentice's Prize*.[39] But they would have bound the playwrights especially in the production of *The Late Lancashire Witches*, a play whose origins, contexts, and content exerted significant new pressures that would have appeared to jeopardize those very commitments.

TOILS AND TROUBLES

There were several pressures that would have made writing a play about the Lancashire witches a complicated undertaking. These pressures were all ramifications of the position of the commercial stage vis-à-vis the cultural politics of the early 1630s refracted by the specific setting and symbolic meaning of Lancashire, and they involved the topic of witchcraft itself, particularly as it was regulated in the provinces, as well as the institutional status of the theater, including the vexed position of the dramatist as purveyor of both popular and royal entertainment during the height of Charles I's "personal rule." It was to these pressures, which called into question the integrity of the dramatists' enterprise, that the collaboration of Heywood and Brome responded.

The belief in and persecution of witchcraft, though not as intense as in Europe, was a volatile issue in early modern England.[40] Witchcraft lay at the intersection of ideological and juridical debates of the period, and its changing status over the course of the sixteenth and seventeenth centuries measured a crisis of belief which had confronted the English population in a variety of ways since at least the Reformation.[41] But the case of Lancashire in the 1630s presented unique issues and difficulties. The affair was structured by many of the intense, competing social and juridical interests of the period, particularly government regulation in the provinces and the contested territory between skeptical inquiry and popular belief in comprehending and adjudicating local customs and grievances. The scare began late in 1633, when a twelve-year-old boy named Edmund Robinson, having neglected his daily chores, explained to his angry father that he had been captured by witches, taken to an old castle, and kept "hostage" while being forced to eat, drink, and watch the curious entertainments of the witches' meal.[42] Young Robinson was to admit some seven months later that this was a story of his own devising, the work of a young imagination bred by fears of parental chastisement as well as popular fables of an earlier Lancashire witch scare in 1612.[43] But at the time, his accusations catalyzed a surge of charges in the county so that by January 1633/4, approximately thirty men and women had been accused of witchcraft and put in jail in Lancaster. The accused were tried at the March 1634 assizes in Lancaster, and seventeen were found guilty by local jurors.

The circuit judges, however, were disturbed by the convictions, and though they returned the supposed witches to prison, they reported their concerns back to London. While the alleged witches remained in prison, the king and the Privy Council took a decisive interest in the affair, which, bearing the signs of a larger witch "infestation," was a threat taken seriously—though for different reasons—by skeptics as well as believers. Secretaries Coke and Windebank ordered Henry Bridgeman, the bishop of Chester, to examine seven of the accused and send them to London for further inquiry. Three of the seven died before being transported to London, but four were taken to the city in June 1634, where they, as well as the Robinson boy and his father, were interrogated by the Privy Council and examined by doctors and matrons for the bodily marks believed to signify a human's relations with the supernatural. The royal physician, William Harvey, supervised the doctors and matrons. Wallace Notestein considers Harvey's involvement to be the most salient point in the affair, a sign of an increasingly rational, empirical approach on the part of magistrates to witchcraft accusations and trials. "Probably by this time [Harvey] had come to disbelieve in [witchcraft]," he suggests. "One can but wonder if Charles, already probably aware of Harvey's views, had not intended from his first step in the Lancashire case to give his physician a chance to assert his opinion."[44]

But Charles and his council's involvement here illustrates not only philosophical skepticism but politically pragmatic interventionism as well. The Lancashire witch scare brought the attention of administrators to activities in a region whose regulation had been persistently difficult for the central government. As B. W. Quintrell has explained of the northern province in Charles's period, "it took the Privy Council many years to acquire a clear conception of Lancashire," and even then little could be done to "strengthen [Lancashire's] links with central government."[45] In other words, the goal of the king and his council in summoning the case to London was neither necessarily nor intentionally to usher in a new age of skeptical empiricism, what J. A. Sharpe describes as the "slackening" of "the desire to prosecute witches at the courts and the willingness to execute them . . . among the elite by 1630s."[46] Rather they were interested in the scare because it exceeded the capacities of provincial justice and afforded them an opportunity to intercede on behalf of central authority, to regulate law enforcement on the periphery—to bring the outskirts *in*. Their interest here was as much in adjudication as in theological or philosophical tolerance.[47] However enlightened the causes and effects, the interest was thus in part a form of royal intervention. Indeed, although James and Charles had been involved in witchcraft cases before, they had never requested the accused or witnesses to attend them in London.[48]

I have discussed this case at length in order to suggest the potential interests at stake for writers undertaking a contemporaneous play about the trial. Because, whether or not they were conscious of these particular ramifications, dramatists approaching this material scheme would have necessarily been implicated in the relations it presented between central, royal government and sociocultural activity in the provinces. This is due to the literal and symbolic significance of the setting of Lancashire for the theater community.

Lancashire had long held a place in the popular imagination as a remote, unsophisticated, and superstitious area as well as an undisciplined Catholic breeding ground. Although William Camden in his *Brittania* (1607, 1637) commended the bustling Lancastrian town of Manchester and praised the region for its aristocratic families that with "provident moderation [and] simplicity" stood "contented with their owne estate," the district was nevertheless seen as an "ungovernable" place relatively untouched by the effects of the Reformation.[49] Dramatic presentations often treated the region comically. In *The Devil Is an Ass* (1616), for instance, Ben Jonson capitalizes on a popular association of Lancashire with occultism in order to emphasize the "real" evil of London. When the naïve devil Pug asks to be sent to the city to practice his tricks, Satan simply scoffs at the request, telling Pug that his tame witchery does not measure up to the secular sins of London. "The State of Hell must care / Whom it employs, in point of reputation, / Here about London. You would make, I think, / An agent to be sent, for Lancashire."[50] Whereas Jonson gestures to Lancashire in order to comment on London, Middleton in his *Inner Temple Masque* (1619) takes the region as his object and mocks its Catholic affiliations:

> A foolish Fasting-Day,
> An unseasonable coxcomb, seeks now for a service;
> Has hunted up and down, has been at court,
> And the long porter broke his head across there;
> He had rather see the devil; for this he says,
> He ne'er grew up so tall with fasting-days.
> I would not, for the price of all my almanacs,
> The guard had took him there, they'd ha' beat out
> His brains with bombards. I bade him stay till Lent,
> And now he whimpers; he'd to Rome, forsooth,
> That's his last refuge, but would try awhile
> How well he should be us'd in Lancashire.[51]

Other forms of literature—letters and travelogues—remarked on and perpetuated the region's Catholic stereotype. Thomas Potts's *Wonderful Discoverie of Witches in the Countie of Lancaster* (1612), chronicling the 1612 scare, "published to the world" the shire's dubious honor of trying nineteen men and women for witchcraft, a number "knowen to exceed all others at any time heretofore."[52] A visitor to Lancashire in 1604 wrote that the inhabitants "sign themselves with the sign of the cross on the forehead at all prayers and blessings, and therefore they call it a blessing therewith to bless themselves when they first enter into the church, and in all their actions, even when they gape."[53] In his demonological tract *The Mystery of Witchcraft*, the Protestant clergyman Thomas Cooper explained that the 1612 haunting in Lancashire occurred in an area of "grosse ignorance and popery."[54] The London lawyer Richard James remarked of his journey to Lancashire in 1637: "Churches farre do stand / In lay mens hands, and chappells have no land / To cherish learned Curates, though Sir John / Doe preach for foure pounds unto Haselingdon."[55] In different ways and with different purposes, then, various seventeenth-century writers record a stereotype of Lancashire's backwardness and recusancy.[56]

This regional identity bore an important and material relation to the professional drama at the time. For Lancashire played a role in debates about popular and royal festivity which called attention not only to the precarious status of various "sports" in post-Reformation England, but also to the potential complicity of such sportive entertainment and monarchical interests. Lancashire's "rural" reputation, as we have seen, associated it with pre-Reformation forms of worship and celebration, and in 1617 the association was concretized with the issuing of the Stuart Book of Sports. After passing through and observing Lancashire in 1617, James I issued the order that, to the consternation of the "godly," gave royal sanction and support to popular recreation. On progress south from Scotland, James had stopped in Lancashire, where he witnessed local protests against godly restrictions on festive celebration. The king responded with a declaration specifically for Lancashire magistrates, which ordered them to permit some forms of festive revelry in the hope that moderate tolerance of popular pastimes would win conformity to the national church. The declaration, which was extended to the entire country in 1618, documented and cemented monarchical support of popular, as well as elite, revelry. At the same time, it also put Lancashire in a kind of synecdochal relationship to the principle of royal regulation of popular pastimes and festivity.

This relation was exacerbated precisely at the time of the Lancashire witch affair. In 1634, in between the original arrest of the witches and the performance of the play, Charles reissued his father's declaration as his own Book of Sports in response to a conflict over Sunday feasts in Somerset. His declaration begins with an interpretation of his father's original as a "prudent consider[ation]" of the need for recreation lest "if these times were taken from them, the meaner sort who labour hard all the week should have no recreations at all to refresh their spirits." It then reprints and supplements the earlier document, telling assize justices to "see that no man do trouble or molest any of our loyal and dutiful people, in or for their lawful recreations" and charging the clergy to ensure that "publication of this our command be made. . . . through all the parish churches of their several dioceses respectively."[57] These injunctions, simultaneous consolidations and allocations of royal authority, display Charles's uncanny ability to enact unaccommodating decisions that alienated and polarized the country. David Cressy notes that "while upholding the strictest ecclesiastical calendar, the Caroline regime also gave encouragement to activities . . . [known] to be pagan in origin and licentious in practice, offending the godly on both moral and theological grounds. The King's Book of Sports, promulgated but only lethargically promoted by James I, was reissued by Charles I . . . as part of a national programme."[58] That national program, in its endorsement of festive as well as ceremonial practices inside and outside the church, was incompatible with Protestant doctrine as well as fiscal responsibility, and rather than promoting domestic harmony, it ended up aggravating ideological conflict.[59]

This ideological conflict spilled over from the political domain into the cultural field of the theater. Charles's reissuing of the Book of Sports gave royal sanction to public as well as court playing, the latter having already been a widely acknowledged indulgence of the king and queen, again making tangible and concrete the affiliation between monarchy and local festivity.[60] Such an affiliation, though it might seem advantageous for popular dramatists, put them instead in difficult, awkward positions, for it implicitly forced their profession into an association with the crown and the influx of courtier drama it supported, an influx that, as the authorial feuding of the second Poets' War suggests, was perceived as antithetical to other theatrical commitments.[61] For a playwright such as Heywood, who advocated the function of the drama in teaching the court (as he wrote in his *Apology*, "What English Prince should hee behold the true portrature of that famous King *Edward* the third . . . and would not bee suddenly Inflam'd with so royall a spectacle, being made apt and fit for the like achievement?"), the former position would have jeopardized not only the moral "place" of the stage but also its dedication to the old "fashion" of the stage against the newer "punies."[62]

But a rejection of the association—that is, a rejection of court interest in the theater—could be equally compromising, for it could be construed as a rejection of the dramatists' own enterprise. A model of this kind of reaction was available in the specter of William Prynne and his shrill antitheatrical invective *Histriomastix* (1633), which cost the author his ears. Prynne's work took the theater to task not only for its anarchic licentiousness and impiousness, the customary antitheatrical complaint, but also for its ideological connection to a profligate king and capricious queen. Whereas earlier antitheatrical documents had presented themselves, however disingenuously, as supporters of the monarch, concerned about the threat posed by the drama to the national order she or he desired, Prynne attacks the stage as an accomplice in the monarchy's general dissipation.[63]

Dramatists of the period show themselves to be rattled by the endless complaints of the book. Heywood in particular attacks Prynne and his treatise by name in the prefaces to his published plays of the early 1630s. The dedication to *The English Traveller* praises plays in spite of Prynne: "So highly were they respected in the most flourishing state of the Roman Empire; and if they have been vilefied of late by any Separisticall humorist, (as in the now Questioned Histriomastix) I hope by the next Terme to give such satisfaction to the world, vindicating many particulars in that worke maliciously exploded and condemned, as that no Gentleman of qualitie and judgment, but shall therein receive a reasonable satisfaction."[64] He treats him again in the epistle to the reader of *A Mayden-head Well Lost* (1634): "Neither can this be drawne within the Criticall censure of that most horrible *Histriomastix*, whose uncharitable doome hauing damned all such to the flames of Hell, hath it selfe already suffered a most remarkable fire here vpon Earth."[65] Of course, Heywood had been a longtime defender of the theater against its opponents, so his counters to Prynne were, in some ways, not unusual. But the vehemence of his response seems to be due in part to a need to disavow the fact that Prynne's critique of the proximity of crown, court, and drama was simply a more strident and hysterical version of his and his cohorts' own. A play like Massinger's *Roman Actor* (1629), in which the thespian protagonist is killed because of court interest in (not disdain for or censorship of) his plays, dramatizes the specific issue at stake: the potentially fatal connection between the actor and the ruler who supports him.[66] Such a play underscores how perplexing were the conditions of the Caroline drama, and it suggests that writing about Lancashire, a geographical symbol of this perplexity in the increasingly polarized political and cultural milieu of the 1630s, might have been especially vexing. It brings into sharp, conscious focus the general forces competing to "place" the stage according to their own interests.[67]

Heywood and Brome may have felt the weight of a particular force, issuing not from the monarch himself but from his aristocratic opposition in the Privy Council. Philip Herbert, earl of Pembroke, a council member and Lord Chamberlain, is believed by contemporary critics to have taken an active interest in the witchcraft affair, commissioning *The Late Lancashire Witches* from the King's Men for his own purposes. The earl hoped, these critics claim, to discredit Archbishop William Laud, who was known to be skeptical of the occult, by convincing the London public of the witches' culpability. Herbert Berry, for instance, assumes that Pembroke "made a bargain" with the King's Men, offering them "the first use of spectacular material" from the royal interrogations so that they would perform a play that, in direct opposition to Laud, depicted the witches as both real and guilty. Berry thus reads *Witches* as a "statement for the prosecution," a play that, following the earl's directives, unequivocally condemns the witches of Lancashire.[68] The fact that the Master of Revels intervened on behalf of the King's Men to prevent other companies from "intermingleing some passages of witches in old playes to yᵉ prʲiudice of their designed Comedy of the Lancashire witches" seems to buttress the claim.[69]

Berry assumes that if or because the earl of Pembroke commissioned the play, the King's Men's writers embraced that commission wholeheartedly, dramatizing the affair in the way Pembroke endorsed—that is, as a declaration of the reality and threat of witchcraft and thus as an affront to Laud (and therefore the king). But such a reading relies too heavily on suspect assumptions about the transparent relationship between a play's patron and its substance and political affiliation.[70] For, given the variety of pressures surrounding the witch trial, which made a definitive authorial position on the case difficult, it is just as possible that the dramatists would have perceived such sponsorship as a burden or imposition on their work—a burden related to, or symbolic of, the series of other pressures connected with the play.[71] If the earl of Pembroke did indeed have a hand in orchestrating *Witches*, such patronage would represent only the climactic demand in a chain of related constraints influencing the production of the Lancashire witch play. Heywood and Brome's response to this demand was to refuse to deliver an unequivocal statement about the witches' existence or guilt.[72] Instead, their play, by depicting a comic version of the witches, emphasizes and exposes the tendentious investments that motivate judicial approaches to witchcraft; it thus renders judgment on the witches impossible.

THINGS IMPROBABLE AND IMPOSSIBLE

Magic and witchcraft were, of course, staples of the early theater. The tradition included plays such as Robert Greene's *Friar Bacon and Friar Bungay* (1589), which used magicians' tricks to represent and then repudiate clerical subversiveness, and *Dr. Faustus* (1590) and *Macbeth* (1604–5), which invoked the occult to figure forth contemporary religious and philosophical struggles between skepticism and faith, iconoclasm and idolatry, predestination and free will. During the reign of James, whose *Daemonologie* (1597) proved his interest in the connection between the occult and divine right, witchcraft persisted as an important trope for bids for patronage as well as political and social critique. Ben Jonson featured witches in the antimasque to his masque for Queen Anne, *The Masque of Queens* (1609). Plays such as Middleton's tragedy *The Witch* (1613?) capitalized on the images of the occult to portray a corrupt court, while Dekker, Ford, and Rowley's *Witch of Edmonton* (1621) presented witchcraft as an effect of the erosion of local social relations. *The Late Lancashire Witches*, in contrast to these plays' epistemological questioning and caustic political critiques or social commentaries, displays witchcraft as a form of festive inversion.

There is evidence that at least one educated theatergoer noticed this particular tone and its divergence from that of other plays. In a description of *Witches*, sent as part of a newsletter to his patron Sir Robert Phelips, the secretary Nathaniel Tomkyns shows himself charmed if unchallenged by the play. He describes the plot and its effects:

> The subject was of the slights and passages done or supposed to be done by these witches sent from thence hither and other witches and their familiars; Of ther nightly meetings in severall places: their banqueting with all sorts of meat and drinke conveyed vnto them by their familiars vpon the pulling of a cord: the walking of pailes of milke by themselues . . . the transforming of men and weomen into the shapes of seuerall creatures and especially of horses by putting an inchaunted bridle into ther mouths: their posting to and from places farre distant in an incredible short time: the cutting of a witch-gentwoman's hand in the forme of a catt, by a soldier turned miller, known to her husband by a ring thereon, (the onely tragicall part of the storie:) the representing of wrong and putatiue fathers in the shape of

meane persons to gentmen by way of derision: the tying of a knott at a
mariage to cassate masculine abilitie, and ye conveying away of ye good
cheer and bringing in a mock feast of bones and stones thereof and ye
filling of pies with liuing birds and yong catts &c: And though there be
not in it (to my understanding) any poeticall Genius, or art, or language, or
iudgement to state or tenet of witches (which I expected,) or application to
vertue but full of ribaldrie and of things improbable and impossible; yet in
respect of the newnesse of ye subiect (the witches being still visible and in
prison here) and in regard it consisteth from the beginning to the ende of
odd passages and fopperies to provoke laughter, and is mixed with diuers
songs and dances, it passeth for a merrie and excellent new play, *per acta est
fabula.*[73]

Tomkyns approves the work as it "passeth for a merrie and excellent new play,"
and he attributes its commercial good fortune to its contemporaneity (the
"newnesse of ye subject").[74] But in addition to its topicality and sensational-
ism, the play appeals to Tomkyns because it defeats his playgoing expectations,
especially those for a learned, didactic treatment of witchcraft. Although journalistic dramas, according to Diane Henderson, attracted spectators by
"us[ing] historical cases . . . to produce entertainment as well as hortatory conclusions," *Witches* is here perceived as far from exemplary.[75] In the place of
instruction, Tomkyns finds "ribaldrie and things improbable and impossible";
in place of artistic decorum, "odd passages and fopperies to provoke laughter."
Heywood and Brome's comic relief serves a purpose: by turning witchcraft
into a "home-spun medley" (*Witches*, 479–80) the dramatists expose the self-
interest that motivates *both* superstitious belief in *and* empirical skepticism of
witchcraft—and the way that these seemingly exclusive epistemologies col-
lude in witchcraft regulation.

Such self-interest is revealed most forcefully when the writers expand on
their sources and depict the behaviors of invented characters. The first scene,
for instance, is not part of the original Lancashire affair. In it three gallants,
Arthur, Shakestone, and Bantam, are hunting a rabbit. The scene combines
the high revelry of the hunt with overtones of witchery: the chase has gone
awry, complains Arthur, because the hare has been stolen by a witch. Incited
by his claim, the men argue about the cause of the hare's disappearance in
rapid statements that shuttle between conviction and distrust:

> ARTHUR. Was ever sport of expectation,
> Thus crost in th'height.
> SHAKESTONE. Tush, these are accidents, all game is subject to.
> ARTHUR. So you may call them
> Chances, or crosses, or what else you please,

But for my part, Ile hold them prodigies,
As things transcending nature.
. . . .
SHAKESTONE. Somewhat strange, but not as you inforce it.
ARTHUR. Make it plaine
That I am in an error, sure I am
That I about me have no borrow'd eyes.
They are mine owne, and matches.
. . . .
SHAKESTONE. Perhaps some Foxe had carth'd there . . .
And so her scape appeare but Naturall,
Which you proclaime a Wonder.   (1–47)

One gallant subscribes, while the other objects, to the idea of witchcraft. Their
beliefs are different but their motives are the same: both characters rationalize
the loss of the hare in order to protect their performance in the hunt. Arthur
believes in witchcraft because it explains his failure; Shakestone rejects the
occult because such a denial gives him leverage over Arthur. Ironically both
abandon the chase, as well as their positions on witchcraft, when a new character, Whetstone, arrives. Whetstone is a fop, and when he champions a belief
in witches, the other three immediately abandon both their hunt and their
conversation. "It is a way to call our wits in question, / To have him seene
amongst us," they say as they sneak away from him (77–78). More important
than arguments either for or against witchcraft is the gallants' concern for their
reputations.

Their reputations are threatened later in the play, and again by witchcraft.
The play's central witch, Mistress Generous, is Whetstone's aunt, and she
exacts revenge from his tormentors by punishing the gallants with hallucina-
tory visions that challenge their ancestry. She reveals to Arthur and Shakestone
that they were begotten by a servant and a local tailor, respectively, and she
produces for Bantam the apparition of the "pedant in [his] fathers house,"
suggesting that, as Whetstone interprets, "one morning, when your mothers
husband rid early to have a *Nisi prius* tryed at *Lancaster* Syzes, hee [the pedant]
crept into his warme place, lay close by her side, and then were you got"
(2126–28). All three gallants, vulnerable to attacks on their pedigrees, are
disturbed by the visions, and their rebuttal is to insist that the visions are
forms of witchcraft—but only in order to discredit and condemn them. The
gallants claim that Mistress Generous's predictions are the effects of conjuring,
and are thus *not* the truth. They also propose to prosecute her, because witchcraft demands trial and elimination. Backed by his friends, Arthur gleefully

exposes Mistress Generous to her husband, delighting especially in the prospect of a display of sensory evidence: "But Gentlemen, shall we try if we can
by examination get from them something that may abbreviate the cause unto
the wiser in Commission for the peace before wee carry them before 'em?"
(2702–5). Arthur combines, ironically, a superstitious conviction in witchcraft
with empiricist tactics to prosecute it.

Like Arthur, the character Doughty rapidly changes his convictions; he
shifts with ease between excesses of belief and skepticism. When he enters the
play, he is firmly convinced that the Seely family, thrown topsy-turvy with
servants and children ruling the parents, has been haunted. But as soon as
comforting patriarchal order has been restored, Doughty reverses his opinion.
"I feare nothing now you have your wits againe," he says, maintaining that
"there is no such thing" as "sprite or goblin" and questioning other believers:
"Art thou mad to dreame of Witchcraft?" (1196–7, 1344–5, 1375).

Ironically Doughty's skeptical conversion is interpreted by the other characters as *evidence* of the very witchcraft he disavows. "He's as much changed
and bewitched as they I fear," Arthur says of him (1376). Nor does Doughty
maintain his skepticism for long; it lasts only until he loses his mistress Mal
and witnesses another marriage turned upside-down. At this point he returns
to his old convictions, which offer him the most effective mechanism for
explaining his own and others' failures in love and lovemaking: "Witchery,
witchery, more witcherie still flat and plaine witchery. Now do I thinke upon
the codpeece point the young jade gave him at the wedding: shee is a witch,
and that was a charme, if there be any in the World" (1904–7). The former
skeptic thus turns believing prosecutor, dedicating himself, like Arthur, to a
judicial process that answers both positions. He promises to "worry all the
Witches in *Lancashire*" till they are "seized on by the tallons of Authority"
(2206–7, 2696–7). Doughty, vacillating between total belief and total distrust, represents the fleeting skepticism and fleeting conviction that are the
products of personal fear and jealousy. His quick conversions, combined with
the pleasure he derives from harrying the women and cooperating with authority, compromise either stance.

Doughty's obverse is Master Generous, husband to the witch Mistress Generous and another character absent from the source material. An innkeeper
whom other characters praise as "the sole surviving sonne / Of long since
banisht hospitality," Generous represents an older brand of rural liberality and
beneficence combined with an enlightened, rational skepticism (205–6). At
the start of the play, he is certain of his wife's fidelity and unconvinced of

witchcraft. Generous responds with equanimity to accusations of witchcraft: "They that think so dreame, / For my beliefe is, no such thing can be" (291–92). But with a twist on a traditional cuckold plot, Generous is taunted into anxiety not about his wife's sexual fidelity but about her interest in the occult. When his servant insists that the wife has been trying to entangle him (the servant) in witchcraft scenarios, Generous quickly adopts a belief in witches.

Generous's attempts to cope with this information organize the second half of the play. In one of the most fascinating scenes, Generous accuses his wife of witchcraft and, after she confesses in lugubrious tones, magisterially and magnanimously forgives her:

> GENEROUS. The more I strive to unwinde
> My selfe from this *Meander*, I the more
> Therein am intricated; prithee woman
> Art thou a Witch?
>
> MISTRESS GENEROUS. It cannot be deny'd, I am such a curst Creature.
>
> GENEROUS. Keep aloofe, and doe not come too neare me, O my trust;
> Have I since first I understood my selfe
> Bin of my soule so charie, still to studie
> What best was for it's health, to renounce all
> The workes of that black Fiend with my best force
> And hath that Serpent twin'd me so about,
> That I must lye so often and so long
> With a Divell in my bosome?
> . . . .
>
> MISTRESS GENEROUS. Tinctured in blood, blood issuing from the
>   heart,
> Sir I am sorry; when I looke towards Heaven
> I beg a gracious Pardon; when on you
> Me thinkes your Native goodnesse should not be
> Lesse pittiful than they: 'gainst both I have err'd
> From both I beg attonement.
> . . . .
>
> GENEROUS. Rise, and as I doe, so heaven pardon me;
> We all offend, but from such falling off,
> Defend us.   (1742–54, 1791–96, 1808–10)

Generous's accusation reproduces the commonplace link between the witch and the devil, but it extends the notion by foregrounding the link's threat to personal integrity. Rich with rhetorical formulations of imperiled selfhood and desperate repentance, this sequence of admission and absolution allows Generous to reclaim his endangered identity by magnanimously accepting his wife's remorse. But Generous's display is called into question immediately since Mistress Generous betrays her confession and absolution by running off with her sister witch Mal, to whom she explains her duplicitous apology:

> Some passionate words mixt with forc't tears
> Did so inchant his eyes and eares
> I made my peace, with promise never
> To do the like; but once and ever
> A Witch thou know'st. Now understand
> New businesse wee tooke in hand.
> My husband packt out of the towne
> Know that the house, and all's our owne.   (2046–53)

Does her husband's prior forgiveness—and the sense of self it refurbished—count if it has been offered to, accepted, and then abandoned by the unrepentant? If this question presents the central interpretive paradox of both the practice and the theory of confession, the play quickly renders the point moot as Generous reveals to the audience that he never completely pardoned his wife anyway. He tells his friends that although he spoke of forgiveness, he remained suspicious and continued to spy on his wife, the surest sign of his loss of faith in her, if not in witchcraft. So when he discovers her missing from bed early in the morning, he tracks her down to her midnight meeting with her coven, and in a wonderful literalization of seventeenth-century "gaol delivery," he hands her over with a mixture of sadness and satisfaction to the authorities:

> My heart hath bled more for thy curs'd relapse
> . . . But wherefore should I preach to one past hope?
> Or where the divell himselfe claimes righte in all.
> Seeke the least part or interest? Leave your Bed,
> Up, make you ready; I must *deliver you*
> *Into the hand of Justice.*"   (2526–32)

Generous shuttles between rejection of and belief in witches insofar as the two poles conform to his sinking marital fortunes and dwindling goodwill. So although he starts out as a rare emblem of an older generation and geography of munificence, he ends the play as the instrument of a newer regime eager to serve a series of higher authorities: first the local commission of the peace, and ultimately, as the audience would have been aware owing to the contemporary case, the prerogative courts.

Generous's change to ungenerous conviction, like Arthur's and Doughty's, characterizes a provincial male personality that neither sustains epistemological doubt nor commits to a course of belief and action. Instead Arthur, Doughty, and Generous waver between positions until they willingly cede responsibility to what Doughty calls "the tallons of Authority." It may be more than a point of irony to note here that during the second half of Charles's rule, Lancashire, in contrast to most other regions splintering from the central government, actually became more conformable to the crown. Its needs were seen as their needs. B. W. Quintrell suggests that after initial antagonism to Charles's 1631 Book of Orders, Lancashire magistrates became increasingly amenable to following statutes and to reporting their activities back to the Privy Council: "Between 1634–1638 Lancashire produced more reports for the Council than any other county. . . . It looks very much as though the requirements of the Book of Orders chimed with what Lancashire JPs at last recognized as necessary for their county."[76] The writers of *Witches* did not have the retrospective vantage point from which to secure this view, but they do expose in their play just such tendentious judicial and magisterial alliances.

In this case the alliance was not based on a mutual belief in the witches' guilt: the circuit judges from London doubted the Lancashire justices and jury, as did the king and majority of his council, who overturned the judgment of the Lancashire jury. But here the difference is precisely the point. Although the council and local jurors disagreed on the particular decision, they nevertheless shared a commitment to a regulatory juridical process: they agreed on bringing the witches in, first to the Lancashire assizes, then to London.[77] The play, that is, especially in the characters of Arthur, Doughty, and Generous, dramatizes the embrace of legal routine and the self-interest that motivates it. Rather than establishing what Berry calls a "case for the prosecution," *Witches* shows that the prosecution and the defense are mutually implicated.

This mutual implication is extended in the witch scenes, which are imaginatively culled from the real incident, and in which the dramatists portray witchcraft as festive revelry, turning *maleficia* into sport. The effect is to qualify *both* sport and the occult by noting their points of contact: the interruption of the chase, for instance, reveals hunting as no more valiant than a search for lowly witches, while it shows witchcraft as no more elevated—or dangerous— than interference with a gallant's play. And in other scenes the dramatists align witchcraft not with aristocratic pretensions (like Middleton's *Witch*) or social ostracism (like *Edmonton*) but with popular indulgences, particularly feasting and festivity, capitalizing on the ambiguous status of popular entertainment to defer, rather than establish, the witches' guilt or innocence.[78]

The play's witches disrupt the order of things, and their behavior appears to some, like Doughty, as dangerous. But their disorder is also associated with festive celebration, making it a positive symbol of communal spontaneity and release.[79] In Doughty's words: "This is quite upside downe, the sonne controlls the father, and the man overcrowes his masters coxcombe, sure they are be-witched. . . . Sure all the Witches in the Country, have their hands in this home-spun medley" (409–11, 479–80). Doughty's response is a frightened one, but his description of the witchcraft as a "home-spun medley" also asso-ciates the witches with permissive recreation. The playwrights emphasize this possibility in other ways as well. For instance, whereas most witches were accused of destroying crops or livestock, these witches of Lancashire are held accountable for stealing meals *already made*. Some take a wedding cake from the marriage feast for the Seelys' servants. Mal Spencer makes her milk pail move and takes a round-trip visit to London in a single evening to get special Miter wine. In the scene most closely modeled on Lancashire court testimony and Edmund Robinson's claims, two witches, including Mistress Generous, spirit a young boy off to their festive gathering. The celebration invokes the supernatural only to turn it into the human and homely. The witches eat and recount stories: of the animals on which they've traveled, of the tricks they've played successfully, of the sexual partners they have had or hope to take. The feast and its conversation are deliberately earthy, indulging carnal appetites in a way both debased and yet poignant for its simplicity and the sense of scarcity it conjures. In contrast to either the refined courtly banquet, the Rabelaisian repast, or even the frightening witches' brew, the party here is on the order of makeshift gluttony. The witches spend most of their time singing ballads for entrees: "Pul for the Poultry, Foule & Fish / For emptie shall not be a dish. . . . This meat is tedious, now some Farie / Fetch what belongs unto the Dairie" (1535–40).

Rather than endorsing or denying the witches or their craft, these scenes make the coven's activities seem not so much illegal as recreational. The witches claim that their interest is only in generating laughter. In their first appearance the witches exchange their plans for the evening's activities:

> MEG. What new devise, what dainty straine
> More for our myrth now then our gaine,
> Shall we in practice put.
> . . . .
> Before we play another game,
> We must a little laugh and thanke
> Our feat familiars for the pranck
> They played us last.
> . . . .

MEG. Now let us laugh to thinke upon
The feat which we have so lately done,
In the distraction we have set
In *Seelyes* house; which shall beget
Wonder and sorrow 'mongst our foes,
Whilst we make laughter of their woes.
. . . .
GIL. But to be short,
The wedding must bring on the sport.
                    (526–33, 548–66)

Their revelry is explicitly termed *sport*, a term that takes on increasingly explicit metatheatrical meaning over the course of the play.

The term is picked up and extended by Mistress Generous when she plans to charm the gallants with false vision of their fathers. She announces that she intends to "celebrate to *sport*: / Tis all for mirth, we mean no hurt" (2080–81; emphasis added). And she pursues the charm more like a play than a bewitching. In order to "bring a new conceit to passe," she orders Whetstone to

Retire the Gallants to some privat roome,
Where call for wine, and junckets what you please,
Then thou shalt need to do no other thing
Than what this note directs thee, observe that
And trouble me no further.   (2066–70)

Mistress Generous figures herself as designer of a plot or "trick" to be performed for her audience of gallants. She and her group of witches come the closest in this play to "playwright figures"—characters whose behavior and actions are analogous to the work of the dramatist—and it is in such self-conscious theatricality that their appeal, rather than their guilt, rests.

These witches are comedians whose activities are a species of Caroline urban wit: as in Mistress Generous's display of false fathers, they dupe the gallants and reveal their pretensions. At the play's opening, one of the witches proposes that they "dance to day / To spoyle the Hunters sport" (571–72). As they parcel out their assignments, they anticipate the theatricality of their endeavor, and Maud decides that she will assume the position of spectator. Meg asks, "But where will *Mawd* bestow her selfe to day?" and Maud replies, "O' th' Steeple top; Ile sit and see you play" (598–99). Their witches' sport, then, is to sport with the sports of the gentry. They repeat their dramatic mischief later in the play when they interfere with the wedding dances. One of the coven causes the musicians to play "every one a severall tune," so that the song becomes a cacophony of incoherent sound. Doughty complains of this collaborative failure against which the witches' success looks brighter: "I bad them play the beginning o' the World, and they play, I know not what" (1396–97). Their last enterprise before their capture is tormenting a boastful miller-turned-soldier who brags he is not afraid of witches. Although the soldier paves the way for their apprehension by the authorities, the witches fright and fight with him in a manner that discredits his valor. In the context of a variety of Caroline comedies that favored the clever underdog over the aristocrat or wealthy merchant, the witches can be seen to possess some of the qualities of less ambiguously triumphant wits, like Fairfield in James Shirley's *Hyde Park*.[80] The pastimes of these shrewd urban characters are games that critique the festive emptiness or the excesses of courtly pretenders. Similarly, the witches' sport relies on this paradigm of witty resistance to blunt the spectacle of the law that seizes them in the end.

While the male characters approve the capture of the witches by officials, the witches practice crafts that—akin not only to *maleficia* but also in various ways to festive play—complicate the play as a simple endorsement of their guilt or innocence. As we have seen, the issue of sports and pastimes was a vexed one at this time, and by invoking it here, in relation to the witches, the playwrights make the case for or against the witches particularly ambiguous. Their Lancashire games—delight in eating, drinking, and piping—represent an extreme side of the indulgent play invited, if not explicitly approved, by the Stuart Book of Sports. To sanction them signaled a tacit confirmation of Charles's 1634 reissue of the Sports Book and its ideological implications. Nevertheless, to object to these simple forms of delight would have represented a zealous rejection of play, particularly stage play. That is, to reject or condemn the witches and their comic enterprise would be to reject *Witches* as a play, as an entertainment, as a pastime. The playwrights thus leave their audience, necessarily complicit with the festive impulse simply by having attended the theater, not with an absolute message about the witches but with information that could be used either to condemn or to defend them. Indeed, this contradictory effect is heightened further by the fact that the play was performed before the Privy Council decision was made, or at least publicized, a point to which the playwrights gesture in their epilogue, the final exercise in forestalling judgment:

> Now while the Witches must expect their due
> By lawfull Justice, we appeale to you
> For favourable censure; what their crime

May bring upon 'em, ripenes yet of time
Has not reveal'd. Perhaps great mercy may
After just condemnation give them day
Or longer life. We represent as much
As they have done, before Lawes hand did touch
Upon their guilt; But dare not hold it fit,
That we for Justices and Judges sit.
And personate their grave wisdomes on the Stage
Whom we are bound to honour; No, the Age
Allowes it not. Therefore unto the Lawes
We can but bring the Witches and their cause,
And there we leave 'em, as their Divels did,
Should we go further with 'em? Wit forbid;
What of their storie, further shall ensue,
We must referre to time, our selves to you.   (2803–20)

The indeterminacy of this ending is intimately connected with the joint production of the play—joint production, that is, by a pair of writers whose
profile violates many of the assumed characteristics of collaborative teams. I
am suggesting that at one level the pair's incongruity stands as a key to
interpreting *Witches*: it makes the play impossible to read unequivocally, challenging any straightforward assumptions that the play would necessarily follow single-mindedly the interest of a noble sponsor. But I am also arguing that
at another level the dramatists' unusual pairing actually helped make this
resistance possible. That is, whether intentionally or not, the affiliation of
Heywood and Brome, dramatists highly invested in the autonomy of the theatrical institution not only against its detractors but also against courtly encroachment, facilitated the ambiguity that marks their play. The mechanics of
this facilitation are past recall now. There is no explicit evidence documenting
the way in which Heywood and Brome came to share responsibility for this
play. Were they hand-picked and paired by the company or its patron since
Brome had written before about northern counties (in *The Northern Lasse*) or
since Heywood pretended to a knowledge of witches (in *Hierarchie*)? Or did
they volunteer to work and to work together? Regardless of the auspices of
their pairing, however, the unique arrangement they present—of competing
biographies, associations, styles—needs to be understood as a response to, a
simultaneous mirroring and attempted deflection of, the novel pressures associated with writing for the Caroline stage and for this witch play in particular.
It also needs to be understood as a powerful statement, in an apparently mar-
ginal play, about what playwrights may have perceived as the endangered
integrity of the theatrical institution in the Caroline period.

Conclusion
Companies in Collaboration

R ather than continuing to pursue the trajectory of joint authorship into
the drama of the Interregnum or Restoration, I turn back in this conclu-
sion to consider another kind of collaborative activity prior to the closing of
the theaters in 1642—that of the acting companies. In the previous chapters I
have aimed to account for the pairings of particular writers, and have raised
and tried to answer a series of questions about the motivations as well as the
implications of these pairings. To conclude, however, I want to consider the
pairing not of dramatists but of dramatic companies, investigating how a
corporate as well as an individual ethos could operate in instances of joint
work.

A number of theater historians have focused on the existence and influence
of "company identity" in the world of the early modern stage, on the way each
acting company would have established "its own style, its own textual procedures, its own sense of purpose, and its own impact on audiences and other
acting companies."[1] Such an emphasis shifts attention from the role of the
individual playwright to the place of the acting group in determining the
choice and meaning of texts; at the same time, it preserves notions of distinct,
if corporate, theatrical personality. My point here is not simply to assign to the
"company" an agency or intentionality usually ascribed (or, more recently,
denied) to the individual writer or player.[2] Rather it is to pursue again the
strategies and potential stakes, especially in terms of audience affiliation and
identification, for groups of actors and shareholders working together. In what
follows, then, I speculate on, without trying to answer definitively, some inter-

pretive questions and challenges posed by company collaboration, defining collaboration as activity that involves multiple troupes performing together on a particular play or for a prescribed period of time, maintaining and returning to their discrete identities when the work is finished. I focus on Thomas Heywood's *Ages* plays, particularly his *Iron Age* (1632), which, as he writes, was "Publickely Acted by two Companies, vppon one Stage at once and haue at sundry times thronged three seuerall Theaters."[3]

This kind of collaboration at the company level has analogues in varieties of shared work by Elizabethan troupes. According to one model, players moved between companies, often permanently or with the expectation of permanence, but also in temporary arrangements, as when Robert Wilson from the Queen's Men and Robert Browne from Worcester's went to play with a branch of Leicester's Men in the Low Countries in 1585. Something closer to a version of company collaboration occurred when players moved as a group, as did a subset of the Admiral's Men—Robert Shaw, William Bird, Richard Jones, and Thomas Downton—who left Henslowe's Rose in 1597 for Pembroke's Men at the Swan, only to be forced to return to Henslowe, under contract, in the fall of that year. Henslowe's accounts for October 1597 preserve the sense of two distinct company identities inhabiting the Rose together, as he documents the date when "be gane my lord admerals & my lord of penbrockes men to playe at my howsse" and a loan to the actor Robert Shaw "to by [*sic*] a boocke for the company of my lorde admeralls men & my lord of penbrockes."[4] In addition to the peregrinations of individuals or sets of players, entire troupes are known to have merged. While Andrew Gurr cautions against a too ready acceptance of theories of company "amalgamation" for the situation of the Admiral's and Strange's Men in the early 1590s, troupes did join forces explicitly, as Oxford's and Worcester's Men did in 1602, when they started to play under one roof and one name.[5]

In addition to such movement and merging, provincial and London records indicate activities that more closely resemble a model of mutual playing, whereby troupes came together for a particular performance or at a particular venue. Touring branches of the Queen's Men, according to Scott McMillin and Sally-Beth MacLean, "entered into occasional collaborations with other acting companies," including the Children of the Chapel and Sussex's Men.[6] The Admiral's Men may have played with Strange's "at the same town, possibly in a shared performance, at Ipswich on 7 August 1592," as well as with the actors of Derby's and Lord Stafford's.[7] Whether the troupes were actually sharing performances or simply venues remains a question; as Gurr notes, "The provincial evidence for two playing companies merging for a joint show is tricky," because "there is rarely enough in the records to register whether a single payment is for a single performance or just the total sum paid to different companies for different plays."[8] For the children's companies, it seems as though joint productions led to, or were part of the process of, fusion or amalgamation. The Children of the Chapel played together with the Windsor Chapel choir in 1567–68 and again in 1577, after which time "the two groups seem to have merged, presumably to become part of [Richard] Farrant's semi-detached enterprise at his new playhouse in Blackfriars."[9] This merged company played at court with the children of Paul's on New Year's Day 1584 in a performance of John Lyly's *Campaspe* and again with them in March for *Sappho and Phao*. The joint performances are memorialized in the published plays' title pages, which indicate that the dramas were "played by her maiesties children, and the children of Paul's." The two groups of children continued to play together at Paul's, under the direction of Thomas Giles with Lyly as deputy and playwright, until the children were prevented from playing in London in 1590.[10]

In hindsight, these instances of communal company activity within the fluid world of London-centered playing can be seen as early permutations of the more circumscribed, distinct collaborative operation behind *The Iron Age*, in which two troupes acted "vppon one Stage at once" before returning to their respective houses and repertories. This latter joint work must be understood in the context of the particular theatrical conditions of the early 1610s (*The Iron Age* was published in 1632 but is believed to have been composed and performed as part of the *Ages* sequence, and thus sometime between 1610 and 1613). These conditions, as opposed to the Elizabethan examples I have cited, included the licensing of several companies under royal patronage, the standardizing of company-playhouse connections (begun formally in 1594), the emergence of the indoor playhouse as a venue for adult companies, and the establishment of predictable—if flexible—repertories and audiences according to social class as well as aesthetic preference.

These conditions are of particular interest in considering the collaboration behind *The Iron Age*, since it likely involved the King's and Queen Anne's companies, whose performances and crowds were beginning to diverge in substantial ways precisely at the time of its debut.[12] Fellow playwrights such as John Webster call attention to substantive issues of venue and audience when, in his letter to the reader in the published edition of *The White Devil* (1612) performed by the Queen's players at the Red Bull, he complains that the play was "acted, in so dull a time of winter, presented in so open and black a theatre, that it wanted . . . a full and understanding auditory." Perhaps the problem was accounted for by the staging of his next play, *The Duchess of Malfi* (performed 1612–14), by the King's Men at the Blackfriars. William Turner, in his *Dish of Lenten Stuffe* (1612), remarks on what recent scholars define as the difference between the Queen's repertory of citizen and "favored nation" plays and the King's tragedies of court and state when he acknowledges that the Bankside players "teach idle trickes of love" whereas the "Bull will play the man."[13] Given this context, I try now to map possible motives for and effects of a theatrical performance that asked two companies to join, perhaps even as they maintained, their discrete corporate identities.

The most obvious ground for the collaboration behind *The Iron Age* is casting demand. Like *The Silver Age* before it, which was performed, according to Revels accounts, by the "Queens players and the Kings men" in 1612, the *Iron Age* involves a large roster of significant characters. There are fifty-two speaking parts named in *Silver* as well as an assortment of "servingmen" and "swaines," and one of its scenes demands at least thirty characters on stage at one time. *Iron* features fewer identified roles than *Silver*—there are twenty-nine speaking parts in addition to roles for attendants, arms bearers, guards, soldiers, and gentlewomen—but one of the play's central scenes includes a banquet with a "lofty dance of sixteen Princes," requiring at least twenty-one different characters on stage at once. And at the end of act 2, scene 1, Priam invites Agamemnon, Ajax, and Achilles as well as "twenty of your chiefe selected Princes" to a banquet with the Trojan army, which he suggests numbered at least as many. It is unlikely that forty-six men crowded onto the stage, but the line explicitly asks that the play be thought of in expansive terms.

Such copiousness is part and parcel of the larger vision of the *Ages* sequence, a flamboyant survey of mythological lore running from the clash of the Olympians and Titans in *The Golden Age*, through Jupiter's dogged pursuit of mortal women in *The Silver Age*, to the labors of Hercules in *The Brazen Age* and the collapse of classical culture as a result of the Trojan War in *The Iron Age*. Kathleen McLuskie attributes the theatrical sweep to Heywood's desire to meld for his audience a variety of dramatic genres, including the masque, revenge play, and the cuckold play: "As well as the physical action of the fights, songs and dances, adapted from the elaborate shows of earlier court entertainments, the plays draw eclectically on the styles of the contemporary drama. . . . The sheer numbers of actors on stage, the range of their skills and the variety of costumes create a sense of opulence which was central to the appeal of commercial theatre."[15]

But saying that joint playing was motivated by the need to fill large ambitions and rosters only leads to more questions. As Gurr asks of the large-cast history plays of the 1590s, "Which came first, the larger companies or the larger plays?"[16] In other words, was Heywood inspired to create his spectacle by the promise of a performance by paired companies, one of them being his own? Or did his play present a challenge to which two companies rose? The distinction is important: the first version suggests a writer responding to a dramatic opportunity, the latter suggests a writer initiating it.[17] And what exactly was the rationale for large-cast plays in the first place? McLuskie assumes audience taste for the extravagant, for the large-scale banquets and masques Heywood's *Ages* plays provided, and collaborative playing might have accommodated this demand. Heywood himself seems to suggest that the impulse was as much nostalgic as it was topical: the prologue to *Silver*, spoken by the figure of the blind Homer, suggests that the series of plays is an effort to revive the chronicle tradition with more classical but still fresher material:

> Since moderne Authors, moderne things haue trac't
> Serching our Chronicles from end to end.
> And all knowne Histories haue long bene grac't,
> Bootlesse it were in them our time to spend
> To iterate tales oftentimes told ore,
> Or subiects handled by each common pen;
> . . . .
> Why should not *Homer*, he that taught in *Greece*,
> Vnto this iudging nation lend like skill.
> And into *England* bring that golden Fleece,
> For which his country is renowned still.[18]

If there were such thematic and aesthetic rationales for large-cast plays, could the playwright or his fellow actors have imagined other reasons—reasons at the level of performance and production? There are multiple possibilities. For *Silver*, which was performed at court, perhaps collaboration was a request made farther up the patronage chain, from one or both of the companies' royal sponsors who wanted to see them together. Or perhaps it was based on other models of joint acting at court, particularly the presence of professional companies and aristocratic amateurs occupying the same space, if at different times, in the masque. For *Iron*, which seems designed for public display only, the motivation may have been sheer novelty: the chance for both companies to perform with different actors at a different venue, to test or combine the range of their theatrical properties (both plays make serious demands for various descents and other machinery), with the Queen's Men benefiting from the prestige of an alliance with King's and a performance at the Globe or Black-friars. Or perhaps it was an opportunity for the troupes to engage in a round of professional one-upmanship, to display vividly their specific styles and to register their distinctions with diverse crowds. These last two options are the most resonant, and they depend on conflicting assumptions about the way acting companies operated in the period. The penultimate suggestion relies on the premise that the companies were friendly and supportive, mutually inter-ested in the other's success, while the final suggestion is grounded in a vision of companies as fundamentally competitive, seeking to advance themselves at the hands or expense of other groups.

My argument here is that a production of *The Iron Age* could capitalize on the possibilities of *both* inter-company camaraderie and inter-company com-petitiveness if it were played with each company assuming one of the sides in the famous conflict. Such staging would display the mutual theatrical engage-ment of both companies while visibly reinforcing their distinctions—to the potential benefit as well as detraction of both. This suggestion is, of course, speculative; and one can just as easily imagine a performance that mixed dif-ferent company members on both sides, with equally interesting motives and effects. But my hunch is that the subject of the Trojan War, with its obvious division of characters into competing camps, gave Heywood and the actors an opportunity to engineer a performance that would ostentatiously stage a com-parison between the troupes.[19] Recognizing and assessing this comparison, then, would have been an intimate part of the play's appeal to different audi-ences at each of its performances at "three seuerall Theatres," believed to have been the Red Bull, the Curtain, and either the Globe or Blackfriars.[20] I look now at some of the ways in which the play calls verbal and visual attention to the presence of two competing troops—and thus perhaps to two competing troupes—as well as the potential effects and implications of such a comparison for audiences.

The published play's dramatis personae, which lists "the party of the *Troians*" and "the party of the *Grecians*" in two columns separated by a vertical line, indicates that, at least in retrospect, Heywood or his printer, Nicholas Okes, was uniquely attuned to the division of *The Iron Age* into camps. Al-though *The Silver Age* and *Brazen Age* both separate their published character lists into columns (as do the texts of Heywood's *Fair Maid of the West* [1631, printer Richard Royston] and *Love's Mistress* [1640, printer John Raworth]), no other Heywood text published before *The Iron Age* organizes columns of characters by nation or faction instead of by order of appearance. There is no model for such a cast list in the play's closest kin, Shakespeare's quarto and folio *Troilus and Cressida* (1609, 1623).[21]

The opposition between camps continues in the text itself. It is perhaps most striking when set against Shakespeare's *Troilus and Cressida*, in which comparisons, often designed to invalidate the possibility of comparison altogether ("what's aught but as 'tis valued?"), are made more often *within*, rather than between, the sides. For instance, *The Iron Age* begins earlier than Shakespeare's *Troilus*, starting before the theft of Helen and thus giving Paris, upon arrival in Sparta, a chance to woo Helen by contrasting himself with Menelaus; Paris is, he claims, "the properer man" (1.2.209). The Greeks of Heywood's drama, that is, tend to measure themselves against the Trojans, and vice versa; Shakespeare's warriors focus on their status within their *own* camps, even if that status is ultimately revealed as insubstantial. Of course, Shakespeare's play depends on the fundamental quarrel between Trojans and Greeks, but his rhetorical energy is spent on internal verbal jousting within the Greek camp (in 1.3), the Trojan camp (in 2.2), and between Ulysses and Achilles (in 3.3). In Heywood's play, Trojans and Greeks meet, opposed and armed, as early as the second act; it is not until late in Shakespeare's fourth act that "all of Troy" arrives for their first full interview with their enemy. (The end of Heywood's act 2, that is, matches Shakespeare's act 4, scene 5.) And while both plays feature a significant "parade" scene, modeled on the epic procession, Shakespeare's pageant of of act 1, scene 2 displays the Trojans only, while Heywood conspicuously features *both* camps in the marches, dances, and banqueting tableaux of act 3, scene 1.

Indeed, this elaborate scene foregrounds dramaturgically the mutual presence and opposition of the camps when, Hector and Ajax's duel having ended in a draw, Priam invites the Greeks to the banquet to which Shakespeare's text only gestures. The armies meet at the city wall, and, according to a very explicit stage direction, "Enter all the Greekes on one side, all the Troians on the other: Euery Troian Prince intertaines a Greeke, and so march two and two, discoursing, as being conducted by them into the Citty" (3.1). At the feast, Hector brings added attention to the paired arrangement, ordering the armies, "Ey so, now sit, a *Troian* and a *Greeke*" (3.1.34). As the meal progresses, the camps fall to fighting; the quickly escalating argument demands that each side respond in unison to the other group. When Hector says that Diomed is the "boldest *Greeke*; / That euer menac'd *Troy* excepting none," Heywood calls for "All Greekes" to ask, "None?" and "All Troians" to reply, "None" (3.1.89–92). The moment is orchestrated so that both camps speak as one "character," and as one character against the other. The scene ends with revels, "a lofty dance of sixteene *Princes*, halfe *Troians* halfe *Grecians*" (3.1.146), exploiting Jacobean tastes for the masked dance while, equally important, exhibiting visually and kinetically each army in opposition to the other. Efforts such as these suggest that the play was designed to accent a performance by two troupes—that Heywood and the companies were manipulating the joint appearance—and that they expected it to achieve specific dramatic effects based on the assumption of audiences especially conscious of company rosters and repertories.

What might those effects have been, then, and what are their implications? Would the joint performance have generated fond feeling between the companies, stressing their shared conditions and aspirations, emphasizing, as the play itself does, the similarities of men at war (or play)? Or would it have exacerbated or fomented competitiveness between the two troupes, whether that competitiveness stemmed from their different status at court, the different strengths of their leading players, or their different visions of what constituted attractive or appealing theater? The character Thersites hints, cynically, at both of these possibilities when he comments on the banquet scene, "See here's the picture of a polliticke state, / They all imbrace and hugge, yet deadly hate" (3.1.10–11).

And how would these dynamics have affected the playgoing experience? Would it have tapped into already existing audience allegiances? That is, was the performance designed to make audiences sympathize with one side or the other depending on their feelings about a given company? If, for instance, the King's Men played the Trojan army—a conjecture based on the fact that their patron indulged in tracing his ancestry through Brutus to Aeneas—would a Bankside audience have favored that faction over the other? Would a Red Bull audience have thus sympathized with the Greek army? Or would the play, rather, have facilitated migration from a favored theater to another, challenging playgoers to move with "their" company to a different venue and thus mixing up usual or expected audience composition? Would the performance of *The Iron Age* thus break down or augment audience affiliation with a particular company? Finally, would joint playing have been profitable financially, in terms of revenue generated? Or could it have been designed for profit in terms of "cultural capital"—for making different actors known to more patrons, or even simply to more or other actors?

By laying out these questions, I mean to suggest ways of broadening the investigation of collaborative work while maintaining the methodological premises and commitments that characterized the earlier chapters of this book. There I developed a "case study" methodology that, while not endorsing a view of the proprietary, autonomous early modern author, nevertheless sought to understand the behavior of dramatists as agents operating, both consciously and unconsciously, within a set of institutional practices and protocols. The discussion centered on their professional as well as psychic investments in working with one another, and how those investments might have been translated into the texts themselves. In pursuing those investments and their dramatic effects, the case histories challenged reigning explanations for joint work and offered fresh perspectives on traditional concerns for Renaissance drama criticism and theater history. The aim was to show with new complexity the possible associations between the court, its patrons, and the stage; to show how subtly dramatists could hint at conditions of production in multiple kinds of metadrama; and to show how broad a vocabulary is needed to describe relations between professional men of the theater.

In this final chapter I have suggested questions for approaching other kinds of collaborative work, like that between companies. These questions would pursue a different angle of analysis by probing the potential effects of joint operations on the audience as much as the motivations of composers and performers. But such a view of collaborative work will nevertheless continue to demand from interpreters sensitivity to the tenaciousness as well as the permeability of Renaissance notions of individual, professional, and corporate identities and the ways these notions influenced and were themselves inflected by joint enterprises.

NOTES

INTRODUCTION

1. See Bentley, *Profession of Dramatist in Shakespeare's Time*, 199.

2. Samuel Schoenbaum warns that "while recognizing joint-authorship as a fact of Elizabethan theatrical life, we must guard against exaggerating its importance; many dramatists preferred to work singly" (*Internal Evidence*, 225).

3. Streitberger, "Personnel and Professionalization"; Gurr, *Shakespearian Playing Companies*, 5.

4. For some book-length studies of early modern manuscript cultures, see Peter Beal, *In Praise of Scribes*; Marotti, *Manuscript, Print*, and *John Donne*; Goldberg, *Writing Matter*; Love, *Scribal Publication*. For criticism on literary communities, see Summers and Pebworth, *Literary Circles*. For a survey and assessment of these studies as well as shorter articles, see my bibliographic essay "Early Modern Collaboration," esp. 612–15.

5. Baldwin, *Organization and Personnel*, 161. E. A. J. Honigmann and Susan Brock, in their publication of playhouse wills, reinforce this focus on theatrical "camaraderie." These theater wills reveal that men and women associated with the drama "inevitably married into each others' families. . . . [They] must have been familiar with the history of the theatre from the inside over several generations" (*Playhouse Wills*, 6).

6. Cox and Kastan, intro. to *New History*, 2.

7. Gurr, *Shakespearian Playing Companies*, 15.

8. Brooks, *Playhouse to Printing-House*, 1–2.

9. These critics thus share tendencies with scholars of non-dramatic texts who are expanding notions of joint work. See, for instance, Stephen Dobranski, who discusses Milton's associations with printers and publishers "as a 'collaboration,' by which I mean a *co*-laboring or working together. Milton benefited from the advice and assistance of acquaintances both during the imaginative creation of his works and during the practical process of putting his writing into print" (*Milton*, 9).

10. The piecemeal efforts of Robert Daborne in submitting to Philip Henslowe in installments various scenes and acts for the lost *Machiavel and the Devil* is only one of

many recorded incidents that would qualify any such notions. See *Henslowe Papers*, 63–82.

11. For definitions and critical evaluation of both external and internal approaches, see Taylor, "Canon and Chronology," 69–93.

12. Hoy, "Shares of Fletcher"; Schoenbaum, *Internal Evidence*; Masten, "Beaumont and/or Fletcher." Hoy relies on the playwrights' differing use of alternative forms (e.g., "have" versus "hath" or "you" versus "ye") to determine authorship; his method was influential throughout the 1960s and 1970s.

13. Hope, *Authorship*, 6.

14. For an overview of the past and future of the field, see Holmes, "Evolution of Stylometry," an effective guide to the technologies as well as implications of statistical computing for authorship studies. MacD. P. Jackson offers a glimpse of the possibilities for authorship studies with the advent of new electronic databases of plays in "Editing, Attribution Studies." See also Taylor, "Middleton and Rowley."

15. For an example of statistical analysis, see Hoorn et al., "Neural Network Identification." The authors suggest that they have devised a way of determining authorship without respect to meaning: "For the proper determination of authorship, the dualism of the sign is not so indissoluble. If a machine can identify an author correctly, then it is impossible to maintain that speech . . . *must* be analysed with regard to meaning" (312). W. van Peer critiques this approach for engaging "in an act of reification" that neglects the literary ("Quantitative Studies," 302). For a critique of the metaphor of a stylistic "fingerprint," see Burrows, "Not Unless You Ask Nicely," 91.

16. Wilson, *Theaters of Intention*, 1.

17. Masten, *Textual Intercourse*, 19.

18. Ibid., 2, 37.

19. Ibid., 7, 2, 20–21.

20. For a similar critique, see Brooks, *From Playhouse to Printing-House*: "[Masten's] effort to locate the production of texts within the discourses of a 'sex gender system' necessarily obscures other bodies of evidence pertaining to the material, institutional, and theatrical practices that sustained playwriting in the period" (156).

21. Consider James Bednarz, quoting Stephen Orgel: "Even if we agree . . . that 'virtually all theatrical literature' is 'basically collaborative in nature,' that does not mean that poets and players were not given specific credit for their specific contributions" (*Shakespeare and the Poets' War*, 14).

22. I emphasize London here because that city is the focus of my study. Although recent scholarship has demonstrated the prevalence and importance of touring for the companies—and thus for the writing of plays—London provides the specific milieu for the writers I consider.

23. For the theater as an anthropological phenomenon, Mullaney, *Place of the Stage*; Bristol, *Carnival and Theater*; and Montrose, *Purpose of Playing*. For examples of work on business mentalities, see Gurr, "Money or Audiences;" Ingram, *Business of Playing*. For analyses of audience composition, see Gurr, *Playgoing in Shakespeare's London*, which mitigates the more extreme claims of both Alfred Harbage (*Shakespeare and the Rival Traditions*) and Ann Jennalie Cook (*Privileged Playgoers*). For relations between government and theater, see Barroll, *Politics, Plague, and Shakespeare's Theater*.

24. Bourdieu, *Theory of Cultural Production*, 132–39. Because Bourdieu's work focuses on the cultural practices of nineteenth-century as well as contemporary France, he tends to attribute a greater degree of conscious awareness of a professional cultural field to his authors than is warranted for Renaissance dramatists. But his model of "position-taking" seems especially useful for understanding the early modern theater, since it affords Renaissance dramatists and other cultural producers the possibility of symbolic strategizing.

25. See, for instance, McLuskie, "Plays and Playwrights."

26. Perry, *Making of Jacobean Culture*, 2.

27. Carson, *Companion to "Henslowe's Diary*," 58.

28. Bradley, *From Text to Performance*, 79.

29. McMillin and MacLean, *Queen's Men*.

30. *Henslowe Papers*, 72. The letter is dated June 5, 1613.

31. Consider Peter Stallybrass's argument that the relationship between the players and the Drapers' Company fueled the success of the early modern theater ("Worn Worlds"). A revised version of the essay titled "The Circulation of Clothes and the Making of the English Theater" appears in Stallybrass and Jones, *Renaissance Clothing*, 175–206.

32. Streitberger, "Personnel and Professionalization," 347.

33. Halasz, *Marketplace of Print*, 27, 47; Knutson, *Playing Companies*, 7.

34. Archer, *Pursuit of Stability*, 100.

35. For a version of this kind of argument which compares the relation of John Fletcher and William Shakespeare to the chivalric quarreling of Palamon and Arcite in *The Two Noble Kinsmen*, see Hedrick, " 'Be Rough with Me.' "

36. Rappaport, *Worlds within Worlds*.

37. See Unwin, *Gilds*, 318, for a discussion of this trend and its relationship to the development of monopolies.

38. Ashton, *City and Court*, 47.

39. See the conflicting interpretations in Kahl, *Development of London Livery Companies*, and Ward, *Metropolitan Communities*.

40. *Profitable and Necessarie Discourse*, B4.

41. Kahl, 2.

42. Grassby, *Business Community*, 367.

43. Ashton, *City and Court*, 31.

44. An emphasis on this kind of role for the guilds in theatrical life is thus distinct from that of Knutson, who tends to idealize guild relations and to see them as analogous to, rather than in complex relations with, aristocratic structures of clientage. In stressing the potential for cooperation rather than conflict between companies, Knutson "separate[s] further the commercial policies of the companies from the personal or ideological quarrels of players and poets." She argues that "commerce among the playing companies was built on patterns of fraternity, the roots of which were feudal hierarchies such as kinship, service, and the guild" (7–8).

45. Streitberger, 347.

46. Gurr, *Shakespearian Playing Companies*, 37–38.

47. Orgel, *Impersonations*, 65; Kahl, 17. Kahl continues: "The authority of the guilds to supervise manufacture and trade was proportionate to their political influence; the relative weight of the guilds depended upon their social prestige. A livery hall, the acquisition of property, the distribution of charity, the entertainment of the aldermen, mayor, royal princes, and the king gave the guilds and companies the social position and influence by which they could gain public recognition. The guilds, therefore, preoccupied with acquiring these attributes of a long and revered tradition, sought a formal and permanent structure to facilitate the accumulation of wealth and prestige. The institution which took shape was the livery company whose peculiar character was its corporate nature conferred by royal charter" (17).

48. For historical accounts of the legal senses of the terms "incorporation," "charter," "patent," and "license," see *Dictionary of Law* and *Harrap's Dictionary of Law*.

49. Kahl, 16.

50. See Westfall, *Patrons and Performance*. Playing companies were not responsible for paying for their charter or for the impositions levied by the monarch, as were other

companies, and thus the less organized their enterprise, the less vulnerable it was to government imposts. And affiliation with nobility or royalty through patronage, no matter how much a "legal fiction," may have been more desirable for social, traditional, and professional reasons than autonomous civic status. (The term is Stallybrass's in "Worn Worlds," 293.)

51. I thank Nora Johnson for suggesting this term and the ideas it connotes.

52. See Knutson, "Falconer to the Little Eyases."

53. See Rackin, *Stages of History*, 19.

54. Thompson, editor's intro. to Bourdieu, 17.

55. Knutson, *Repertory*, 101.

CHAPTER ONE. SCENES OF COLLABORATIVE PRODUCTION

1. Book-length studies include Beal, *In Praise of Scribes*; Burt, *Licensed by Authority*; Crane, *Framing Authority*; Dobranski, *Milton, Authorship, and the Book Trade*; Dutton, *Mastering the Revels*; Halasz, *Marketplace of Print*; Love, *Scribal Publication*; Marotti, *Manuscript, Print*; Rose, *Authors and Owners*; Wall, *Imprint of Gender*; Woodmansee, *The Author, Art, and the Market*.

2. Dekker, *Guls Horne-Booke*, C2v.

3. Carson, *Companion to "Henslowe's Diary,"* 57–58.

4. Carson, "Collaborative Playwriting," 14–15.

5. Ibid., 19–22.

6. *Henslowe's Diary* records one payment to the three writers: "lent unto the company the 18 of aguste 1598 to bye a Boocke called hoote anger sone cowld of mr porter mr cheattell & bengemen Johnson in full payment" (96).

7. For historicizing approaches to the absence in the early modern theater of intellectual property "rights," see Masten, "Playwrighting," 358. See also Thomas, "Eschewing Credit." For the absence of copyright in the period more generally, see Loewenstein, "Authentic Reproductions."

8. For a summary of the history of the boy companies, see Gurr, *Shakespearian Playing Companies*, 218–29 and 337–65. For dates of closure and reopening, see Gair, *Children*, 110–18.

9. For a list of boy company plays and their authorial ascriptions, see Shapiro, *Children of the Revels*, 261–68. I address disagreements with these ascriptions as they arise.

10. See Gair, *Children*, 82–94; Shapiro, *Children*, 28–29.

11. See Gair, *Children*, 78.

12. Although, after 1610, prices at the indoor theaters ranged between 6d. and 2s. 6d., as opposed to the amphitheaters' range of 1d. to 1s., the prices for children's performance, at least before 1600, ranged from 2d. to 6d. See Gurr, *Shakespearean Stage*, 12; Gair, *Children*, 88–89. On individual style, see Finkelpearl, *Marston*. Gair attributes the revival of playing at Paul's to the interests of John Marston and William Stanley, sixth earl of Derby, who were at Middle Temple and Lincoln's Inn, respectively, in the late 1590s (*Children*, 116). It is worth noting that writing for performances by and at the Inns of Court was often collaborative, as texts such as *Tancred and Gismond, Gorboduc*, and *Jocasta* attest. For this reason it might seem counterintuitive to assert that an Inns audience would facilitate the work of a single playwright. But dramatic writing for the Inns, including collaborative writing, was a different proposition from scripting professional plays for public consumption. Of course, there are similarities between these venues in terms of method and intent, but the movement from the enclosed and fundamentally amateur world of the law schools to the verifiably market-oriented world of company theater cannot be underestimated, especially when that difference

was being assessed by the professional dramatists and not the Inns men themselves (see chapter 2). Collaborative writing at the Inns served primarily pedagogical and recreational purposes largely specific to the training of lawyers and gentlemen, a different agenda from those of either public or private professional theaters. And consider the emphasis on personal style in Jasper Heywood's praise of the Inns in an unpaginated preface to *Thyestes*: "In Lyncolnes Inne and Temples twayne, Grayes Inne and other mo, / Thou shalt them fynde whose paynfull pen / thy verse shall florishe so, / That Melpomen thou wouldst well weene / had taught them for to wright, / And all their works with stately style, / and goodly grace t'endight. / There shalt thou se the selfe same Northe, / whose woorke his witte displayes, / And Dyall dothe of Princes paynte, / and preache abroade his prayse. / There Sackuyldes Sonetts sweetely sauste / and featly fyned bee, / There Nortons ditties so delight,. There Yelvertons doo flee. . . . There heare nthou shalt a great reporte, / of Baldwyns worthie name, / Whose Myrrour dothe of Magistrates, / proclayme eternall fame."

13. For capacity, see Gair, *Children*, 67, and Gurr, *Stage*, 196.

14. Chambers, *Elizabethan Stage*, 2:50.

15. Jonson, *Fountaine of Selfe-Loue, or Cynthias Revels*, A2. When the third actor loses the draw for the prologue, he makes a threat: " 'Slid, I'll do somewhat now afore I goe in, though it be nothing but to reuenge myself on the *Author*: since I speake not his *Prologue*. Ile go tell all the Argument of his *Play* aforehand, and so stale his *Inuention* to the *Auditory* before it come forth" (A2v). Of course, such a threat only strengthens, however ironically, the notion of the author here.

16. Harbage, *Shakespeare*, 57. Harbage's specific differentiation here seems of merit, even while the overarching claims in his book about a "war" between theaters is less acceptable. For a discussion of the "impressment" of boys, see Orgel, *Impersonations*, 66.

17. Bourdieu, *Distinction*, 94.

18. Bly, *Queer Virgins*, 116–44.

19. Halpern, *Poetics*, 33. For personal style more generally, see Whigham, *Ambition and Privilege*.

20. Marotti, *John Donne*, 13.

21. Ibid., 14.

22. For the exploitation of a player's celebrity, see Alexandra Halasz's discussion of Richard Tarlton in *Marketplace*, 66–67.

23. See Mann, *Elizabethan Player*, 54–73. The fact that many of these actors were also playwrights only enhances the point.

24. Weever, *Epigrammes*, E6.

25. *Return from Parnassus* 1.2.198–99. All subsequent citations are given in the text.

26. Wright, "Excerpta"; emphasis added.

27. The sequence and shape of the Poetomachia, which I consider a real, if manufactured, event of the Elizabethan stage, is cogently evaluated by Cyrus Hoy in his introduction to *Satiromastix*. See Hoy, *Introductions*, 1:179–95. More recently, James Bednarz has provided a compelling chronology of the plays and a discussion of their implications in *Shakespeare and the Poets' War*.

28. Jonson, *Poetaster*, 4:3.4.321.

29. Roslyn Knutson argues that the Poets' War is largely a historiographic invention. See "Falconer to the Little Eyases."

30. Bednarz, "Representing Jonson," 23. See also Michael Steggle, who discusses the Poets' War as "situated at the fault lines of early professional drama, taking part not just in interpersonal conflicts but in crucial intellectual and practical struggles over the nature and future of that drama" (*Wars of the Theatres*, 11).

31. Marlowe, *Tamburlaine*, prologue, 5.

32. Shakespeare, *Love's Labor's Lost* 4.196.

33. Cicero, *De oratore* 1.39; Scaliger, *Select Translations*, 3.

34. Hoskyns, *Directions*, 39.

35. Ibid., 40.

36. Brinsley, *Ludus Literarius*, 114.

37. For discussions of the ideology of double translation, see Kerrigan, "Articulation of the Ego," and Sanders, *Gender and Literacy*, 1–56.

38. Jonson, *Discoveries*, 574.

CHAPTER TWO. "WORK UPON THAT NOW"

1. For the the effect of the succession on the dramatists and their understanding of their craft and their testing of its boundaries, see Clare, *Art*, 71–79.

2. See Van Fossen, intro. to Chapman, Jonson, and Marston, *Eastward Hoe*.

3. Schelling, intro. to Chapman, Jonson, and Marston, *Eastward Ho*, xi, xiii.

4. Leinwand, *City Staged*, 115.

5. Hoskyns, *Directions for Speech and Style*, 2.

6. Jonson, *Cynthia's Revels* 3.1.34–37. This passage is not in the quarto of 1601.

7. Dekker, *Guls Horne-Booke*, E4v.

8. Middleton and Rowley, *The Spanish Gipsie*, D8v.

9. Gainsford, *Rich Cabinet*, Q3. For the effects of improvisation, see Mann, *Elizabethan Player*, 68.

10. Such an argument, of course, challenges implicitly the notion that the gathering of commonplaces reflects "a theory and practice of reading, writing, education, and social mobility that developed alongside and in partial resistance to the individualistic, imitative, imaginative, and aristocratic paradigms for selfhood and authorship that tends to be associated with the English Renaissance" (Crane, *Framing Authority*, 4).

11. See Wells, "Jacobean City Comedy." For a discussion of *Westward Hoe* as the first of its genre at the private theaters, see Manley, *Literature and Culture*, 443.

12. See Levin, "Notes towards City Comedy," 126. Most other recent critics are equally hostile to the three plays, usually on moral grounds. Some complain that the plays are *too* moral, others that they are *amoral*. For the first view, see Leinwand; *City Staged*; for the latter, see Hoy, *Introductions*, 2: 159–60.

13. For a sustained discussion of the plays' competing views of London, see Van Fossen's discussion of the way *Eastward* "parodies *Westward Hoe* to show its shallowness of vision of the city; it itself offers a dialectic to see beneath the surface to the cause of social and artistic disorder" (2).

14. See also Gurr, *Playgoing*, 53–80; Gair, *Children*, 72–73. For an early assertion of the difference between public and private theaters, see Harbage, *Shakespeare and the Rival Traditions*, which lauds the native spirit of the public theaters. Compare Cook, who asserts the "dominance of one sort of playgoer over all others: he was the privileged playgoer" (*Privileged Playgoers*, 8).

15. In Collier, *Annals*, 1:275.

16. Jonson, *Cynthia's Revels*, induction, 132–41.

17. Sturgess, *Jacobean Private Theatre*, 48–49, 64.

18. Bentley, *Profession of Player*, 198.

19. Based on attributions in Harbage, *Annals of English Drama*.

20. See Finkelpearl, *John Marston*; Marotti, *John Donne*.

21. See Gair, *Children*, 99–151.

22. Based on attributions in Shapiro, *Children*, 261–66. I do not include here plays

for children's troupes other than Paul's and the Blackfriars' Boys (also Queen's Revels Boys).

23. I do not include *Satiromastix* (1602, Paul's and Chamberlain's) as a collaborative play, although a number of scholars have suggested that this contribution to the so-called war of the theaters was crafted by both Dekker and Marston. I side with Cyrus Hoy here, who sees Marston as helping to get Dekker access to Paul's or lending general creative, but not collaborative, support: "[There has been] a general assumption that Marston aided him in the play. This is possible so far as a contribution to the dramatic portraiture and the satiric strategies are concerned, but Marston had nothing at all to do with the actual writing of the play" (*Introduction*, 1:191).

24. See *Henslowe's Diary*, 218, 219-20.

25. Forker, *Skull*, 73.

26. Genette, *Palimpsests*, 35-36.

27. For an aesthetic-structural discussion of consecutive plays, see Hunter, "*Henry IV*." For more recent work on the use of sequels and prequels to capitalize on the commercial success of a given play, see Roslyn Knutson's general discussion of the strategies of the acting companies and her specific acknowledgment of the ways serial plays "exploited *narrative* dependency" (*Repertory*, 50; emphasis added).

28. Henslowe, for instance, gave the Admiral's Men money to buy *The First Civil Wars in France* from Dekker and Drayton on September 29, 1598. By October 8, just a little over a week later, Henslowe was giving money to the company for the purchase of "divers thinges for the playe called the first severelle warres of france." We can assume this first installment was performed sometime after October 11 of that year, the last time Henslowe makes an entry for props for it, and before November 3, when Henslowe gives money for the company to purchase *The Second Part of the Civil Wars*, again from Dekker and Drayton. But even before Henslowe pays for "divers thinges" for this installment, he has already "lent unto Robert shawe the 18 of November 1598 to lend unto mr dickers in earnest of A boocke called the 3 pte of the syvelle wares of france." Henslowe pays for props for the second part on the day *after* the purchase of the third part. Interestingly enough, on January 20, 1598/9, Henslowe paid Dekker three pounds in advance for the "firste Intreducyon of the syvell wares of france"—that is, a prequel to the first installment paid for in September (*Henslowe's Diary*, 98-103). "Firsts" could come "last" on the Renaissance stage.

29. Hunter, "*Henry IV*," 237.

30. Knutson explains the phenomenon of serial plays as the result of the "company's apparent belief that several similar plays of unremarkable quality were more profitable than a singular masterpiece" (*Repertory*, 50).

31. Ibid., 97.

32. Gair, *Children*, 134.

33. Gair calls *Antonia and Mellida* and *Antonia's Revenge* a "self-consciously balanced organization of two parts" (intro. to *Antonio's Revenge*, x). For the composition, performance, and publication dates of *Bussy D'Ambois* and *The Revenge of Bussy D'Ambois*, see Parrott, "Date," and Ure, "Date." Both conclude that *Bussy* was written by Chapman in 1604 and revised by Chapman with Nathan Field between 1610 and 1612, and that *Revenge* was written either immediately before or after that revision.

34. Shapiro, *Rival Playwrights*, 6.

35. For a compelling discussion of the play as organized around accreditation and indebtedness, see Leinwand, *Theatre, Finance, and Society*, 42-55.

36. Chapman, Jonson, and Marston, *Eastward Hoe*, prologue, 1-9. All subsequent citations are to the Van Fossen edition and are given in the text.

37. On place, see Cohen, "Function of Setting."

38. Fleming, "Graffiti," 347.

39. As Jonson formulated, "Language most shows a man; speak that I may see thee." See Jonson, *Discoveries*, 8:625.

40. Agnew, *Worlds Apart*, 4.

41. See *Conversations with Drummond*, 598.

42. Van Fossen, 18.

43. I rely here on Van Fossen: "A few individual passages in the play have also been traced to specific sources . . . Hakluyt's *Principal Navigations* and More's *Utopia* . . . Rabelais's *Pantagruel* and Florio's *Second Fruits*. . . . Three additional kinds of direct borrowing may be treated . . . quotations, corruptions, or parodies of songs, ballads, and play ends. . . . Gertrude sings two unidentified snatches as well as passages from sophisticated songs by Campion and Dowland" (13–14).

44. Ibid., 16–17.

45. Appendix 2 in *Eastward Hoe*, ed. Van Fossen, 221.

46. See Van Fossen, who partitions the play by acts but decides that everyone had a hand in writing the Slitgut scene (1–12).

47. See Fleming; Crane, 3–6.

48. Hoy, *Introductions*, 2:147.

49. Forker, 98.

50. Dekker and Webster, *Northward Hoe*, 4.1. 44–58. All subsequent citations are given in the text.

51. Frederick Fleay made the identification first. See *Biographical Chronicle*, 2:270. See also Chambers, *Elizabethan Stage*, 3:295–96. Allardyce Nicoll makes the strongest positive identification, even suggesting that Bellamont is important in Chapman's biography: "It has to be stated categorically that Dekker's Bellamont stands apart as an almost unique creation and that concerning the validity of the identification with Chapman there can be not the slightest doubt. Its certainly lies beyond question. . . . A reading of [Chapman's] works alone may leave us puzzled, and the puzzlement is increased when we look at the various documentary records which have come down to us; but with the picture of Bellamont all seems to be brought within the design of a single, if complex, personality" ("Dramatic Portrait," 215–16).

52. See Sisson, *Lost Plays*, 12–79.

53. See Jonson, *B. Ion.*

54. Critics favor either *Westward* or *Northward* for different reasons. Leinwand approves of *Westward*, finding "the structure of [Northward] more disjointed than its predecessor" (*City Staged*, 50). Larry Champion, by contrast, maintains the organizational superiority of *Northward*: "The structure of the first is fundamentally flawed and contributes directly to the [poor] quality of dramaturgy. The second, structurally sound, tonally and morally consistent, and reasonably witty, deserves a better fate than merely to be considered a sequel" ("*Westward-Northward*," 252). Hoy, too, favors *Northward* (*Introductions*, 2:247).

CHAPTER THREE. BEAUMONT, FLETCHER, AND SHAKESPEARE

1. For a discussion of the acquisition of Blackfriars by the King's Men, see Bentley, "Shakespeare." For a somewhat exaggerated account of Beaumont, Fletcher, and Massinger as writers for the gentry once the King's Men acquired Blackfriars, see Wallis, *Beaumont, Fletcher, and Company*. For the effects on the repertory of the King's Men after their acquisition of Blackfriars, see Bliss, "Tragicomic Romance."

2. Bly, *Queer Virgins*, 116–43.

3. See Gossett, "Masque Influence."

4. Gossett, *Influence of the Jacobean Masque*, 12.

5. Masten, *Textual Intercourse*, 101.

6. McMullan, *Politics of Unease*, 132. According to McMullan, "In his analyses of political life, especially the political life of the country, Fletcher appears aware of the essentially collaborative nature of rule, the inadequacy of absolutism, and the correspondent need for a politics of involvement. . . . [M]any of his plays demonstrate the potential energy of popular unrest in the face of failed responsibility, and they dramatize the dangers inherent in political instability. The politics represented in and by these plays are at once collaborative, consensual, and conservative, seeking wider involvement in political processes and rejecting absolutist claims, yet resting on an established hierarchical framework: exactly the kind of politics in favor at the Huntingdons' seat at Ashby-de-la-Zouche. But it is not only his patronage environment but also his professional practice as a playwright that orients Fletcher toward a politics of involvement, a politics of collaboration" (132).

7. Recent criticism has argued against classic readings of the masque as devoted only to the idealization of the monarch. See Bevington and Holbrook, intro. to *Politics of the Stuart Court Masque*, 1–13.

8. Performances by professional theater companies are one example of the connection. See Dillon, *Theatre, Court, and City*, 1–42. See also Jean MacIntyre for a summary of the "players participation in court revels" (*Costumes and Scripts*, 234).

9. Limon, *Masque*, 27–28.

10. See Knowles, "Insubstantial Pageants."

11. See Parry, *Golden Age*, Smuts, *Court Culture*; Barroll, *Anna of Denmark*; Astington, *English Court Theatre*.

12. Langbaine, *Account*, N6.

13. See Lytle and Orgel, *Patronage in the Renaissance*; Evans, *Ben Jonson*; Peck, *Court Patronage*.

14. See Welsford, *Court Masque*, 41; Young, *Tournaments*.

15. Young, 42.

16. Orgel, *Jonsonian Masque*, 63.

17. See Knowles, passim.

18. See Barroll, *Anna of Denmark* and "Inventing the Stuart Masque."

19. See Finet, *Finetti Philoxenis*; Sullivan, *Court Masques*; Orrell, "Savoy Correspondence, 1604–1618" and "Savoy Correspondence, 1613–75."

20. Such a definition is distinct from Stephen Orgel's discussion in *Illusion of Power* of the way masque performances were built to glorify the position of the monarch and thus to ensure that all other "identifications" revolved around him.

21. Bourdieu, *Distinction*, 7.

22. Whigam, "Interpretation," 625; emphasis added.

23. MacIntyre, 53.

24. Welsford, 3–145.

25. Hammer, "Upstaging the Queen," 52.

26. Ibid., 58.

27. Ibid. Hammer, focused on the presentations of 1595, does not pursue further this idea of "replacement." I would suggest that the "replacement" involved incorporation: masques "took over" the place of chivalric display partly by including such demonstrations (as in *Oberon*) in their own stories.

28. *Masque of Flowers* 1.4–7.

29. Jonson, *Masque of Queenes* 1.4–5, 774–75.

30. Jonson, *The Characters of Two Royall Masques*, B4.

31. Bourdieu, *Distinction*, 170.

32. See Knowles, 109.

33. Quoted in Sullivan, *Court Masques*, 95.

34. Quoted in Nagler, *Source Book*, 153.

35. Unsigned letter in Winwood, *Memorials*, 3:179.

36. Quoted in Jonson, *Ben Jonson*, 10:519.

37. Campion, *Lord Hay's Masque*, ll. 133–35.

38. James Knowles discusses the contrast in "Insubstantial Pageants." But even as he differentiates the relative "openness" of country house masques in comparison to performances at court, he suggests their emphasis on personal identification that I am linking with court performances as well: "Although these country-house masques might be quite elaborate . . . the pivotal moment depends less on the revelation of an architectural wonder than on the fiction, or on the symbolic meanings attached to the presence of the guests" (121).

39. Marston, *Lorde and Ladye Huntingdon's Entertainment*, 147–48.

40. Ibid., 149.

41. Astington, 194.

42. Jonson, *Ben Jonson*, 10:404.

43. Quoted ibid., 10:446.

44. Quoted ibid., 10:446–47.

45. Birch, *James I*, 1:87.

46. Jonson, *Ben Jonson*, 10:497.

47. Finet, B2v, C2v.

48. See Dudley Carleton's description of the Spanish ambassador at *The Masque of Blackness*: "At Night we had the Queen's Maske in the Banquetting-House, or rather her Pagent. . . . The *Spanish* and *Venetian* Ambassadors were both present, *and sate by the King in State*; at which Monsieur *Beaumont* quarrells so extreamly, that he saith *the whole Court is Spanish*. But by his Favour, he should fall out with none but himself, for they were all indifferently invited *to come as private Men, to a private Sport*; which he refusing, the *Spanish* Ambassador willingly accepted, and being there, seeing no Cause to the contrary, he put off *Don Taxis*, and took upon *El Senor Embaxadour*, wherein he outstript *our little Monsieur*. He was privately at the first mask, and sate amongst his Men disguised; at this he was taken out to dance, and footed it like a lusty old Gallant with his Country Woman. He took out the Queen, and forgot not to kiss her Hand, though there was Danger it would have left a Mark on his Lips" (Winwood, *Memorials*, 2:44).

49. Dekker, *Guls Horn-booke*, E3. Although strategies of recognition and identification were an essential part of public or professional drama, they were usually contained within the fiction of the play, a point I discuss further later in this chapter.

50. Raylor, *Essex House Masque*, 133.

51. Hammer, 44.

52. Chamberlain, *Letters*, 75.

53. For my attributions, see McGee and Meagher, "Checklist, 1603–1616," and "Checklist, 1614–1625." Of course, I do not mean to suggest that my grouping is comprehensive. Consider also Jonson's remark that "next himself only Fletcher and Chapman could make a masque" (*Discoveries*, 596).

54. See the dedications in Daniel, *Vision*, A3, and Jonson, *Characters*, C2v.

55. Jerzy Limon distinguishes between the *multiple* authors of the masque as it was performed before an audience and the masque as it was recounted by a single individual and published for popular consumption: "It seems clear that the masque-in-performance and the printed literary masque not only belong to different systems, but also that their authorship is not the same. The first type of masque always has several

authors (not to mention all those who actually performed), the second is the creation
. . . of an individual" (*Masque*, 28). For my study, this distinction seems unnecessary.
Even if the published text was indeed the work of one guiding or shaping hand, insofar
as it was an attempt to represent a performance and the conditions motivating it, it
provides a picture of the multiple contributors behind the show.

56. See Philip Edwards's introduction to *A Book of Masques*, 127. See also Fredson
Bowers's intro. to Beaumont and Fletcher, *Dramatic Works*, 120–24.

57. Jonson, *Characters*, A3v, A4v.

58. The literature on Jonsonian "self-fashioning" is vast. See, among others, Helgerson, *Self-crowned Laureates*; Fish, "Author-Readers."

59. Quoted in Sullivan, 246, 199.

60. *Calendar of State Papers Domestic*, 9:172.

61. Daniel, *Tethy's Festival*, ll. 54–58.

62. Daniel, *Panegyrike*, H6v.

63. Chapman, *Memorable Masque*, ll. 188–99.

64. Campion, *Lord Hay's Masque*, in *Court Masques*, ll. 588–605.

65. In Nichols, *Progresses*, 2:136.

66. For a further discussion of the ideologies at stake in the confluence of court and
civic revels, see Wright, "Rival Traditions," esp. 197–99.

67. See McGee and Meagher, "Checklist, 1603–1616." Some masks, manor shows,
and entries in the checklists are attributed to multiple writers, like the entertainments
in 1606 for Christian IV, attributed to Jonson, Henry Roberts, and Marston, or the
coronation triumph for James I in 1604, attributed to Thomas Dekker, Ben Jonson,
Stephen Harrison, John Webster, and Thomas Middleton. Jonson published a version
of the event as *B. Jon: His Part of King James His Royal Entertainment* (1604) and included
only his own contributions, while Thomas Dekker gave an account of the entire entry
in *The Magnificent Entry* (1604), putting his name only on the title page.

68. See *Calendar of Dramatic Records*, 99.

69. Tannenbaum, "Fletcher Autograph," 38; emphasis added.

70. Beaumont and Fletcher, *Comedies and Tragedies*, A4v.

71. Ibid., D1.

72. Aubrey, *Brief Lives*, 21.

73. Finkelpearl, *Court and Country Politics*, 18. Finkelpearl opposes readings that
join the two on the basis of shared backgrounds, which he says were "so different that
friendship, much less harmonious collaboration, might well have been impossible.
Theirs is a story of parallels that event converged" (8). Wallis writes that "gentlemen
by birth, by education and by literary and dramatic tastes, Fletcher and Beaumont had
used their eyes and ears well at the private theatres and the Globe, had written their
own first ventures for Pauls and Blackfriars, had acquired by trial and error a keen sense
of what elements of stagecraft appealed to Jacobean playgoers, and finally, for the
King's Men, had hit upon the formulae which brought into being a new brand of
entertainment for the gentry" (174).

74. The argument that follows demonstrates how this interest invests the entire
play, making it irrelevant who wrote which parts. For a summary of the decomposition
of the text, see T. W. Craik's intro. to his edition of Beaumont and Fletcher, *The Maid's
Tragedy*, 1–2.

75. Between 1611 and 1613, their *Cupid's Revenge* (1608), *Philaster* (1608), and *A
King and No King* (1611) were all performed at least once at court. See Chambers,
Elizabethan Stage, 4:125–28.

76. Lee Bliss sees their later plays becoming steadily more "comic [in] emphasis"
("Pastiche," 252). Craik also sees in the deadly duel at the play's end an inversion of

the usual disguise technique of comedy "to produce a tragic irony of pathos" (intro., 21).

77. Consider Sarah Sutherland's chapter on *The Maid's Tragedy* in her *Masques in Jacobean Tragedy*, 62–74; see also Neill, " 'The Simetry, Which Gives a Poem Grace.' "

78. Beaumont and Fletcher, *Maid's Tragedy*, ed. Craik, ll.5–10. All subsequent citations are from this edition and are given in the text.

79. Jonson, *Hymenaei*, ll. 12–16.

80. Gossett, *Influence*, 204.

81. See Beaumont, *Masque of the Inner Temple and Gray's Inn*, ll. 134–40.

82. Puttenham, *Art of English Poesie*, E1–E2v.

83. These scenes might thus be said to fit Gossett's definition of a "masque element": an aspect of a play that echoes the idea or genre, if not the form, of the masque (*Influence*, 12).

84. Blau, "Absolved Riddle."

85. See Sommerville, *Politics and Ideology*, 69–77.

86. For a sustained discussion on the relation of *The Maid's Tragedy to Hamlet*, see Davies, "Beaumont and Fletcher's *Hamlet*."

87. Quoted in Jonson, *Ben Jonson*, 10:553.

88. Barroll, *Anna of Denmark*, 83.

89. There has not been enough attention given to the erotics (both same and opposite sex) of the masque, to the possibilities of sexual innuendo and real activity. The banquets before and after the masques were also scenes of voluptuousness. Masques themselves hinted at the sexual potential of the masque even as they idealized or platonized it. Thus William Browne in his *Inner Temple Masque* instructs the men to dance: "Choose now among this fairest number / Upon whose breasts love would for ever slumber; / Choose not amiss, since you may where you will, / Or blame yourselves for choosing ill. / Then do not leave, though oft the music closes, / Till lilies in their cheeks be turn'd to roses" (*Masque of the Inner Temple*, ll. 449–54). Francis Lenton's anagrams in his *Innes of Court Anagrammatist* (1634) on the names of the participants in James Shirley's *Triumph of Peace* (1634) demonstrate an audience member's understanding of the ribaldry. Making an anagram of one dancer, John Farwell's name, into "We fall on Hir," Lenton writes that if, during the masque, "my Mistresse chance to slide, / And (willing) trips downe on her side, / I know not how to doe her honour, / But to imitate, and fall upon her" (D3v).

90. "Overdetermined" is a useful term to connote the regularity with which the masques ended with some form of a "taking-out" or dancing performance and the paying of homage to king or queen.

91. Finkelpearl, "Two Distincts," 184.

92. See Hope, *Authorship*, 83–89; Potter, intro. to Shakespeare and Fletcher, *Two Noble Kinsmen*, 16–23.

93. See Finkelpearl, "Two Distincts," 185–86.

94. All three masques, though most explicitly Beaumont's, are echoed in the play. The pyramid at the play's close, Potter suggests, is resonant with Campion's climactic obelisk (68); and the play's country dancers, whose mad morris is virtually lifted from Beaumont's antimasque, also can be seen to reflect Chapman's characters, who "come hither with a charge to do these nuptials, I hope, very acceptable service" (*Memorable Masque*, ll. 375–76). The play begins with a wedding procession and ends with an offstage joust that is preceded by "spectacular religious rites at exotic altars" (Potter, 101). All these ritual moments, as the medieval, Chaucerian analogue of the Jacobean masque, recall the staged ceremonies of February 1613/14. The play thus "integrate [s] masque elements into [its] fabric," as Gossett has explained (*Influence*, 129). The

density of such elements means that the play feels "at certain times . . . masque-like" even if it does not contain an inset masque as *The Maid's Tragedy* does (Gossett, *Influence*, 131).

95. Chapman, *Memorable Masque*, ll. 188–99.

96. Quoted in Sullivan, 225–26.

97. *Calendar of State Papers Domestic*, 9:172.

98. Quoted in Sullivan, 76.

99. Hedrick, "Be Rough with Me," 45, 47, 48.

100. Shakespeare and Fletcher, *Two Noble Kinsmen*, ed. Potter, 1.2.35–40. All subsequent citations are from edition and are given in the text.

101. Finkelpearl, "Two Distincts," 191.

102. See Potter, 68. Consider also Finkelpearl, who points out that "the Spartan harshness of the *four* executions does not, significantly, derive from Chaucer" ("Two Distincts," 192).

103. Orgel, "Poetics." See also Jonathan Goldberg on the "mysteries" of state in *James I and the Politics of Literature*.

104. For audience "engagement," see Cartelli, *Shakespeare*. The careers of William Kemp and Robert Armin, or the display of Richard Burbage and Nathan Field in the fifth act of Jonson's *Bartholmew Fair*, testify to the reciprocal relation of actors' real and stage personae.

105. Earle, *Micro-cosmographie*, E3v.

106. MacIntyre, 225–26, 224.

107. See Yachnin, "Powerless Theater." He extends the argument in *Stage-wrights*.

108. The Inns of Court masques performed for the 1613 wedding, for instance, involved elaborate land and water processions which recognized performers as well as producers. See Philip Edward's intro. to *The Masque of the Inner Temple and Gray's Inn*, in *A Book of Masques*, 129.

CHAPTER FOUR. *THE CHANGELING* AND THE
PERVERSION OF FELLOWSHIP

1. For the most detailed, though sometimes strained, account of the topical dimensions of the play, see Bromham and Bruzzi, *"The Changeling."*

2. Neill, "Hidden Malady," 114, 107.

3. Patterson, intro. to *Collected Works of Middleton*. I thank Annabel Patterson for letting me read her essay in manuscript.

4. Ricks, "Moral and Poetic Structure," 291.

5. Consider Jean MacIntyre: "After some years in which three adult companies and two boy companies met an increased demand for dramatic entertainment, even so canny and experienced a manager as Henslowe seems to have thought there was 'room for one more,' and so backed Lady Elizabeth's Men despite the demise of the boy companies not long before. Attempts by others (such as the Beestons) to set up new companies followed for another quarter century, but these companies were never so stable as the ones surviving from Elizabeth's days. In the 1620s two of these Elizabethan survivors went under; although actors were ready enough to form new combinations, their companies mostly proved ephemeral" (*Costumes and Scripts*, 321–22).

6. Gurr, *Shakespearian Playing Companies*, 128–29.

7. Baldwin, *Organization*, 161. See also Honigmann and Brock, *Playhouse Wills*, 1–10. Steven Rappaport defines livery companies as "incorporated societies . . . which were principally social organizations or components of the economic structure, but they retained important political and social functions" (*Worlds*, 177, 183).

8. See Ingram, *Business of Playing*, 182–218.

9. See Grassby, *Business Community* and *Kinship and Capitalism*. See also Rappaport; Archer, *Pursuit*.

10. See Honigmann and Brock, 1–30.

11. Ibid., 107, 142–43.

12. Beaumont, *Knight*, induction, 103–5.

13. *Lingua*, Fl.

14. *Conversations with Drummond*, 598.

15. Nungezer, *Dictionary*, 124.

16. MacD. Jackson ("Late Webster") argues that the play should be attributed to Webster, Rowley, and Heywood.

17. Rowley and Webster, *Cuckold*, 3:37.

18. Shakespeare, *Hamlet*, in *The Riverside Shakespeare*, 3.2.277–78.

19. *Dramatic Records*, 5, 74.

20. *Dramatic Records in the Declared Accounts*, 5, 68, 69, 74.

21. Massinger, *The Roman Actor*, 2.1.412–13.

22. Taylor, *Armado,* B3v, C1.

23. Dekker and Middleton, *Roaring Girl* 5.1.290.

24. Rowley, *Search*, A4.

25. Middleton, *Triumphs*, A2.

26. Jonson, *Bartholomew Fair*, 53–55.

27. *Henslowe and Alleyn*, 86–87.

28. Ibid., 57.

29. In Cooke, *Greenes Tu Quoque*, A2.

30. *Henslowe and Alleyn*, 144.

31. For a general discussion showing that artisanal life could be depicted only in gentle terms, see Stevenson, *Praise*.

32. For an overview of this genealogy, see Mills, *One Soul*.

33. Montaigne, *Essaies*, 21.

34. Dorke, A3.

35. Breme, *Mirrour*, B4, B5v–B6.

36. Bacon, *Essays*, 139, 141.

37. Churchyard, *Sparke of Friendship*, C1.

38. Masten, *Textual Intercourse*, 35.

39. Ibid., 2.

40. Shannon, *Sovereign Amity*, 50.

41. Breme, B4.

42. See Najemy, *Between Friends*, 22. Najemy specifically uses the terms of humanist epistolary conventions to explain the relationship of Machiavelli and Vettori.

43. Bawcutt, intro. to *The Changeling*, xlii.

44. Jackson, *Studies*, 125. T. H. Howard-Hill has accepted this attribution in the entry on Rowley in the *Dictionary of Literary Biography*.

45. For *The Spanish Gypsy,* see Jackson, *Studies*, 131; for *Game at Chess*, see Gurr, *Playing Companies*, 374.

46. Daalder, intro. to *The Changeling*, xiv.

47. See Bentley, *Jacobean and Caroline Stage*, 5:1015–16. Bentley points out that Rowley enjoyed an established reputation in the theater, but as a player rather than playwright: his "popular standing . . . is suggested by manuscript verses in which his name is linked with [the actors] John Lowin, Nicholas Tooley, and Joseph Taylor" (5: 1016, 1018). Rowley's name appears in articles of agreement along with Robert Pallant, Joseph Taylor, Robert Hamlen, John Newton, and others. See *Henslowe Papers*,

90–91. Gurr suggests that Rowley, with John Newton, represented the Palsgrave's company, which had formerly been Prince Henry's company (*Playing Companies*, 121). This does not make sense, however, as Rowley had been associated from 1609 with Charles's troupe, even when they were still the Duke of York's company.

48. Bentley, *Jacobean and Caroline Stage*, 4:858.

49. Corrigan, "Middleton," 287.

50. Information on Middleton and Rowley comes from Bentley, *Jacobean and Caroline Stage*. For Middleton, see 4:860–61; for Rowley, see 5:1016.

51. Information on plays and venues comes from ibid., 3:14, 305–433; Chambers, *Elizabethan Stage*, 3:215–36; McMullan, *Politics of Unease*, 267–69.

52. "The majority of the playwrights mentioned in [Henslowe's] diary were independent agents selling their talents wherever they could," Carson, *Companion to "Henslowe's Diary,"* 54–56, 64). As Carson points out, the writers' link was often through Henslowe.

53. Rowley is known to have worked once with John Day and John Wilkins on *The Travels of Three English Brothers* (1607), once with Thomas Heywood on *Fortune by Land and Sea* (1608), once with John Ford and Thomas Dekker on *The Witch of Edmonton* (1621), once with John Fletcher on *The Maid in the Mill* (1623), once with John Webster on *A Cure for a Cuckold* (1625), and once with Webster, Ford, and Dekker in *Keep the Widow Waking* (1625). Middleton has been shown to have collaborated once with Webster in *Anything for a Quiet Life* (1621), once with Dekker, Michael Drayton, Anthony Munday, and Webster on *Caesar's Fall* (1599, lost), and twice with Dekker on *1 The Honest Whore* (1602) and *The Roaring Girl* (1612). See Bentley, *Jacobean and Caroline Stage*, 5:1016–18, 4:860–64. For additional information about *Keep the Widow Waking*, see Sisson, *Lost Plays*, 80–124.

54. Dorke, Blv.

55. Middleton and Rowley, *A Fair Quarrel* 1.1.71.

56. Rowley, *A New Wonder*, A2v.

57. Bueler, "Rhetoric of Change," 112.

58. The main plot is usually attributed by critics to Middleton, while the subplot is considered Rowley's (see, for instance, Bawcutt, intro. xlii). Such distinctions between who wrote what are less important in a play of such deep linguistic integrity than the fact that both authors use the same words to make their characters misrecognize themselves and one another.

59. Middleton and Rowley, *The Changeling*, 1.1.26–28. All subsequent citations are given in the text.

60. Jardine, *Reading Shakespeare*, 115.

61. For the position that friendship is precluded by the inequality of the sexes, see Shannon.

62. For an extended discussion of humanist and Protestant ideologies of companionate marriage and the way dominant social models "construct[ed] marital equality on the basis of women's sexual control and men's wealth" and "still trie[d] to legitimate the hierarchies of class and gender which sustained the Tudor religious order," see Wayne, intro. to Tilney, *Flower of Friendship*.

63. Cicero, *De amicitia*, A5–A5v.

64. Ibid., A6.

65. Bly, *Queer Virgins*, 131.

66. Perkins, *Discourse of Conscience*, 3, 6.

67. For a full explication of the "O" and orgasm, see Garber, "Insincerity of Women," 364.

68. Taverner, *Proverbes*, I5.

CHAPTER FIVE. *THE LATE LANCASHIRE WITCHES* AND JOINT
WORK ACROSS GENERATIONS

1. Laird Barber, intro. to Brome and Heywood, *Late Lancashire Witches*, 1. Despite
assertions that the play was a Heywood composition from 1612 revised by Brome (see
Jackson, "Late Webster," 307), I follow Barber, as well as Brome's biographer Catherine
Shaw (*Richard Brome*, 108–9), in treating the piece as jointly written from its inception.
See also Martin, "Is *The Late Lancashire Witches* a Revision?"

2. McLuskie, "Plays," 170, 169.

3. Gurr writes, "Under Charles [I] playgoing became socially more respectable
than it had ever been and as a result the different playing companies found their social
and cultural allegiances diverging from one another further than ever" (*Shakespearian
Playing Companies*, 139).

4. For social pressures on Caroline playwrights' aesthetics, see Kaufmann, *Richard
Brome*, 12–13.

5. McLuskie, "Plays," 169. McLuskie's theory begs the question of what constitutes a "successful" collaboration. She seems to believe that it involves coherence of
plot and tone; for instance, she praises the Beaumont and Fletcher collaborations especially for their unity of tone and smoothness (175). Whether these are appropriate
criteria for judging theatrical success on the early modern stage is debatable, but I am
more concerned with the benchmark she sets for effective writing groups: their members should be similar or equivalent in personal temperament and professional experience. Cf. Philip Finkelpearl, who argues for wide variations in collaborative writers'—
particular Beaumont and Fletcher's—political persuasions (*Court and Country* and
"Beaumont, Fletcher").

6. I am dating the notoriously slippery "start" of the commercial theater in London to the 1560s. See Gurr, *Shakespearian Playing Companies*, 24; and *Shakespearian
Stage*, 113–55. For a discussion of the importance of 1576 as the start of the commercial
theater, see De Grazia, "World Pictures."

7. See Nungezer, *Dictionary*, 190–92; Clark, *Thomas Heywood*; Heywood, *English
Traveller*, dedication, ll. 2–3.

8. The license reads "A new Comedy, a *Fault in Friendship*, by Young Johnson and
Broome alld 2 Oct. 1623, for Princes Company, I/i" (Bawcutt, *Control and Censorship*,
145). One must of course wonder whether this was a collaborative effort or a writing
error that turned "Young Brome" into "Young Johnson and Broome."

9. His writing career continued, however, into the Interregnum.

10. For an interpretation of the relationship between Shakespeare and Fletcher and
how it affected *The Two Noble Kinsmen*, see Frey, "Collaborating with Shakespeare." For
Fletcher and Massinger, Hoy, "Massinger as Collaborator."

11. Bentley, *Stage*, 3:436.

12. The writers' contemporaries notice this implicitly: they published Brome's
plays through the Interregnum, a time when the (re)printing of plays such as the
Beaumont and Fletcher *Folio* was meant to recall, nostalgically, pre-Cromwell days,
whereas Heywood's plays, which underwent multiple (re)printings (often at his behest)
in the 1620s and 1630s, were not (re)printed at all between 1642 and 1660. See
Bentley, *Stage* 3: 49–92; 4: 553–86.

13. Brome, *Love-Sick Court*, F3.

14. Brome, *The Damoiselle*, A2.

15. Heywood, *Hierarchie*, S1–S1v.

16. Although there are clearly other stage writers missing from this list, compiled
as it is largely of writers whose names were open to "nick-naming," it seems to me

significant that Heywood should neglect his recent collaborator in a text published just a year after their collaborations (I discuss their other collaborations later in this chapter), I would read the absence of Brome, who was often called "Dick" in other poets' commendatory epistles, as a sign of Heywood's classifying him with another, later category of poets; Heywood does not think of Brome alongside these other stage names.

17. Brome, *Northern Lasse*, A4v, emphasis added.

18. In Beaumont and Fletcher, *Comedies and Tragedies*, G1.

19. C. G. [Charles Gerbier?], "To Censuring Critics on the Approved Comedy, *The Antipodes*," in Brome, *Antipodes*, 218–19.

20. In Hall, *Jovial Crew*, 5.

21. Brome, *Weeding of Covent-Garden*.

22. Jonson, *Bartholomew Fair*, induction, 5–6.

23. Jonson, *Ben Jonson*, 3:ix. *The New Inn* was a "flop" at Blackfriars in 1629 at the same time Brome's lost play *The Lovesick Maid* was so successful that the King's Men afterwards gave Master of the Revels Sir Henry Herbert a £2 gratuity. Jonson published *The New Inn* in 1631 with an "Ode to Himself" (written in 1629) that some have read to include a jab at Brome through a pun on "sweepings": "No doubt some mouldy tale, / Like *Pericles*, and stale / As the shrieve's crusts, and nasty as his fish-/ *scraps*, out of every dish, / Thrown forth, and raked into the common tub / May keep the play club: / There, sweepings do as we / For who the relish of these guests will fit / Needs set them but the alms-basket of wit" (ll. 21–30).

24. Heywood, *Hierarchie*, S2v, S3.

25. Gurr, *Shakespearian Playing Companies*, 137. See also Kaufmann: "The enthusiastic and interested (while artistically narrow and demanding) attitude of the court succeeded in influencing not merely the spectacles and plays designed for the courtier group, but also effected a sharper alignment of dramatic intention elsewhere" (18).

26. Gurr, *Shakespearian Playing Companies*, 151. Gurr departs here from Peter Beal, who reads the situation as a "historically . . . significant issue of an opposition in aesthetic matters between two social groups: between the standards of amateur gentlemen poets in the court circle who tended to patronize the fashionable Blackfriars theatre, and the standards of professional writers employed by the more 'popular' Cockpit theatre" ("Massinger," 202). Instead, Gurr emphasizes the fray *within* the Blackfriars audience rather than *between* the two theaters.

27. Brome, *Jovial Crew*, 14.

28. See Freehafer, "Brome," 368.

29. Kaufmann, 18.

30. Heywood, *English Traveller*, dedication, ll. 8–9, 14–15.

31. Baines, *Heywood*, 7.

32. Heywood, *Pleasant Dialogues*, R4v.

33. Heywood, *If You Know Not Me*, A2.

34. Brome, *Weeding*, A1.

35. Martin Butler discusses Brome's appeal to a "third" class of theatergoer in the Caroline period, the "elite gentry," as opposed to either a courtly or grounding audience (*Theatre and Crisis*, 100–40). I suggest here that his view of the audience and the role of the theater was more "popular" than Butler's notion.

36. Heywood, *Apology*, F3v. Baines compares Heywood's *Apology* with Sir Philip Sidney's *Apology for Poetry* (156).

37. Brome, *English Moor*, F5v.

38. See Jackson Cope's detailed reading in *Theatre and the Dream*.

39. The Stationers' Register entry reads, "Mr. Mosely. Entered for his Copies Two

plaies called. The Life & Death of Sr. Martyn Skink. wth ye warres of ye Low Countries. by Rich. Broome. & Tho: Heywood. & The Apprentices Prize" (Bentley, *Stage*, 4:58). Bentley conjectures that both plays were written and performed in 1634, around the same time as *Witches*. Kaufmann agrees with the date for *Martin Skink*, 180). There is no other external evidence for this date, however.

40. See Larner, *Enemies of God*, 15; Sharpe, *Witchcraft in Early Modern England*, 12.

41. Intellectual and social historians have provided various ways of understanding the ideological investments in and implications of witchcraft in early modern England. Keith Thomas (*Religion*) and Alan MacFarlane (*Witchcraft*) offer anthropologically inflected explanations of popular belief in the occult as a way for preindustrial societies to deal with inexplicable natural disasters and rapidly changing socioeconomic conditions. Stuart Clark has discussed witchcraft in epistemological terms by explaining its role in supporting the stark binarisms of early modern political philosophy ("King James's *Daemonologie*"). More recently, historians have focused on the dynamics, rather than functionality, of witchcraft belief, particularly at the village level—on the ways these beliefs negotiated differences in class, age, and gender, and on the ways it framed issues of authority and social order both before and after legal proceedings were initiated. See Annabel Gregory on the changing role of accusations that are nevertheless continually "associated with a belief that investment in social relations is essential for survival and success" ("Witchcraft," 63. See also J. A. Sharpe, who in his work on witchcraft in seventeenth-century Yorkshire suggests that "witches were frequently regarded as frightening and powerful. The witch was capable of killing or crippling with a touch or an ambivalent phrase. Behind such incidents there lurks a whole history of fears, of the building of reputations, of interpersonal tensions" (*Witchcraft in Seventeenth-Century Yorkshire*, 11).

42. The most complete narrative of the incident is in Notestein, *History of Witchcraft*, 146–64. See also *Calendar of State Papers Domestic*, 1634/5: 26, 52, 77, 98, 129, 141.

43. Lancashire had witnessed at least two other witchcraft scares during the reigns of Elizabeth and James. The first was in 1599, the second in 1612. The latter involved several of the people, at that time children, who were to be involved in the scare of 1633/4, including the senior Robinson, who gave testimony at the 1612 trial. For the 1599 trial, see Notestein, 70–75. For the 1612 trial, see Notestein, 121–27. See also Potts, *Wonderfull Descoverie*. The boy's story echoes aspects of the 1612 scare, particularly in his description of the witches' feast.

44. Notestein, 154.

45. Quintrell, "Government in Perspective," 37.

46. See Sharpe, *Instruments*. He proves his statement using the Lancashire affair, saying if it had not been for elite skepticism, the event "could have been a serious outbreak" (126).

47. Despite the intervention, which overturned the earlier assize findings, there is no record of a reversal of the earlier decision, and the women were returned to the Lancashire prison, where they, like the others, died.

48. See Notestein, 63–162.

49. Camden, *Brittania*, 748.

50. Jonson, *Divell*, 1.1.29–33.

51. Middleton, *Inner-Temple Masque*, 143.

52. Potts, A4v, B1.

53. Quoted in Haigh, *Reformation*, 222.

54. Quoted in Sharpe, *Instruments*, 86.

55. Richard James, *Iter Lancastrense*, in Heywood and Brome, *Late Lancashire Witches*, 230–31. All subsequent citations are given by line number in the text.

56. Historians have confirmed the bases for this contemporary stereotype, depicting Lancashire as an emblem of religious extremism that derived from social practice rather than doctrinal conviction. The reputation was acknowledged and promulgated by various sectors of the population. Quintrell explains that northern regions were recognized by their own inhabitants as well as the rest of the populace as "distinctive" largely because it was a political and financial advantage for both groups to stress their differences. The "strangeness" of the northern territories, he writes, "carrying with it a hint of poverty and the need for special consideration was obviously an asset, even if it exaggerated differences between . . . London and more distant regions" (36). Haigh depicts Tudor Lancashire as a place "partially insulated from the rest of England by attitude and geography, [where] economic and social change proceeded only slowly. Where traditional social structures and economic patterns faced . . . no challenge, there can have been no momentum towards religious change, and the stability of life must have produced a temper antipathetic to any alteration" (97).

57. Gardiner, *Constitutional Documents*, 99, 103.

58. Cressy, *Bonfires*, 35.

59. Even Kevin Sharpe, whose approach to Charles I is extremely favorable, admits that "perhaps more than any other of his injunctions [the Book of Sports] raised opponents who were not natural enemies to the [Anglican] church and forced them to a radical choice that presaged the choice many were to have to make in 1642: that between conscience and obedience" (*Personal Rule*, 359).

60. See Gurr, *Shakespearian Playing Companies*, 137–58. For Henrietta Maria's interest in masquing, see Veevers, *Images*.

61. The declaration was a central part of what has been called the Stuart "politics of misrule," the licensing of certain forms of popular recreation in order to control Catholic recusancy and guarantee broader compliance with government regulation of church and state. Leah Marcus (*Politics of Mirth*) offers the most complete study of the phenomenon of the phenomenon of the "carnivalesque" in relation to this very specific piece of legislation and in terms of its effect on writers' sense of their own as well as royal authority. She maintains that the Sports Book represented a particular kind of encroachment by the central government on cultural activity, one that redefined popular festivity in a way that ironically made license and lawlessness a form of "submission to authority." But the decree also alienated more austere as well as more militant members of the Protestant community, as the declaration seemed to bring the national church closer and closer to old forms of ceremony as well as ungodly behavior. For writers of the Jacobean period, Marcus sees the Book of Sports as ultimately productive: it "did not guarantee the subjection of the artists. . . . [I]t seems to have made them more wary, more defensive of their own autonomy. Even as they wrote in praise of 'public mirth,' many developed strategies for preserving their own liberty" (8). As she herself sees in Jonson's relationship to Charles I, the situation is more complex during the Caroline period.

62. Heywood, *Apology*, B4.

63. Though see Butler for a discussion of Prynne's complicated stance vis-à-vis the king: even as he "fulminate[d] against Charles's church, [his pamphlets] run thick with protestations of loyalty" (*Theatre and Crisis*, 88–89).

64. Heywood, *English Traveller*, ll 21–28.

65. Heywood, *Mayden-head*, A3.

66. In the play, there are members of the Roman senate who reject playing for

more traditional reasons. But the real threat to the theater comes from the emperor and his new wife, who enjoy it. See also Annabel Patterson (*Hermeneutics*, 116) for a discussion of James Shirley's similar concerns with the court in *The Triumph of Peace* (1634).

67. Heywood's contribution to the collection of poems celebrating the Cotswold Games (*Annalia Dubrensia*) suggests his continuing interest in this matter.

68. Berry, "Globe Bewitched," 222, 218. See also Gurr, *Shakespearian* Playing Companies, 146–48.

69. Bawcutt, *Control and Censorship*, 189.

70. These same assumptions also inform readings of *Sir John van Olden Barnavelt* and *A Game at Chess* in which scholars take for granted that patronage or protection of a play would have been met with uniform approval and would have translated into a production that unproblematically echoed a patron's interests. Consider F. J. Levy's discussion in "Staging the News."

71. This does not mean, of course, that these playwrights were always averse to sponsorship; Heywood's *Love's Maistresse* (1636), a masque for Queen Henrietta Maria, makes this abundantly clear. In this case, however, the stakes, as I have shown, were quite different.

72. Gurr gestures to this possibility, but only in an offhand manner: "[The play] lacked any kind of satire, unless the very breadth of the comedy was an oblique comment on Pembroke's commission, a refusal either by Heywood and Brome or by the company to take it at all seriously" (*Shakespearian Playing Companies*, 148). My reading does take seriously the strength of the players' possible rejection of patronage.

73. Quoted in Berry, 212–13.

74. *Witches'* consecutive three-day run, still a rarity in 1634, confirms its success. See Gurr, *Shakespearian Playing Companies*, 85.

75. Henderson, "Theater and Domestic Culture," 175.

76. Quintrell, "Government in Perspective," 55.

77. For the prevalence of social negotiation before taking a case to the courts, see Holmes, "Women: Witnesses and Witches."

78. Frances Dolan claims that this approach degrades female agency by "present[ing] witchcraft as trivial [rather than] deeply threatening" while allowing the witches to be "trivialized yet still [held] legally accountable" (*Dangerous Familiars*, 201. But the turning of witchcraft into sport, I suggest, actually challenges such accountability. In keeping with other impulses of the play, the dramatists' comic "trivialization" makes the witches "witty," thereby protecting them from judgment.

79. For the seminal account of the politics of the carnivalesque, see Bakhtin, *Rabelais and His World*. For applications and reformulations of Bakhtinian terms to the early modern world or the early modern theater, see Stallybrass and White, *Politics and Poetics of Transgression*, and Bristol, *Carnival and Theater*.

80. See Miller, "Historical Moment."

CONCLUSION

1. McMillin and MacLean, *Queen's Men*, xii.

2. Consider Mary Bly's explanation of "product control" at the Whitefriars theater: "I may seem to be making a simple replacement, substituting for an 'author figure' the Whitefriars syndicate, and moving blithely into an investigation of *their* intent, treating Whitefriars texts as if the plays were single-authored and as if such an intent were recoverable. In fact, I propose a much more diffuse concept of writing. . . . I do not wish to pry apart Whitefriars scripts, bestowing fragments on [authors], but

instead to widen the configuration of Whitefriars authors to those never mentioned on the Whitefriars title-pages" (*Queer Virgins*, 121).

3. Heywood, *Iron Age*, 24–26. All subsequent references are cited in the text.

4. *Henslowe's Diary*, 21, 60, 72. By 1598 he is no longer registering the distinction.

5. Gurr, "Chimera of Amalgamation." Chambers prints the full Privy Council letter to the Lord Mayor, which submits that a third company, an addition to the established Chamberlain's and Admiral's men, be allowed to play in London, specifically at the Boar's Head. The wording of interest concerns the merging, here made to seem mutually acceptable, of Worcester's and Oxford's, "by reason that the seruants of our verey good L. the Earle of Oxford, and of me the Earle of Worcester, being ioyned by agrement togeather in on [one] Companie . . ." (*Elizabethan Stage*, 4:334).

6. McMillin and MacLean, 62.

7. Gurr, *Shakespearian Playing Companies*, 234.

8. Ibid., 235–36.

9. Ibid., 223.

10. See Shapiro, *Children of the Revels*, 18. See also Gurr, Shakesperian Playing Companies, 222–23.

11. A. M. Clark gives a persuasive chronology of the five plays (*Golden, Silver, Brazen*, and the two parts of *Iron*), dating them all between 1610 and 1613; (*Thomas Heywood*, 62–67). See also Reynolds, *Staging*, 5–7. Arlene Weiner, in her introduction to an edited version of *The Iron Age*, argues that it was the first, rather than last, of the sequence, and preceded rather than followed Shakespeare's *Troilus and Cressida*. Particularly because of the play's elaborate use of masques and other court revels which echo the interests of plays such as *The Tempest*, the play is best dated to the second decade of the seventeenth century. My reading will also suggest that Heywood's manipulation of company collaboration becomes more refined between *Silver* and *Iron*.

12. In the absence of further evidence, scholars have assumed that *The Iron Age* was jointly acted by the troupes that teamed together for *Silver Age*, which we know from court records to have been performed by the King's and Queen's companies (see *Malone Society Collections*, 13:49). Questions about motive and effect of joint playing would remain the same regardless of company.

13. Quoted in Gurr, *Playgoing*, 235.

14. See Weiner's notes to *The Iron Age*, 208.

15. McLuskie, *Dekker and Heywood*, 16, 18.

16. Gurr, "Amalgamation," 85.

17. There is, of course, a middle ground, in which opportunity and a writer's interest coincide with and reinforce, rather than initiate, each other.

18. Heywood, *Siluer Age*, B1.

19. A drama dealing with two competing factions did not, of course, necessarily have to be played by two companies; Shakespeare's *Troilus and Cressida* is the most obvious example. My point here is that Heywood and the companies were in a position to seize on the topic as an *occasion* for joint work.

20. See Clark, 64–65.

21. In a survey of all professionally acted plays published for the first time between 1610 and 1632, and not in collection or translation, none conspicuously divides the dramatis personae into two labeled columns, differentiated by a line, which group together sets of characters. There are, of course, character lists divided into two columns, sometime separated with a vertical line, and often meant to pair characters with their actors (as in James Shirley, *The Wedding* [1629, printer Nicholas Okes], or Philip

Massinger, *The Roman Actor* [1629, printer Bernard Alsop and Thomas Fawcet]). But none are labeled according to the fiction of the play, and most seem to be space savers, with no special order to the columns except by hierarchy or appearance. Title pages were consulted based on published plays in *Bibliography of English Drama*. *A Maiden-head Well Lost*, published after *Iron* and also printed by Nicholas Okes, does divide the cast by *family* (the house of Florence and the house of Milan). The title page specifically labels it as a play performed by Queen Henrietta's Men; there is no indication that it is a collaboratively acted play.

SELECTED BIBLIOGRAPHY

Aers, Lesley, and Nigel Wheale. *Shakespeare in the Changing Curriculum*. London: Routledge, 1991.

Agnew, Jean-Christophe. *Worlds Apart: The Market and the Theater in Anglo-American Thought*. Cambridge: Cambridge University Press, 1986.

Anglo, Sydney, ed. *The Damned Art: Essays in the Literature of Witchcraft*. London: Routledge & Kegan Paul, 1977.

———*Annalia Dubrensia*. London, 1636.

Archer, Ian. *The Pursuit of Stability: Social Relations in Elizabethan London*. Cambridge: Cambridge University Press, 1991.

Aristotle. *Nicomachean Ethics*. In *Introduction to Aristotle*. Ed. Richard McKeon. New York: Random House, 1947.

Ashton, Robert. "Caroline Politics, 1625–1640." In Worden, 79–85.

———. *The City and the Court, 1603–1643*. Cambridge: Cambridge University Press, 1979.

Astington, John. *English Court Theatre, 1558– 1642*. Cambridge: Cambridge University Press, 1999.

Aubrey, John. *Brief Lives*. Ed. Oliver Lawson Dick. Ann Arbor: University of Michigan Press, 1962.

Austin, Warren. *A Computer-Aided Technique for Stylistic Discrimination: The Authorship of "Greene's Groatsworth of Wit."* Nacogdoches, Tex.: U.S. Department of Health, Education and Welfare, 1969.

Bacon, Sir Francis. *The Essays*. Ed. John Pitcher. New York: Penguin Books, 1985.

Baines, Barbara. *Thomas Heywood*. Boston: Twayne, 1984.

Bakhtin, Mikhail. *Rabelais and His World*. Trans. Helene Iswolsky. Bloomington: Indiana University Press, 1984.

Baldwin, T. W. *Organization and Personnel of the Shakespearean Company*. Princeton: Princeton University Press, 1927.

Barber, Laird. Introduction to Brome and Heywood, 1–98. New York: Garland Press, 1979.

Barish, Jonas. *The Anti-theatrical Prejudice*. Berkeley: University of California Press, 1981.

Barroll, J. Leeds. *Anna of Denmark, Queen of England: A Cultural Biography*. Philadelphia: University of Pennsylvania Press, 2001.

———. "Inventing the Stuart Masque." In Bevington and Holbrook, 121–43.

———. *Politics, Plague, and Shakespeare's Theater: The Stuart Years*. Ithaca: Cornell University Press, 1991.

Barroll, J. Leeds, et al., eds. *The Revels History of Drama in English*. Vol. 3. *1576–1613*. London: Methuen, 1975.

Barthes, Roland. *Image, Music, Text*. Trans. Stephen Heath. New York: Hill and Wang 1977.

Barton, Ann Righter. *Shakespeare and the Idea of the Play*. New York: Barnes and Noble, 1962.

Bawcutt, Nigel. *The Control and Censorship of Caroline Drama: The Records of Sir Henry Herbert, Master of the Revels*. Oxford: Clarendon Press, 1996.

———. Introduction to Middleton and Rowley, *The Changeling*, xv–lxviii.

Beal, Peter. "Massinger at Bay: Unpublished Verses in a War of the Theatres." *Yearbook of English Studies* 10 (1980): 190– 203.

———. *In Praise of Scribes: Manuscripts and Their Makers in Seventeenth-Century England*. Oxford: Clarendon Press, 1998.

Beaumont, Francis. *The Knight of the Burning Pestle*. Ed. Michael Hattaway. New York: W. W. Norton, 1986.

———. *The Masque of the Inner Temple and Gray's Inn*. Ed. Philip Edwards. In *A Book of Masques*, 125–48.

Beaumont, Francis, and John Fletcher. *Comedies and Tragedies*. London, 1647.

———. *Cupid's Revenge*. Ed. Fredson Bowers. In *Dramatic Works*, 2:315–448.

———. *The Dramatic Works in the Beaumont and Fletcher Canon*. Gen. ed. Fredson Bowers. 10 vols. Cambridge: Cambridge University Press, 1966–99.

———. *A King and No King*. Ed. George Walton Williams. In *Dramatic Works*, 2:167–314.

———. *The Maid's Tragedy*. Ed. T. W. Craik. Manchester: Manchester University Press, 1988.

———. *The Maid's Tragedy*. Ed. Howard Norland. Lincoln: University of Nebraska Press, 1968.

———. *The Maides Tragedy*. London, 1619.

———. *The Maids Tragedie*. London, 1630.

———. *Philaster*. Ed. Andrew Gurr. London: Methuen, 1969.

———. *The Scornful Lady*. Ed. Cyrus Hoy. In *Dramatic Works*, 2:449–566.

———. *The Works of Beaumont and Fletcher*. Ed. Alexander Dyce. 10 vols. London, 1843; reprint, Freeport, N.Y.: Books for Libraries Press, 1973.

Beckwith, Sarah. "The Power of Devils and the Hearts of Men: Notes toward a Drama of Witchcraft." In Aers and Wheale, 143–61.

Bednarz, James. "Representing Jonson: *Histriomastix* and the Origin of the Poets' War." *Huntington Library Quarterly* 54 (1991): 1–30.

———. *Shakespeare and the Poets' War*. New York: Columbia University Press, 2000.

Beier, A. L., David Cannadine, and James Rosenheim. *The First Modern Society: Essays in English History in Honour of Lawrence Stone*. Cambridge: Cambridge University Press, 1989.

Beier, A. L. and Roger Finlay. *London: The Making of the Modern Metropolis*. London: Longman, 1986.

Bentley, Gerald Eades. *The Jacobean and Caroline Stage*. 7 vols. Oxford: Clarendon Press, 1941–68.

———. *The Profession of Dramatist in Shakespeare's Time, 1590–1642*. Princeton: Princeton University Press, 1971.

———. *The Profession of Player in Shakespeare's Time, 1590–1642*. Princeton: Princeton University Press, 1984.

———. "Shakespeare and the Blackfriars Theatre," *Shakespeare Survey* 1 (1948): 38–50.

Bernard, Richard. *A Guide to Grand-Jury Men with Respect to Witches*. London, 1627/8.

Berry, Herbert. "The Globe Bewitched and *El Hombre Fiel*." *Medieval and Renaissance Drama in England* 1 (1984): 211–30.

Bevington, David. "Inventing the Stuart Masque." In Bevington and Holbrook, 121–43.

———. *Tudor Drama and Politics*. Cambridge: Harvard University Press, 1969.

Bevington, David, and Peter Holbrook, eds. *The Politics of the Stuart Court Masque*. Cambridge: Cambridge University Press, 1998.

Bevington, David, Richard Strier, and David L. Smith, eds. *The Theatrical City: Culture, Theater, and Politics in London, 1576–1642*. Cambridge: Cambridge University Press, 1995.

A Bibliography of English Printed Drama to the Restoration. Ed. W. W. Greg. 4 vols. London: Oxford University Press, 1951.

Fleay, Frederick G. *A Biographical Chronicle of the English Drama, 1559–1642*. 2 vols. London, 1891.

Birch, Thomas, ed. *The Court and Times of James I*. 3 vols. London, 1848.

Blau, Herbert. "The Absolved Riddle: Sovereign Pleasure and the Baroque Subject in the Tragicomedies of John Fletcher." *NLH* 17 (1986): 539–54.

Blayney, Peter. "The Publication of Playbooks." In Cox and Kastan, 383–422.

Bliss, Lee. "Pastiche, Burlesque, Tragicomedy." In Braunmuller and Hattaway, 237–63.

———. "Tragicomic Romance for the King's Men, 1609–1611: Shakespeare, Beaumont, and Fletcher." In Braunmuller and Bulman, 148–64.

Blisset, William, Julian Patrick, and R. W. Van Fossen. *A Celebration of Ben Jonson*. Toronto: University of Toronto Press, 1973.

Bly, Mary. *Queer Virgins and Virgin Queans on the Early Modern Stage*. Oxford: Oxford University Press, 2000.

A Book of Masques, in Honour of Allardyce Nicoll. Cambridge: Cambridge University Press, 1967.

Bourdieu, Pierre. *Distinction: A Social Critique of the Judgement of Taste*. Trans. Richard Nice. Cambridge: Harvard University Press, 1984.

———. *Language and Symbolic Power*. Ed. John B. Thompson. Trans. Gino Raymond and Matthew Adamson. Cambridge: Harvard University Press, 1991.

———. *A Theory of Cultural Production*. Trans. Randal Jackson. New York: Columbia University Press, 1993.

Bradley, David. *From Text to Performance in the Elizabethan Theatre: Preparing the Play for the Stage*. Cambridge: Cambridge University Press, 1992.

Braunmuller, A. R. "The Arts of the Dramatist." In Braunmuller and Hattaway, 53–90.

Braunmuller, A. R., and James Bulman, eds. *Comedy from Shakespeare to Sheridan: Change and Continuity in English and European Drama*. Newark: University of Delaware Press, 1986.

Braunmuller, A. R., and Michael Hattaway, eds. *The Cambridge Companion to English Renaissance Drama*. Cambridge: Cambridge University Press, 1990.

Bray, Alan. "Homosexuality and the Signs of Male Friendship in Elizabethan England." In Goldberg, *Queering*, 40–61.

———. *Homosexuality in Renaissance England*. London: Gay Men's Press, 1982.

Breme, Thomas. *A Mirrour of Friendship*. London, 1584.

Brennan, Michael. *Literary Patronage in the Renaissance: The Pembroke Family*. London: Routledge, 1988.

Brinsley, John. *Ludus Literarius or the Grammar Schoole*. Ed. E. T. Campagnac. Liverpool: University of Liverpool Press, 1917.

Bristol, Michael. *Carnival and Theater: Plebeian Culture and the Structure of Authority in Renaissance England*. New York: Methuen, 1985.

Brome, Richard. *The Antipodes*. In *Three Renaissance Travel Plays*. Ed. Anthony Parr. Manchester: Manchester University Press, 1995.

———. *The Damoiselle*. In *Five New Plays*. London, 1653.

———. *The English Moor*. In *Five New Playes*. London, 1659.

———. *The Jovial Crew*. Ed. Ann Haaker. Lincoln: University of Nebraska Press, 1968.

———. *The Love-Sick Court*. In *Five New Playes*. London, 1659.

———. *The Northern Lasse*. London, 1632.

———. *The Weeding of the Covent-Garden*. In *Five New Playes*. London, 1659.

Brome, Richard, and Thomas Heywood. *The Late Lancashire Witches*. Ed. Laird Barber. New York: Garland, 1979.

Bromham, A. A., and Zara Bruzzi. *"The Changeling" and the Years of Crisis, 1619–1624*. London: Pinter Publishers, 1990.

Brooks, Douglas. *From Playhouse to Printing House: Drama and Authorship in Early Modern England*. Cambridge Studies in Renaissance Literature and Culture 36. Cambridge: Cambridge University Press, 2000.

Browne, William. *The Masque of the Inner Temple*. Ed. R. F. Hill. In *A Book of Masques*, 179–206.

Bruster, Douglas. *The Drama and the Market in the Age of Shakespeare*. Cambridge: Cambridge University Press, 1992.

Bueler, Lois. "The Rhetoric of Change in *The Changeling*." *ELR* 14 (1984): 95–113.

Burrows, J. F. "Not Unless You Ask Nicely: The Interpretive Nexus between Analysis and Information," *Literary and Linguistic Computing* 7 (1992): 91–109.

Burt, Richard. *Licensed by Authority: Ben Jonson and the Discourses of Censorship*. Ithaca: Cornell University Press, 1993.

Butler, Martin. *Theatre and Crisis, 1632–1642*. Cambridge: Cambridge University Press, 1984.

A Calendar of Dramatic Records in the Books of the Livery Companies of London, 1485–1640. Oxford: Malone Society, 1954.

Calendar of State Papers, Domestic Series. Vols. 5 and 7. London: Longman, Green, Longman and Roberts, 1862.

Camden, William. *Brittania*. London, 1634.

Campion, Thomas. *The Lord Hay's Masque*. In Lindley, 18–34.

———. *The Lord's Masque*. Ed. I. A. Shapiro. In *A Book of Masques*, 95–124.

Capp, Bernard. *English Almanacs, 1500–1800: Astrology and the Popular Press*. Ithaca: Cornell University Press, 1979.

Carroll, D. Allen. Introduction to *Greene's Groatsworth of Wit*. Ed. D. Allen Carroll. Binghamton, N.Y.: Medieval and Renaissance Texts and Studies, 1994. 1–38.

Carson, Neil. "Collaborative Playwriting: The Chettle, Dekker, Heywood Syndicate." *Theatre Research International* 14 (1989): 13–23.

———. *Companion to "Henslowe's Diary."* Cambridge: Cambridge University Press, 1988.

Cartelli, Thomas. *Shakespeare, Marlowe, and the Economy of Theatrical Experience.* Philadelphia: University of Pennsylvania Press, 1991.

Chamberlain, John. *The Chamberlain Letters.* Ed. Elizabeth McClure Thomson. New York: G. P. Putnam's Sons, 1965.

Chambers, E. K. *The Elizabethan Stage.* 4 vols. Oxford: Clarendon Press, 1923.

Champion, Larry. "*Westward-Northward*: Structural Development in Dekker's *Ho* Plays." *Comparative Drama* 16 (1982): 251–66.

———. Chapman, George. *All Fools.* Ed. G. Blakemore Evans. In *Plays*, 1:227–310.

———. *Bussy D'Ambois: A Tragedie.* Ed. John H. Smith. In *Plays*, 2:7–264.

———. *Gentleman Usher.* Ed. Robert Ornstein. In *Plays*, 1: 59–130.

———. *An Humorous Day's Mirth.* Ed. Allan Holaday. In *Plays*, 1:59–130.

———. *The Plays of George Chapman.* Vol. 1. *Comedies.* Gen. ed. Allan Holaday. Urbana: University of Illinois Press, 1970.

———. *The Plays of George Chapman.* Vol. 2. *Tragedies.* Gen. ed. Allan Holaday. Cambridge: D. S. Brewer, 1987.

Chapman, George, Ben Jonson, and John Marston. *Eastward Ho.* Ed. F. W. Schelling. London, 1903.

———. *Eastward Hoe.* Ed. R. W. Van Fossen. Manchester: Manchester University Press, 1979.

Chettle, Henry. *Kind-Hart's Dreame.* London, 1592.

Churchyard, Thomas. *A Sparke of Friendship and Warme Goodwill.* London, 1588.

Cicero, Marcus Tullius. *De Amicitia.* Trans. Harry Edinger. New York: Library of Liberal Arts, 1967.

———. *De Oratore.* Trans. E. W. Sutton. Cambridge: Harvard University Press, 1948.

Clare, Janet. *Art Made Tongue-Tied by Authority: Elizabethan and Jacobean Dramatic Censorship.* Manchester: Manchester University Press, 1990.

Clark, A. M. *Thomas Heywood, Playwright and Miscellanist.* New York: Russell & Russell, 1967.

Clark, Ira. *Professional Playwrights: Massinger, Ford, Shirley, and Brome.* Lexington: University Press of Kentucky, 1992.

Clark, Stuart. "King James's *Daemonologie*: Witchcraft and Kingship." In Anglo, 156–82.

Cogswell, Thomas. *The Blessed Revolution: English Politics and the Coming of War, 1621–1624.* Cambridge: Cambridge University Press, 1989.

———. "Thomas Middleton and the Court, 1624: *A Game at Chess* in Context." *Huntington Library Quarterly* 47 (1984): 273–88.

Cohen, R. A. "The Function of Setting in *Eastward Ho.*" *Renaissance Papers 1973* (1973): 83–96.

Collier, J. Payne. *Annals of the Stage.* 3 vols. London, 1831.

Conversations with Drummond. In *Oxford Jonson*, 595–611.

Cook, Ann Jennalie. *Privileged Playgoers of Shakespeare's London, 1576–1642.* Princeton: Princeton University Press, 1981.

Cope, Jackson. *The Theater and the Dream.* Baltimore: Johns Hopkins University Press, 1977.

Corrigan, Brian Jay. "Middleton, *The Revenger's Tragedy*, and Crisis Literature." *SEL* 38 (1998): 281–95.

Cox, John D., and David Scott Kastan, eds. *A New History of Early English Drama*. New York: Columbia University Press, 1997.

Craik, T. W. Introduction to Beaumont and Fletcher, *The Maid's Tragedy*, 1–46.

Crane, Mary. *Framing Authority: Sayings, Self, and Society in Sixteenth-Century England*. Princeton, N.J.: Princeton University Press, 1993.

Cressy, David. *Bonfires and Bells: National Memory and the Protestant Calendar in Elizabethan and Stuart England*. Berkeley: University of California Press, 1989.

Cust, Richard. "News and Politics in Seventeenth-Century England." *Past and Present* 112 (1986): 60–90.

Danby, John F. *Poets on Fortune's Hill: Studies in Sidney, Spenser, Beaumont, and Fletcher*. London: Faber and Faber, 1952.

Daniel, Samuel. *A Panegyrike Congratvlatorie Deliuered to the Kings Most Excellent Maiestie*. London, 1603.

———. *Tethys' Festival*. In Lindley, 54–65.

———. *The Vision of Twelve Goddesses*. London, 1604.

Day, John. *Ile of Gvls*. Ed. G. B. Harrison. London: Oxford University Press, 1936.

D'Avenant, Sir William. *The Shorter Poems, and Songs from the Plays and Masques*. Ed. A. M. Gibbs. Oxford: Clarendon Press, 1972.

———. *Dramatic Works of William D'Avenant*. London: Sotheran, 1872.

Davidson, Clifford, and C. J. Giankaris, eds. *Drama in the Renaissance: Comparative and Critical Essays*. New York: AMS Press, 1986.

Davies, H. Neville. "Beaumont and Fletcher's *Hamlet*." In Muir, Halio, and Palmer, 173–81.

Davies, John of Hereford. *The Complete Works of John Davies*. Ed. Alexander Grosart. 2 vols. London, 1875.

Davis, Joe Lee. *The Sons of Ben: Jonsonian Comedy in Caroline England*. Detroit, Mich.: Wayne State University Press, 1967.

De Grazia, Margreta. "World Pictures, Modern Periods, and the Early English Stage." In Cox and Kastan, 7–21.

De Grazia, Margreta, Maureen Quilligan, and Peter Stallybrass, eds. *Subject and Object in the English Renaissance*. Cambridge Studies in Renaissance Literature and Cultures 8. Cambridge: Cambridge University Press, 1996.

Dekker, Thomas. *The Dramatic Works of Thomas Dekker*. Ed. Fredson Bowers. 4 vols. Cambridge: Cambridge University Press, 1953.

———. *Guls Horne-Booke*. London, 1604.

———. *Satiromastix*. In *Dramatic Works*, 1:299–395.

———. *The Shoemaker's Holiday*. Ed. Anthony Parr. New York: W. W. Norton, 1990.

Dekker, Thomas, and Thomas Middleton. *The Roaring Girl*. In *Drama of the English Renaissance*. Vol. 2. Ed. Russell A. Frazer and Norman Rabkin. New York: Macmillan, 1976. 333–68.

Dekker, Thomas, and John Webster. *Northward Hoe*. In Dekker, *Dramatic Works*, 2: 405–489.

———. *Westward Hoe*. In Dekker, *Dramatic Works*, 2:311–403.

A Dictionary of Law. Oxford: Oxford University Press, 1994.

Dillon, Janet. *Theatre, Court, and City*. Cambridge: Cambridge University Press, 2000.

Dobranski, Stephen. *Milton, Authorship, and the Book Trade*. Cambridge: Cambridge University Press, 1999.

Dolan, Frances. *Dangerous Familiars: Representations of Domestic Crime in England, 1550–1700*. Ithaca: Cornell University Press, 1994.

Dorke, Walter. *Tipe or Figure of Friendship*. London, 1589.

Dramatic Records in the Declared Accounts of the Treasurer of the Chamber, 1558–1642. Oxford: Malone Society, 1961.

Dutton, Richard. *Mastering the Revels: The Regulation and Censorship of English Renaissance Drama*. Iowa City: University of Iowa Press, 1991.

Earle, John. *Micro-cosmographie*. London, 1623.

Edwards, Philip, et al., eds. *Revels History of Drama in English*. Vol. 4. *1613–1642*. London: Methuen, 1981.

Evans, Robert C. *Ben Jonson and the Poetics of Patronage*. Lewisburg, Pa.: Bucknell University Press, 1989.

Ewbank. Inga-Stina. " 'These pretty devices': A Study of Masques in Plays." In *A Book of Masques*, 405–48.

Field, Nathan. *The Plays of Nathan Field*. Ed. William Peery. Austin: University of Texas Press, 1950.

Finet, John. *Finetti Philoxenis*. London, 1656.

Finkelpearl, Philip. "Beaumont, Fletcher, and 'Beaumont & Fletcher': Some Distinctions. *ELR* 1 (1971): 144–64.

———. *Court and Country Politics in the Plays of Beaumont and Fletcher*. Princeton: Princeton University Press, 1990.

———. *John Marston of the Middle Temple: A Dramatist in His Social Setting*. Cambridge: Harvard University Press, 1969.

———. "Two Distincts, Division None: Shakespeare and Fletcher's *The Two Noble Kinsmen* of 1613." In Parker and Zitner, 184–99.

Fish, Stanley. "Author-Readers: Jonson's Community of the Same." *Representations* 7 (1984): 26–58.

Fleay, Frederick G. *A Biographical Chronicle of the English Drama, 1559–1642*. 2 vols. London, 1891.

Fleming, Juliet. "Graffiti, Grammatology, and the Age of Shakespeare." In Fumerton and Hunt, 315–52.

Fletcher, Anthony, and John Stevenson, eds. *Order and Disorder in Early Modern England*. Cambridge: Cambridge University Press, 1985.

Fletcher, John. *The Faithful Shepherdess*. Ed. Cyrus Hoy. In Beaumont and Fletcher, *Dramatic Works*, 3:483–612.

Fletcher, John, and Nathan Field. *Four Plays, or Moral Representations, in One*. Ed. Cyrus Hoy. In Beaumont and Fletcher, *Dramatic Works* 8:225–344.

Fletcher, John, Nathan Field, and Philip Massinger. *The Queen of Corinth*. Ed. Robert Kean Turner. In Beaumont and Fletcher, *Dramatic Works*, 8:3–111.

Fletcher, John, and Philip Massinger. *The Tragedy of Sir John Van Olden Barnavelt*. In Beaumont and Fletcher, *Dramatic Works*, 8:483–632.

Forker, Charles. *The Skull Beneath the Skin: The Achievement of John Webster*. Carbondale: University of Southern Illinois Press, 1986.

Foucault, Michel. *Discipline and Punish*. Trans. Alan Sheridan. New York: Pantheon Books, 1977.

———. "What Is an Author?" In Harari, 141–60.

Freehafer, John. "Brome, Suckling, and Davenant's Theater Project of 1639," *Texas Studies in Literature and Language* 10 (1968): 367–83.

Frey, Charles. "Collaborating with Shakespeare." In Frey, *Shakespeare*, 31–44.

———, ed. *Shakespeare, Fletcher, and "The Two Noble Kinsmen."* Columbia: University of Missouri Press, 1989.

Fumerton, Patricia. *Cultural Aesthetics: Renaissance Literature and the Practice of Social Ornament*. Chicago: University of Chicago Press, 1991.

Fumerton, Patricia, and Simon Hunt, eds. *Renaissance Culture and the Everyday*. Philadelphia: University of Pennsylvania Press, 1999.

Gainsford, Thomas. *The Rich Cabinet*. London, 1616.

Gair, W. Reavely. *The Children of Paul's: The Story of a Theatre Company, 1553–1608*. Cambridge: Cambridge University Press, 1982.

———. Introduction to Marston, *Antonio's Revenge*, 1–46.

Gallagher, Lowell. *Medusa's Gaze: Casuistry and Conscience in the Renaissance*. Stanford: Stanford University Press, 1991.

Garber, Marjorie. "The Insincerity of Women." In De Grazia, Quilligan, and Stallybrass, 349–68.

Gardiner, S. R., ed. *Constitutional Documents of the Puritan Revolution, 1625–1660*. Oxford: Clarendon Press, 1899.

Genette, Gérard. *Palimpsests: Literature on the Second Degree*. Trans. Channa Newman and Claude Doubinsky. Lincoln: University of Nebraska Press, 1986.

Goldberg, Jonathan. *James I and the Politics of Literature: Jonson, Shakespeare, Donne, and Their Contemporaries*. Baltimore: Johns Hopkins University Press, 1983.

———. *Sodometries: Renaissance Texts, Modern Sexualities*. Stanford: Stanford University Press, 1992.

———. *Writing Matter: From the Hands of the English Renaissance*. Stanford: Stanford University Press, 1990.

———. ed., *Queering the Renaissance*. Durham: Duke University Press, 1994.

Gordon, D. J. *The Renaissance Imagination: Essays and Lectures*. Ed. Stephen Orgel. Berkeley: University of California Press, 1975.

Gossett, Suzanne. *The Influence of the Jacobean Masque on the Plays of Beaumont and Fletcher*. New York: Garland, 1988.

———. "Masque Influence on the Dramaturgy of Beaumont and Fletcher," *Modern Philology* 69 (1972): 199–208.

Grassby, Richard. *The Business Community of Seventeenth-Century England*. Cambridge: Cambridge University Press, 1997.

———. *Kinship and Capitalism: Marriage, Family, and Business in the English-Speaking World, 1580–1740*. New York: Cambridge University Press, 2001.

Greenblatt, Stephen. *Renaissance Self-Fashioning*. Berkeley: University of California Press, 1980.

———. "Shakespeare Bewitched." In Kishi, Pringle, and Wells, 17–42.

Greene, Thomas. *The Light in Troy: Imitation and Discovery in Renaissance Poetry*. New Haven: Yale University Press, 1982.

Gregory, Annabel. "Witchcraft, Politics, and 'Good Neighborhood.'" *Past and Present* 113 (1991): 31–66.

Gurr, Andrew. "The Chimera of Amalgamation." *Theatre Research International* 18 (1993): 85–93.

———. "Money or Audiences: The Impact of Shakespeare's Globe." *Theatre Notebook: A Journal of the History and Technique of the British Theatre* 42 (1988): 3–14.

———. *Playgoing in Shakespeare's London*. 2d ed. Cambridge: Cambridge University Press, 1996.

———. *The Shakespearean Stage, 1574–1642*. Cambridge: Cambridge University Press, 1980.

———. *The Shakespearian Playing Companies*. Oxford: Clarendon Press, 1996.

Haigh, Christopher. *Reformation and Resistance in Tudor Lancashire*. Cambridge: Cambridge University Press, 1975.

Halasz, Alexandra. *The Marketplace of Print: Pamphlets and the Public Sphere in Early*

Modern England. Cambridge Studies in Renaissance Literature and Culture 14. Cambridge: Cambridge University Press, 1997.

Halpern, Richard. *The Poetics of Primitive Accumulation: English Renaissance Culture and the Genealogy of Capital*. Ithaca: Cornell University Press, 1991.

Hammer, Paul J. "Upstaging the Queen: The Earl of Essex, Francis Bacon, and the Accession Day Celebrations of 1595." In Bevington and Holbrook, 41–66.

Hanson, Laurence. "English Newsbooks, 1621–1641." *The Library* 18 (1938): 367–75.

Harari, Josué, ed. *Textual Strategies*. Ithaca: Cornell University Press, 1979.

Harbage, Alfred. *Annals of English Drama, 975–1700*. 3d ed. Rev. Sylvia Wagoneheim. London: Routledge, 1989.

———. *Shakespeare and the Rival Traditions*. New York: Columbia University Press, 1952.

Harrap's Dictionary of Law and Society. Kent: Harrap Books, 1989.

Harrison, G. B. *A Jacobean Journal, 1603–1608*. London: Routledge, 1941.

———. ed. *The Trial of the Lancashire Witches*. London: Peter Davies, 1929.

Haynes, Jonathan. *The Social Relations of Jonson's Theatre*. Cambridge: Cambridge University Press, 1992.

Hedrick, Donald. " 'Be Rough with Me': The Collaborative Arenas of *The Two Noble Kinsmen*." In Frey, *Shakespeare*, 45–77.

Heinemann, Margot. *Puritanism and Theatre: Thomas Middleton and Opposition Drama under the Early Stuarts*. Cambridge: Cambridge University Press, 1980.

Helgerson, Richard. *Forms of Nationhood: The Elizabethan Writing of England*. Chicago: University of Chicago Press, 1992.

———. *Self-Crowned Laureates*. Berkeley: University of California Press, 1983.

Henderson, Diane. "Theater and Domestic Culture." In Cox and Kastan, 173–94.

Henslowe and Alleyn: Being the Diary of Philip Henslowe and the Life of Edward Alleyn. Ed. J. Payne Collier. London, Shakespeare Society, 1853.

Henslowe Papers: Being Documents Supplementary to Henslowe's Diary. Ed. W. W. Greg. London: A. H. Bullen, 1897.

Henslowe's Diary. Ed. R. A. Foakes and R. T. Rickert. Cambridge: Cambridge University Press, 1961.

Hensman, Bertha. *The Shares of Fletcher, Field, and Massinger in Twelve Plays of the Beaumont and Fletcher Canon*. 2 vols. Salzburg: Insitut für Englische Sprache, Universität Salzburg, 1974.

Heywood, Jasper. *Thyestes*. London, 1560.

Heywood, Thomas. *An Apology for Actors*. London, 1612.

———. *The Dramatic Works of Thomas Heywood*. 6 vols. Reprint, New York: Russell and Russell, 1964.

———. *The English Traveller*. In Robert Jackson Hudson, *A Critical Edition of Thomas Heywood's "The English Traveller."* Ann Arbor: University Microfilms, 1962.

———. *Gynaikeion: or, Nine Books of Various History. Concerning Women*. London, 1624.

———. *The Hierarchie of the Blessed Angells*. London, 1635.

———. *If You Know Not Me, You Know Nobody*. London, 1639.

———. *The Iron Age*. Ed. Arlene Weiner. New York: Garland, 1979.

———. *A Mayden-head Well Lost*. London, 1634.

———. *Pleasant Dialogues and Dramma's*. London, 1637.

———. *Silver Age*. London, 1613.

———. *The Wise Woman of Hogsdon*. In *Dramatic Works*, 5:275–353.

Heywood, Thomas, and Richard Brome. *The Late Lancashire Witches*. Ed. Laird Barber. New York: Garland, 1979.

Hirschfeld, Heather. "Early Modern Collaboration and Theories of Authorship," *PMLA* 116 (2001): 609–22.

Hirst, Derek. *Authority and Conflict: England, 1603–1642*. Cambridge: Harvard University Press, 1986.

Holmes, Clive. "The County Community in Stuart Historiography." *Journal of British Studies* 19 (1980): 54–73.

———. "Women: Witnesses and Witches." *Past and Present* 140 (1993): 45–78.

Holmes, David. "The Evolution of Stylometry in Humanities Scholarship." *Literary and Linguistic Computing* 13 (1998): 111–17.

Honigmann, E. J., and Susan Brock. *Playhouse Wills, 1558–1642*. Manchester: Manchester University Press, 1993.

Hoorn, Johan F., et al. "Neural Network Identification of Poets Using Letter Sequences." *Literary and Linguistic Computing* 14 (1999): 311–38.

Hope, Jonathan. *The Authorship of Shakespeare's Plays*. Cambridge: Cambridge University Press, 1994.

Hope, Jonathan, and Gordon McMullan. *The Politics of Tragicomedy: Shakespeare and After*. London: Routledge, 1992.

Hoskyns, John. *Directions for Speech and Style*. Ed. Hoyt Hudson. Ann Arbor: University Microforms, 1975.

Howard, Douglas, ed. *Philip Massinger: A Critical Reassessment*. Cambridge: Cambridge University Press, 1985.

Howard-Hill, T. H. "Crane's 1619 Promptbook of *Sir John Van Olden Barnavelt.*" *Modern Philology* 86 (1988): 146–70.

Hoy, Cyrus. *Introductions, Notes, and Commentaries to Texts in the Dramatic Works of Thomas Dekker*. 4 vols. Cambridge: Cambridge University Press, 1980.

———. "Massinger as Collaborator: The Plays with Fletcher and Others." In Howard, 117–39.

———. "The Shares of Fletcher and His Collaborators in the Beaumont and Fletcher Canon I–VI," *Studies in Bibliography* 8 (1956): 129–46; 9 (1957): 143–62; 11 (1958): 85–106; 12 (1959); 91–116; 13 (1960); 77–108; 14 (1961); 45–67; 15 (1962): 71–90.

Hunter, G. K. "*Henry IV* and the Elizabethan Two-Part Play." *Review of English Studies* 5 (1954): 236–48.

Hutson, Lorna. *The Usurer's Daughter: Male Friendship and Fictions of Women in Sixteenth-Century England*. London: Routledge, 1994.

Ingram, William. *The Business of Playing: The Beginnings of the Adult Professional Theater in Elizabethan London*. Ithaca: Cornell University Press, 1987.

Jackson, MacD. P. "Editing, Attribution Studies, and 'Literature Online': A New Resource in Renaissance Drama." *Research Opportunities in Renaissance Drama* 37 (1998): 1–16.

———. "Late Webster and His Collaborators: How Many Playwrights Wrote *A Cure for a Cuckold?*" *Papers of the Bibliographical Society of America* 95 (2001): 295–313.

———. *Studies in Attribution: Middleton and Shakespeare*. Salzburg: Institut für Anglistik und Amerikanistik, Universität Salzburg, 1979.

Jackson, William, ed. *Records of the Court of the Stationers' Company, 1602–1640*. London: Bibliographical Society, 1957.

Jardine, Lisa. *Reading Shakespeare Historically*. London: Routledge, 1996.

Jonson, Ben. *Bartholomew Fair*. Ed. George Hibbard. New York: Norton, 1977.

———. *Ben Jonson*. ed. C. H. Herford, Percy Simpson, and Evelyn Simpson. 11 vols. Oxford: Clarendon Press, 1925–52.

——. *B. Ion: His Part of King James his Royall and Magnificent Entertainment*. London, 1604.

——. *The Characters of Two Royall Masques*. London, 1608.

——. *The Complete Masques*. Ed. Stephen Orgel. New Haven: Yale University Press, 1969.

——. *The Complete Plays*. Ed. G. A. Wilkes. 5 vols. Oxford: Clarendon Press, 1982.

——. *Cynthia's Revels*. In *Ben Jonson*, 4:1–84.

——. *Discoveries*. In *Oxford Jonson*, 521–95.

——. *The Divell is an Asse*. In *Ben Jonson*, 6:143–269.

——. *The Fountaine of Self-Loue, or Cynthias Revels*. London, 1601.

——. *The Gypsies Metamorphosed*. In *Ben Jonson*, 7:539–622.

——. *Hymenaei, or the Solemnities of Masque and Barriers at a Marriage*. In *Ben Jonson*, 7:205–41.

——. *The Masque of Queenes*. In *Ben Jonson*, 7:267–319.

——. *The New Inne*. In *Ben Jonson*, 6:383–498.

——. *Oberon*. In *Ben Jonson*, 7:337–56.

——. *The Oxford Ben Jonson*. Ed. Ian Donaldson. Oxford: Oxford University Press, 1985.

——. *Poetaster*. In *Ben Jonson*, 4:185–325.

——. *The Staple of News*. Ed. Anthony Parr. Manchester: Manchester University Press, 1988.

——. *Volpone*. In *Ben Jonson*, 5:1–137.

Kahl, William. *The Development of London Livery Companies*. Kress Library of Business and Economics 15. Cambridge: Harvard University Press, 1958.

Kaufmann, R. J. *Richard Brome, Caroline Playwright*. New York: Columbia University Press, 1961.

Kerrigan, William. "The Articulation of the Ego in the English Renaissance." In Smith, *Freud*, 261–306.

Kishi, Tetsuo, Roger Pringle, and Stanley Wells, eds. *Shakespeare and Cultural Traditions*. Newark: University of Delaware Press, 1994.

Knowles, James. "Insubstantial Pageants: *The Tempest* and Masquing Culture." In Richards and Knowles, 108–25.

Knutson, Roslyn. "Falconer to the Little Eyases: A New Date and Commercial Agenda for the 'Little Eyases' Passage in *Hamlet*." *Shakespeare Quarterly* 46 (1995):1–31.

——. *Playing Companies and Commerce in Shakespeare's Time*. Cambridge: Cambridge University Press, 2001.

——. *The Repertory of Shakespeare's Company, 1594–1613*. Fayetteville: University of Arkansas Press, 1991.

Koestenbaum, Wayne. *Double Talk: The Erotics of Male Literary Collaboration*. New York: Routledge, 1989.

Kyd, Thomas. *The Spanish Tragedy*. Ed. J. R. Mulryne. New York: W. W. Norton, 1989.

Langbaine, Gerard. *An Account of the English Dramatick Poets*. London, 1691.

Laqueur, Thomas. "Crowds, Carnival, and the State in English Executions, 1604–1868." In Beier, Cannadine, and Rosenheim, 305–56.

Larner, Christine. *Enemies of God: The Witch-Hunt in Scotland*. London: Chatto & Windus, 1981.

Leinwand, Theodore. *The City Staged: Jacobean Comedy, 1603–13*. Madison: University of Wisconsin Press, 1986.

———. *Theatre, Finance, and Society in Early Modern England*. Cambridge: Cambridge University Press, 1999.

Lenton, Francis. *The Innes of Court Anagrammatist*. London, 1634.

Levin, Harry. "Notes towards City Comedy." In Lewalski, 126–46.

Levine, Laura. *Men in Women's Clothing: Anti-theatricality and Effeminization*. Cambridge: Cambridge University Press, 1994.

Levy, F. J. "How Information Spread among the Gentry, 1550–1640." *Journal of British Studies* 22 (1982): 11–34.

———. "Staging the News." In Marotti and Bristol, 252–78.

Lewalski, Barbara, ed. *Renaissance Genres: Essays on Theory, History, and Interpretation*. Cambridge: Harvard University Press, 1986.

Limon, Jerzy. *Dangerous Matter: English Drama and Politics in 1623/24*. Cambridge: Cambridge University Press, 1986.

———. *The Masque of Stuart Culture*. Newark: University of Delaware Press, 1990.

Lindley, David, ed. *Court Masques: Jacobean and Caroline Entertainments*. Oxford: Oxford University Press, 1995.

Lingua, or the Combat of the Tongue. London, 1607.

Loewenstein, Joseph. "Authentic Reproductions: The Material Origins of the New Bibliography." In Maguire and Berger, 23–44.

Logan, Marie-Rose, and Peter Rudnytsky. *Contending Kingdoms: Historical, Psychoanalytic, and Feminist Approaches to the Literature of Sixteenth-Century England and France*. Detroit: Wayne State University Press, 1991.

Love, Harold. *Scribal Publication in Seventeenth-Century England*. Oxford: Clarendon Press, 1993.

Lytle, Guy Fitch, and Stephen Orgel, eds. *Patronage in the Renaissance*. Princeton: Princeton University Press, 1981.

MacFarlane, Alan. *Witchcraft in Tudor and Stuart England*. New York: Harper and Row, 1970.

MacIntyre, Jean. *Costumes and Scripts in the Elizabethan Theatres*. Edmonton: University of Alberta Press, 1992.

MacKenzie, D. L. "*The Staple of News* and the Late Plays." In Blisset, Patrick, and Van Fossen, 84–128.

Maguire, Laurie, and Thomas L. Berger, eds. *Textual Formations and Reformations*. Newark: University of Delaware Press, 1998.

Malcolmson, Christina. " 'As Tame as the Ladies': Politics and Gender in *The Changeling*," *ELR* 20 (1990): 320–40.

Malone Society Collections. 15 vols. Oxford: Oxford University Press, 1907–93.

Manley, Lawrence. *Literature and Culture in Early Modern London*. Cambridge: Cambridge University Press, 1994.

Mann, David. *The Elizabethan Player: Contemporary Stage Representations*. London: Routledge, 1991.

Marcus, Leah. *The Politics of Mirth: Jonson, Herrick, Milton, and Marvell and the Defense of Old Holiday Pastimes*. Chicago: University of Chicago Press, 1986.

———. *Puzzling Shakespeare: Local Reading and Its Discontents*. Berkeley: University of California Press, 1989.

Marlowe, Christopher. *Tamburlaine the Great, Parts I and II*. Ed. John Jump. Lincoln: University of Nebraska Press, 1967.

Marotti, Arthur. *John Donne, Coterie Poet*. Madison: University of Wisconsin Press, 1986.

———. *Manuscript, Print, and the English Renaissance Lyric*. Ithaca: Cornell University Press, 1995.

———. "The Transmission of Lyric Poetry and the Institutionalizing of Literature in the English Renaissance." In Logan and Rudnytsky, 21–41.

Marotti, Arthur, and Michael Bristol, eds. *Manuscript, Print, Performance: The Changing Relations of the Media in Early Modern England.* Columbus: Ohio State University Press, 2000.

Marston, John. *Antonio's Revenge.* Ed. W. Reavely Gair. Manchester: Manchester University Press, 1978.

———. *The Lorde and Ladye Huntingdon's Entertainment.* In Nichols, 2: 145–52.

Martin, Robert Grant. "Is *The Late Lancashire Witches* a Revision?" *Modern Philology* 13 (1915): 253–65.

Masque of Flowers. Ed. E. A. J. Honigmann. In *A Book of Masques,* 149–78.

Massinger, Philip. *The Roman Actor.* In *Drama of the English Renaissance II: The Stuart Period.* Ed. Russell. A Fraser and Norman Rabkin. New York: Macmillan, 1976. 716–42.

Masten, Jeffrey. "Beaumont and/or Fletcher: Collaboration and the Interpretation of Renaissance Drama," *ELH* 59 (1992): 337–56.

———. "Playwrighting: Collaboration and Authorship." In Cox and Kastan, 357–82.

———. "Pressing Subjects, or the Secret Lives of Shakespeare's Compositors." In Masten, Stallybrass, and Vickers, 75–107.

———. *Textual Intercourse: Collaboration, Authorship, and Sexuality in Renaissance Drama.* Cambridge Studies in Renaissance Literature and Culture 14. Cambridge: Cambridge University Press, 1997.

Masten, Jeffrey, Peter Stallybrass, and Nancy Vickers. *Language Machines: Technologies of Literary and Cultural Production.* London: Routledge, 1997.

Maus, Katharine Eisaman. *Inwardness and Theater in the English Renaissance.* Chicago: University of Chicago Press, 1995.

McGee, C. E., and John C. Meagher, "Preliminary Checklist of Tudor-Stuart Entertainments, 1603–1616." *Research Opportunities in Renaissance Drama* 27 (1984): 47–126;

———. "Preliminary Checklist of Tudor-Stuart Entertainments, 1614–1625." *Research Opportunities in Renaissance Drama* 30 (1988): 17–128.

McLuskie, Kathleen. "'A Maidenhead, Amintor, at my yeares': Chastity and Tragicomedy in the Plays of John Fletcher." In Hope and McMullan, 92–121.

———. *Dekker and Heywood: Professional Dramatists.* New York: St. Martin's, 1994.

———. "The Plays and the Playwrights, 1613–1642." In Edwards et al., 169–82.

———. "The Poets' Royal Exchange: Patronage and Commerce in English Renaissance Drama." *Yearbook of English Studies* 21 (1991): 53–62.

McMillin, Scott, and Sally-Beth MacLean. *The Queen's Men and Their Plays.* Cambridge: Cambridge University Press, 1998.

McMullan, Gordon. *The Politics of Unease in the Plays of John Fletcher.* Amherst: University of Massachusetts Press, 1995.

McRae, Andrew. *God Speed the Plow: Representations of Agrarian England.* Cambridge: Cambridge University Press, 1996.

Mehl, Dieter. *The Elizabethan Dumb Show.* Cambridge: Harvard University Press, 1966.

Meres, Francis. *Palladis Tamia or Wits Treasury.* In Smith, *Essays,* 308–24.

Middleton, Thomas. *Chaste Maid in Cheapside.* Ed. R. B. Parker. London: Methuen, 1969.

———. *Civitatis Amor.* In *Works,* 7:267–90.

———. *A Game at Chess.* Ed. T. Howard Howard-Hill. Manchester: Manchester University Press, 1993.

————. *Inner Temple Masque*. In *Works*, 7:195–216.

————. *A Mad World My Masters*. Ed. Standish Henning. Lincoln: University of Nebraska Press, 1969.

————. *The Sun in Aries*. In *Works*, 7:333–50.

————. *Triumphs of Honour and Industry*. In *Works*, 7:291–308.

————. *Triumphs of Honour and Virtue*. In *Works*, 7:351–68.

————. *Triumphs of Love and Antiquity*. In *Works*, 7:309–32.

————. *The Triumphs of Truth*. London, 1613.

————. *The Works of Thomas Middleton*. Ed. A. H. Bullen. 8 vols. Boston: Houghton Mifflin, 1886.

Middleton, Thomas, and William Rowley. *The Changeling*. Ed. Nigel Bawcutt. London: Methuen, 1970.

————. *The Changeling*. Ed. Joost Daalder. New York: W. W. Norton, 1990.

————. *A Courtly Masque: The Device Called The World Tost at Tennis*. London, 1620.

————. *A Fair Quarrel*. Ed. George Price. Lincoln: University of Nebraska Press, 1976.

————. *The Old Law*. Ed. Catherine Shaw. New York: Garland Publishers, 1982.

————. *The Spanish Gipsie*. London, 1653.

Miller, Edwin Haviland. *The Profession of Writer in Elizabethan England*. Cambridge: Harvard University Press, 1951.

Miller, Paul W. "The Historical Moment of Caroline Topographical Comedy." *Texas Studies in Language and Literature* 32 (1990): 359–70.

Mills, Laurent. *One Soul in Bodies Twain: Friendship in Tudor Literature and Stuart Drama*. Bloomington, Ind.: Principia Press, 1937.

Mincoff, Marco. "The Social Background of Beaumont and Fletcher." *English Miscellany: A Symposium of History, Literature, and the Arts* 1 (1950): 1–30.

Montaigne, Michel. *Essaies*. Trans. John Florio. Menston, England: Scolar Press, 1969.

Montrose, Louis. *The Purpose of Playing: Shakespeare and the Cultural Politics of the Elizabethan Theater*. Chicago: University of Chicago Press, 1996.

Mooney, Michael. "'Framing' as Collaborative Technique: Two Middleton-Rowley Plays." In Davidson and Giankaris, 300–314.

Muir, Kenneth, Jay Halio, and D. J. Palmer, eds. *Shakespeare, Man of the Theater*. Newark: University of Delaware Press, 1983.

Mullaney, Steven. *The Place of the Stage: License, Play, and Power in Renaissance England*. Chicago: University of Chicago Press, 1988.

Murray, Timothy. *When Theater Becomes a Book*. Ann Arbor: University Microfilms International, 1984.

Nagler, A. M. *A Source Book in Theatrical History*. New York: Dover Publications, 1952.

Najemy, John. *Between Friends: Discourses of Power and Desire in the Machiavelli-Vettori Letters*. Princeton: Princeton University Press, 1993.

Nashe, Thomas. *Nashes Lenten Stuff*. In *The Works of Thomas Nashe*. Ed. Ronald McKerrow. Vol. 3. London, 1910.

Neill, Michael. "The Hidden Malady: Death, Discovery, and Indistinction in *The Changeling*." *Renaissance Drama* 22 (1991): 95–121.

————. "'The Simetry, Which Gives a Poem Grace': Masque, Imagery, and the Fancy of *The Maid's Tragedy*." *Renaissance Drama* 3 (1970): 111–35.

Nichols, J. *The Progresses, Processions, and Magnificent Festivities, of King James the First*. 4 vols. London, 1828.

Nicoll, Allardyce. "The Dramatic Portrait of George Chapman." *Philological Quarterly* 41 (1962): 215–28.

Norland, Howard B. Introduction to Beaumont and Fletcher, *The Maid's Tragedy*, xi–xxvii.

Notestein, Wallace. *A History of Witchcraft in England from 1558–1718*. New York: Russell and Russell, 1965.

Nungezer, Edwin. *A Dictionary of Actors and of Other Persons Associated with the Public Representation of Plays in England before 1642*. New Haven: Yale University Press, 1929.

Orgel, Stephen. *The Illusion of Power: Political Theater in the English Renaissance*. Berkeley: University of California Press, 1975.

———. *Impersonations: The Performance of Gender in Shakespeare's England*. Cambridge: Cambridge University Press, 1996.

———. *The Jonsonian Masque*. Cambridge: Harvard University Press, 1965.

———. "The Poetics of Incomprehensibility." *Shakespeare Quarterly* 42 (1991): 431–37.

Orrell, John. "The London Court Stage in the Savoy Correspondence, 1604–1618." *Theatre Research International* 3 (1978): 157–75.

———. "The London Court Stage in the Savoy Correspondence, 1613–75," *Theatre Research International* 4 (1979): 79–93.

Parker, R. B., and S. P. Zitner, eds. *Elizabethan Theater: Essays in Honor of S. Schoenbaum*. Newark: University of Delaware Press, 1996.

Parr, Anthony, ed. *Three Renaissance Travel Plays*. Manchester: Manchester University Press, 1995.

Parrott, T. M. "The Date of Chapman's *Bussy D'Ambois*," *Modern Language Review* 3 (1908): 126–40.

Parry, Graham. "Entertainments at Court." In Cox and Kastan, 195–212.

———. *The Golden Age Restor'd: The Culture of the Stuart Court, 1603–42*. Manchester: Manchester University Press., 1981.

Patterson, Annabel. *Censorship and Interpretation: The Conditions of Writing and Reading in Early Modern England*. Madison: University of Wisconsin Press, 1984.

———. *The Hermeneutics of Censorship: The Conditions of Writing and Reading in Early Modern England*. Madison: University of Wisconsin Press, 1984.

———. Introduction to *The Changeling*. In *Collected Works of Thomas Middleton*. Ed. Gary Taylor. Oxford: Clarendon Press, forthcoming.

———. *Reading between the Lines*. Madison: University of Wisconsin Press, 1993.

Peck, Linda Levy. *Court Patronage and Corruption in Early Stuart England*. Boston: Unwin Hyman, 1990.

———. ed. *The Mental World of the Jacobean Court*. Cambridge: Cambridge University Press, 1991.

Penniman, Josiah. *The War of the Theatres*. Philadelphia, 1897.

Perkins, William. *Discourse of Conscience* (1596). In *William Perkins, 1558–1602, English Puritanist*. Ed. Thomas Merrill. Nieuwkoop: B. De Graaf, 1966.

———. *The Whole Treatise of the Cases of Conscience*. London, 1614.

Perry, Curtis. *The Making of Jacobean Culture: James I and the Renegotiation of Elizabethan Literary Practice*. Cambridge: Cambridge University Press, 1997.

Potter, Lois. Introduction to Shakespeare and Fletcher, 16–23.

Potts, Thomas. *The Wonderfull Discoverie of Witches in the Countie of Lancashire*. London, 1612.

Prest, Wilfrid R. *The Inns of Court under Elizabeth I and the Early Stuarts*. Totowa, N.J.: Rowman and Littlefield, 1972.

A Profitable and Necessarie Discourse, for the Meeting with the Bad Garbelling of Spices. London, 1591.

Puttenham, George. *The Arte of English Poesie*. London, 1589.

Prynne, William. *Histriomastix*. London, 1634.

Quintrell, B. W. "Government in Perspective: Lancashire and the Privy Council, 1570–1640." *Transactions of the Historic Society of Lancashire and Cheshire* 131 (1982): 35–62.

Rackin, Phyllis. *Stages of History: Shakespeare's English Chronicles*. Ithaca: Cornell University Press, 1990.

Rappaport, Stephen. *Worlds within Worlds: Structures of Life in Sixteenth-Century London*. Cambridge: Cambridge University Press, 1989.

Raylor, Thomas. *The Essex House Masque of 1621*. Pittsburgh: Duquesne University Press, 2000.

Raymond, Joad, ed. *Making the News: An Anthology of the Newsbooks of Revolutionary England, 1641–1660*. New York: St. Martin's Press, 1993.

The Return from Parnassus. In *The Three Parnassus Plays*. Ed. J. B. Leishman. London: Nicholson & Watson, 1949.

Reynolds, George. *The Staging of Elizabethan Plays at the Red Bull Theater, 1605–1625*. London: Oxford University Press, 1940.

Rhodes, Neil. *Elizabethan Grotesque*. London: Routledge & Kegan Paul, 1980.

Richards, Jennifer, and James Knowles, eds. *Shakespeare's Late Plays*. Edinburgh: Edinburgh University Press, 1999.

Ricks, Christopher. "The Moral and Poetic Structure of *The Changeling*." *Essays in Criticism* 10 (1960): 290–306.

Rimbault, Edward, ed. *Early English Poetry, Ballads, and Popular Literature*. London, 1841.

Rose, Mark. *Authors and Owners: The Invention of Copyright*. Cambridge: Harvard University Press, 1993.

Rowley, William. *All's Lost by Lust and A Shoemaker, a Gentleman*. Ed. Charles Stork. Philadelphia: University of Pennsylvania Press, 1910.

———. *A New Wonder, A Woman Never Vexed*. London, 1632.

———. *A Search for Money, or the lamentable complaint for the losse of the wandering Knight, Monsieur l'Argent*. London, 1609.

Rowley, William, and John Webster. *A Cure for a Cuckold*. In *The Complete Works of John Webster*. Ed. F. L. Lucas. Vol. 3. London: Chatto and Windus, 1927.

Rutter, Carol, ed. *Documents of the Rose Playhouse*. Manchester: Manchester University Press, 1984.

Saunders, Eve Rachele. *Gender and Literacy on Stage in Early Modern England*. Cambridge Studies in Renaissance Literature and Culture 28. Cambridge: Cambridge University Press, 1998.

Saunders, J. W. "The Stigma of Print: A Note on the Social Bases of Tudor Poetry." *Essays in Criticism* 1 (1951): 139–64.

Scaliger, Julius Caesar. *Select Translations from Scaliger's "Poetics."* Trans. M. Padelfort. New York: H. Holt, 1905.

Schelling, F. E. Introduction to Chapman, Jonson, and Marston, ix–xxxi.

Schochet, Gordon. *Patriarchalism in Political Thought: The Authoritarian Family and Political Speculation and Attitudes Especially in Seventeenth-Century England*. Oxford: Basil Blackwell, 1975.

Schoenbaum, Samuel. *Internal Evidence and Elizabethan Dramatic Authorship*. Evanston: Northwestern UP, 1966.

Seaver, Paul. "The Artisanal World." In Bevington, Strier, and Smith, 87–100.

———. *Wallington's World*. Stanford: Stanford University Press, 1986.

Shakespeare, William. *The Riverside Shakespeare*. Ed. G. B. Evans. Boston: Houghton Mifflin, 1974.

Shakespeare, William, and John Fletcher. *The Two Noble Kinsmen*. Ed. Lois Potter. Surrey: Thomas Nelson and Sons, 1997.

Shannon, Laurie J. *Sovereign Amity: Figures of Friendship in Shakespearean Contexts*. Chicago: University of Chicago Press, 2002.

Shapiro, James. *Rival Playwrights: Marlowe, Jonson, Shakespeare*. New York: Columbia University Press, 1991.

Shapiro, Michael. *Children of the Revels: The Boy Companies of Shakespeare's Time and Their Plays*. New York: Columbia University Press, 1967.

Sharpe, J. A. *Instruments of Darkness: Witchcraft in England, 1550–1750*. New York: Penguin Books, 1996.

———. "Last Dying Speeches: Religion, Ideology, and Public Execution in Seventeenth-Century England." *Past and Present* 107 (1985): 144–68.

———. *Witchcraft in Early Modern England*. London: Pearson Education, 2001.

———. *Witchcraft in Seventeenth-Century Yorkshire: Accusations and Counter-measures*. York: Bothwick Institute of Historical Research, 1992.

Sharpe, Kevin. *The Personal Rule of Charles I*. New Haven: Yale University Press, 1992.

Shaw, Catherine. *Richard Brome*. Boston: Twayne Publishers, 1980.

Sheen, Erica. "Agent for His Master: Political Service and Professional Liberty in *Cymbeline*." In Hope and McMullan, 55–76.

Shirley, James. *Hyde Park*. London, 1637.

Sisson, C. J. *Lost Plays of Shakespeare's Age*. Cambridge: Cambridge University Press, 1936.

Smith, G. Gregory, ed. *Elizabethan Critical Essays*. London, 1904.

Smith, Irwin. *Shakespeare's Blackfriars Playhouse*. New York: New York University Press, 1964.

Smith, Joseph, ed. *The Literary Freud: Mechanisms of Defense and the Poetic Will*. Psychiatry and the Humanities 4. New Haven: Yale University Press, 1980.

Smuts, R. Malcolm. *Court Culture and the Origins of a Royalist Tradition in Early Stuart England*. Philadelphia: University of Pennsylvania Press, 1987.

———. "Cultural Diversity and Cultural Change at the Court of James I." In Peck, *Mental World*, 99–112.

Sommerville, J. P. *Politics and Ideology in England, 1604–42*. London: Longman, 1986.

Stallybrass, Peter. "Worn Worlds: Clothes and Identity on the Renaissance Stage." In De Grazia, Quilligan, and Stallybrass, 289–320.

Stallybrass, Peter, and Ann Rosalind Jones, *Renaissance Clothing and the Materials of Memory*. Cambridge: Cambridge University Press, 2000.

Stallybrass, Peter, and Allon White. *The Politics and Poetics of Transgression*. Ithaca: Cornell University Press, 1986.

Steggle, Matthew. *Wars of the Theatres: The Poetics of Personation in the Age of Jonson*. Victoria, B.C.: University of Victoria Press, 1997.

Stevenson, Laura. *Praise and Paradox: Merchants and Craftsmen in Elizabethan Popular Literature*. Cambridge: Cambridge University Press, 1984.

Stork, Charles Wharton, Introduction to *William Rowley, His "All's Lost by Lust" and "A Shoemaker, a Gentleman."* Ed. Charles Stork. Philadelphia: University of Pennsylvania Press, 1910. 7–71.

Stow, John. *A Survey of London*. Ed. Henry Morley. Dover, N.H.: Alan Sutton, 1994.

Streitberger, W. R. "Personnel and Professionalization." In Cox and Kastan, 337–55.

Sturgess, Keith. *Jacobean Private Theatre*. London: Routledge and Kegan Paul, 1987.

Sullivan, Mary. *Court Masques of James I*. New York: Knickerbocker Press, 1913.

Summers, Claude, and Ted-Larry Pebworth, eds. *Literary Circles and Cultural Communities*. Columbia: University of Missouri Press, 2000.

Sutherland, Sarah. *Masques in Jacobean Tragedy*. New York: AMS Press, 1983.

Swain, J. T. "The Lancashire Trials of 1612 and 1634 and the Economy of Witchcraft." *Northern History* 30 (1994): 64–85.

Tannenbaum, Samuel. "A Hitherto Unpublished John Fletcher Autograph." *Journal of English and Germanic Philology* 28 (1929): 35–40.

Taverner, Richard. *Proverbes or Adagies gathered out of the Chiliades of Erasmus*. London, 1545.

Taylor, Gary. "The Canon and Chronology of Shakespeare's Plays." In Wells and Taylor, 69–144.

———. "Forms of Opposition: William Shakespeare and Thomas Middleton," *ELR* 24 (1994): 283–314.

———. "Middleton and Rowley—and Heywood: *The Old Law* and New Attribution Technologies." *Publication of the Bibliographical Society of America* 96.2 (2002): 165–217.

Taylor, John. *An Armado, or Navy, of 103 Ships & Other Vessels*. London, 1627.

———. *Carrier's Cosmography*. London, 1637.

Thomas, Keith. *Religion and the Decline of Magic*. New York: Scribner, 1971.

Thomas, Max W. "Eschewing Credit: Heywood, Shakespeare, and Plagiarism before Copyright." *NLH* 31 (2000): 277–93.

Thompson, John B. Editor's introduction to Bourdieu, *Language,* 1–31.

Tilney, Edmund. *The Flower of Friendship*. Ed. Valerie Wayne. Ithaca: Cornell University Press, 1992.

Tiptoft, John, trans. *De Amicitia*, by Cicero. London, 1481.

Unwin, George. *The Gilds and Companies of London*. London: G. Allen & Unwin, 1938.

Ure, Peter. "The Date of the Revision of Chapman's *Tragedy of Bussy D'Ambois*," *Notes and Queries* 197 (1951): 1–2.

Van Fossen, R. W. Introduction to Chapman, Jonson, and Marston, 1–58.

Van Peer, W. "Quantitative Studies of Literature. A Critique and an Outlook." *Computers and the Humanities* 23 (1989): 301–7.

Veevers, Erica. *Images of Love and Religion: Queen Henrietta Maria and Court Entertainments*. Cambridge: Cambridge University Press, 1989.

Wall, Wendy. *The Imprint of Gender:Authorship and Publication in the English Renaissance*. Ithaca: Cornell University Press, 1993.

Wallis, John. *Beaumont, Fletcher, and Company*. New York: King's Crown Press, 1947.

Walton, John K. *Lancashire: A Social History*. Machester: Manchester University Press, 1986.

Ward, Joseph. *Metropolitan Communities: Trade Guilds, Identity, and Change in Early Modern London*. Stanford: Stanford University Press, 1997.

Wayne, Valerie. Introduction to Tilney, 1–96.

Webster, John. *The Duchess of Malfi*. Ed. Elizabeth Brennan. New York: W. W. Norton, 1993.

———. *The White Devil*. Ed. Christina Luckyj. New York: W. W. Norton, 1996.

Weever, John. *Epigrammes in the oldest cut, and newest fashion*. London, 1599.

Wells, Stanley, and Gary Taylor. *William Shakespeare: A Textual Companion*. Oxford: Clarendon Press, 1987.

Wells, Susan. "Jacobean City Comedy and the Ideology of the City." *ELH* 48 (1981): 37–60.

Welsford, Enid. *The Court Masque*. Cambridge: Cambridge University Press, 1927.

Westfall, Suzanne. *Patrons and Performance: Early Tudor Household Revels*. Oxford: Clarendon Press, 1990.

Whigham, Frank. *Ambition and Privilege: The Social Tropes of Elizabethan Courtesy Theory*. Berkeley: University of California Press, 1984.

———. "Interpretation at Court: Courtesy and the Performer-Audience Dialectic," *NLH* 14 (1983): 623–39.

Wiggin, Pauline. *An Inquiry into the Authorship of the Middleton-Rowley Plays*. Boston, 1897.

Wilkinson, D. J. "Performance and Motivation amongst Justices of the Peace in Early Stuart Lancashire." *Transactions of the Historic Society of Lancashire and Cheshire* 138 (1989): 35–66.

Wilson, Luke. *Theaters of Intention: Drama and the Law in Early Modern England*. Stanford: Stanford University Press, 2000.

Winwood, Ralph. *Memorials of Affairs of State in the Reigns of Q. Elizabeth and K. James I*. 3 vols. London, 1725.

Woodmansee, Martha. *The Author, Art, and the Market: Rereading the History of Aesthetics*. New York: Columbia University Press, 1994.

Worden, Blair, ed. *Stuart England*. Oxford: Phaidon Press, 1986.

Wormald, Jenny. "James VI and I, *Basilikon Doron* and *The Trew Law of Free Monarchies*: The Scottish Context and the English Translation." In Peck, *Mental World*, 36–54.

Wright, Abraham. *Excerpta Quaedam per Adolescentem*. BM Add. MS 22608.

Wright, Nancy E. " 'Rival Traditions': Civic and Courtly Ceremonies in Jacobean London." In Bevington and Holbrook, 197–213.

Wrightson, Keith. *English Society: 1580–1680*. New Brunswick: Rutgers University Press, 1982.

Yachnin, Paul. "The Powerless Theater." *ELR* 21 (1991): 49–74.

———. *Stage-Wrights: Shakespeare, Jonson, Middleton, and the Making of Theatrical Value*. Philadelphia: University of Pennsylvania Press, 1997.

Young, Alan. *Tudor and Jacobean Tournaments*. London: George Philip, 1987.

INDEX

acting companies. *See* playing companies
Admiral's Men, 18, 34, 35, 101–2, 146
Aglaura, 125
Agnew, Jean-Christophe, 43
Alleyn, Edward, 95, 101
Anne, Queen, 50, 54, 57, 61, 64, 66, 87, 134
antimasques, 54, 88
Antipodes, The, 121–22, 126
Antonio and Mellida, 36
Antonio's Revenge, 36
Anything for a Quiet Life, 102
Apology for Actors, An, 91, 126, 131
Apprentice's Prize, The, 126
apprentices, 43, 90
Archer, Ian, 168n. 9
Aristotle, 27
Armado, An, 94
Armin, Richard, 167n. 104
Arraignment of Paris, The, 60
Arte of English Poesie, 72
Ashton, Robert, 10
Astington, John, 60, 163n. 11
attribution studies, 2–4, 15; computers in, 3, 156 n.14; socio-linguistics, 3–4; stylometry, 3–4, 15
Aubrey, John, 69
audience: composition of, 21, 171n. 35; expectations of, 22, 53, 88, 145, 150, 152. *See also* playhouses; playing companies

author: agency of, 1, 13, 153; identification of, 3–5, 22, 24, 174n. 2; style of, 13–14, 17, 21, 23–28, 30–31. *See also* attribution studies; authorship; style
authorship: models of, 14, 15, 17–23, 46–47, 159n. 15; theories of drama, 2–6, 16, 51, 53, 69; theories of manuscript, 1, 16, 24; theories of masque, 53, 62–63, 67, 164n. 53, 164n. 55, 165n. 67. *See also* author; collaboration

Bacon, Sir Francis, 55, 63, 78–79, 98
Baines, Barbara, 125
Baldwin, T. W., 2, 91
Bankside, 92, 95, 148
Barber, Laird, 170n. 1
Barkstead, William, 111
Barroll, J. Leeds, 54, 75, 163n. 11
Bartholomew Fair, 95, 119, 123, 156n. 23
Bawcutt, Nigel, 100, 169n. 58
Beal, Peter, 155n. 4, 158n. 1, 171n. 26
Beaumont, Francis, 3, 4, 14, 22, 34, 63, 122, 162n. 1; as collaborator, 3–4, 34, 51, 52–54, 68–77, 86–88, 89, 102–3, 119–20
Bednarz, James, 26, 156n. 21, 159n. 27
Bentley, G. E., 33, 101, 162n. 1, 168–69n. 47, 171–72n. 39

HEATHER ANNE HIRSCHFELD was born and raised in suburban New York. She received her bachelor's degree, magna cum laude, from Princeton University, and her doctorate, with Phi Beta Kappa honors, from Duke University. She has been the recipient of a Folger fellowship as well as awards for teaching and research at the University of Tennessee, where she has been assistant professor of English since 2000. Her articles have appeared in *Genre, Journal of Medieval and Early Modern Studies, Renaissance Drama, Renaissance Papers, PMLA*, and *Shakespeare Quarterly*. She lives in Knoxville, Tennessee, with her cat, Henslowe.